W9-DDD-248

"David Clark has overcome adversities most of us can't even begin to fathom. Morbidly obese, hopelessly addicted to drugs and alcohol, he not only turned his life around but went on to complete the world's toughest footrace, the 135-mile Badwater ultramaraton. Inspiring and engaging, *Out There: A Story of Ultra Recovery*, is a dramatic story about dealing with profound difficulties and having the strength and courage to persist, endure and prevail no matter how badly the odds are stacked against you."

- Dean Karnazes, Endurance athlete and *New York Times* bestselling author

"David Clark is AMAZING! When I first met David I just thought he was a

super-fit athlete and extremely kind man, only to find out that David is a real life example of someone who decided to make a change. Incredibly for him, it was as simple as grabbing his shoes and making a choice to live. I think what makes him extraordinary is he isn't just running a couple miles around the block...oh sure, he may have started there...but he now does ultramarthons. And he doesn't just complete these races—he competes with the best! As a fellow runner and former 320-pound person, now trainer/motivational speaker/weight-loss coach, I know what it takes to do what he does and the impact it has on the lives of others. David, keep up the inspiring work and never forget what brought you here!"

- Rebecca Meyer Wright, NBC's *Biggest Loser*, Season 8 At-Home Winner

Table of Contents

This book is dedicated to all those still out there struggling with addiction.

Out There: A Story of Ultra Recovery

By David Clark

Cover photo: Leadville Race Series

Foreword

by Marshall Ulrich

Speeding towards death, red-lining the engine at full throttle, few people look in the rear view mirror, see the path of destruction they've left behind, slam on the bakes, come to an abrupt stop, and have the strength to head in a new direction. Or do we all have that strength, somewhere deep, down inside?

In *Out There: A Story of Ultra Recovery*, Dave Clark bares his soul in a raw and shocking manner by telling his story of how alcohol and drugs led to isolation and despair. You may think you know bottom, but you don't know the depths that one can sink until you read this first-hand account of the dark places he has been, all the while managing to fool himself—justifying his actions while denying the damage he was doing to himself, his family, his friends, his business partners, everyone around him. From the depths of darkness, Dave was able to see a glimmer of light. A flicker of hope.

At six foot-tall and 320 pounds, Dave stopped on the high speed road of destruction and took the first steps on a treadmill to reclaim his health and his life. The path was not an easy one. He trained and suffered until he could run a 100-mile race, an ultramarathon. Achieving fitness and sobriety, Dave realized the human spirit can overcome the physical pain of running as well as the emotional pain of addiction and that it is possible to restore appreciation and gratitude for support systems that have always been there, even after keeping them out for decades. We all make adjustments and changes in our lives, but even more dramatic than his weight loss and sobriety is the story of how he lifted himself up from the depths of despair to re-invent himself and become whole again. Dave changed his view of the world, and of himself. Now he dedicates himself to inspiring others to overcome any challenge, in part by manning a 24-hour hotline for anyone who is struggling with addition— because he knows that doing for others is more important than watching out for only ourselves.

As an ultrarunner for more than 30 years and as a man who has struggled with my own demons (as we all have), I know it takes a hell of a lot of hard work and fortitude to overcome physical and emotional pain. Yet, while I've heard stories of recovery before, never have I read such a raw and honest account of the depths of darkness and depravity a man can reach. Sometimes it is a difficult story to read, but ultimately it is not a story of destruction. *Out There* is a story of the long trail that winds upward toward enlightenment and fulfillment. Dave shares his story of ultra recovery in order to help others realize that while the spirit may be tarnished, it is not shattered. By taking responsibility for yourself and your actions—while letting others in to help—you can discover that which gleams within. It has been my pleasure to rub elbows with him on that ultrarunning trail, literally and figuratively, and through his profound and ultra uplifting story, I know you will feel the same.

❶
Help!

I opened my eyes and stared at the ceiling for what seemed like an hour before any lucid or tangible awareness materialized. The situation was not a new one. I had been here before. I was experiencing pain from every physical source possible, but this time the pain in my head and the aches in my body couldn't come close to the torturous pounding I was sustaining from my mind—the feeling of failure, of hopelessness, of sheer depression was palpable. Lying on my bed in that moment, I heard a noise. It was an actual audible sound and at first it seemed as if it was coming from far away. It carried with it a powerful tremor that was coming from inside my body. It was a deep, low echo from my core and I felt a dark wave fall over me as it resonated. It made me feel as if there wasn't a single reason I should be alive, like the world itself was requesting for me to just let go. I was utterly alone and devoid of any hope or expectation that things would ever get better.

I believe the noise I heard that day may have been received through my heart, not my ears, but the sound was nevertheless real. The sound was the release of the human spirit; the auditory note struck as the soul concedes, breaks in half and collapses. I was busted up, I was broke and I was broken. I couldn't imagine I would make it to the end of the day.

"I am going to die," I whispered out loud to no one.

I could smell the alcohol, fast food and drugs escaping my 320 pounds of bloated body; it was escaping through my pores.

"I might die today," I repeated. And even though I was only 33 years old and the thought itself seemed heavy, it also seemed ok. Before I could analyze the thought any further, though, the retching started. I jumped from the bed and ran to the bathroom, arriving at the toilet just in time. From my stomach came a horrible stream of bile and blood mixed into a bright yellow and red ray of death that burned my throat on its way up and out. After a series of kneeling, shaking and repeatedly convulsing until I collapsed, the process finally played itself out. My body released into a limp, defeated mass of exhaustion. I wiped the blood and vomit from my mouth as I was sitting on the bathroom floor leaning against the wall behind me.

I stared up to the sky. "Please," I said so softly I barely heard it myself..."Please, help me."

❷
We All Are

Roll the tape—fast forward to the present. On the surface, I seemed mentally sound. I had a job. I was an executive, in fact. I was 38 years old, 6 feet tall, 160 pounds. I had a wife, kids, and a house in the suburbs—the whole cliché. The only thing dispelling the illusion of normalcy was the little tidbit that I had been running for 20 hours non-stop. Only a few months ago I would have laughed until my sides hurt if you'd told me there was any person on the planet—not just capable of doing this, but dumb enough to do it. Yet somehow I made it all the way to this moment. I was an idiot, I knew that. And (I realized recently) that I seemed to enjoy inflicting pain on myself—in some ritual to test the limits of my aging body and diminishing sanity.

As you can guess, I haven't always been a runner. In fact, there was a time when just walking up stairs to use the bathroom or say goodnight to the kids was an extreme test of endurance. Just a short time ago I was 320 pounds, and my only "test of limits" was to see how much whiskey I could drink by myself in one night and still be able to blink. But here I was, running my skinny ass off and trying to do anything to keep myself from quitting in the middle of this 100-mile run. I was miserable and this no longer seemed a good idea at all.

"I don't even like to drive that far."

"I only run if I am being chased by a man with a big knife."

I am treated to these witty quips from my friends and family when they hear about my strange endeavors to run long distances and push to the point of physical breakdown (or sometimes even past that point). Any response I give—creative, humorous or simply honest, merely solidifies my spot in the asylum as far as they're concerned. So I try to smile and look amused, and I usually am. But it's hard—even for the most seasoned distance runner—to communicate the reasoning behind these self-inflicted pain parties. How do you justify all the training, expense and time allocated—all for the privilege of running 100 miles in the middle of nowhere? Could there possibly be a meaningful "one liner" response? I doubt it. In ultra marathons there are no big crowds—no glory, just a long open road to the center of your soul. "Hey dude, let's run for 30 hours."

My all-time favorite question is "Do you get any money for doing this?"

The answer is no. Actually it's worse than no—I pay to do these races.

I usually just shrug my shoulders and tell them I woke up from a coma and wanted to run. That seems to suffice for the time being. The truth is I don't know why I want to run so far. Most likely, I want to run 100 miles because the task itself seems so ridiculous and impossible. Not surprisingly, the answer you receive when you ask a runner "Why do you run?" varies greatly depending on whom you are asking and even when you ask them.

The heroes in most sports are the men and women who can score the most points. The athletes that can jump higher or throw the ball farther get the attention and endorsements. Even in other types of running, such as track and field or marathons, the focus seems to be on the elite athletes and the amazing paces they can maintain during the race. "Can you believe those Africans can run 26 miles at a sub 5-minute mile?" I hear this from co-workers and friends immediately after any nationally televised marathon. In ultra running the heroes finish last. Sure, there are a handful of elites in the field that are on a mission to reach the end before the other competitors, but this is the rare exception. The elite athletes in mainstream sports tend to compete to find out "Who is the better man?" The ultra world consists mostly of runners who push themselves to the brink of failure in an effort to measure the depth of their own strength. They seek to find "What kind of man am I?"

It's been said that if you want to see the world's greatest athletes, go watch the Ironman Triathlon. You will see the top men and women swim 2.4 miles, bike 112 miles and then run a marathon—all in world class times, one after another. The winning time is usually an unimaginable 9 hours or less. However, if you want to see the human spirit in its most pure and inspirational state, stay until midnight just before the 17-hour cut-off at the end of the race. You will see everyday people drag themselves across the finish line in 16 hours and 58 minutes, covered in spit and blood and vomit. Watch as the tears and embraces spread through the crowd as families watch their own "champions" collapse into their arms, victorious and fully released from the struggle. Those are my heroes.

I didn't start off my life as a runner, in fact I am sure that I have said all of the same things that I now hear from those who are troubled or simply confused by my long distance running:

"I have bad knees."

"I am just not a born runner."

"I just don't enjoy running."

"I only run when chased by a man with a knife..." (Yeah, that one again.)

And I certainly wasn't born with a runner's body, either. In fact, being overweight has always been something I was teetering on the edge of, and sometimes I fell right over that edge into "McDonalds Dunkin Donut Land." I wasn't lean as a child. I wasn't obese; I just seemed to hang in the balance somewhere. I was very active. I played a lot of baseball and other sports with my brother and dad, which kept me in reasonable shape. But I was never light and wiry, to say the least.

I was sort of a mischievous child with a heart of gold. At least that's how I choose to describe it. I had good intentions, and the love I had for my mom, dad and brothers was never in question. I did, however, act impulsively whenever adventure presented itself. This resulted in many times when the outcomes of my particular actions seemed to be selfish. The truth is, I used to beat the shit out of myself all the time for even the tiniest inconsiderations that I bestowed on someone else. I always worried whether someone got screwed by getting the smallest piece of cake—or if someone had a bad view of the television set. Whenever we passed stranded motorists on the highway, I always asked my dad if we could stop and help them. I protected kids who were bullied—and got bullied myself for the effort. I was always concerned that everyone felt happy, loved, and that no one felt left out.

This was kind of a pattern for me. I was capable of feeling profound pain when I considered how other people felt or if their feelings were hurt, yet I acted many times without thought of what would happen to me or anyone else as a result of my leap into the fire. One time I decided to take my brand new BB gun and shoot out every windshield in the entire neighborhood from my bedroom window. No thoughts, no worries—seemed like a great idea at the time.

Then there were other times like when my family went to Chuck E Cheese when I was a child, and I saw a kid wandering around the arcade watching other kids play video games. He wasn't playing any games himself and seemed to be sad. I don't think he was there with his family, just a kid from the neighborhood killing time, but I had a huge pocket full of tokens so I approached him. I could not imagine how horrible he must have felt being unable to play games while all the other kids were having fun. I could "feel it" and it hurt my stomach. I offered him my tokens—all of them.

I played sports, I loved baseball in particular, but I played hockey, kickball, tennis, you name it. I was blessed with good eye-hand coordination and did well in almost any athletic endeavor. Although there always seemed to be one or two kids who were a little faster or stronger than I was, I had something a little more unusual. I had the ability to play my very best, when there was the most on line—or more accurately, when I felt I had a chance to defy the odds and do something big. It didn't seem to matter whether it was a playoff game or just a sand lot Saturday afternoon—if the game was on the line, I usually seemed to come up with a big performance.

My very first year of little league baseball, I struck out a batter with bases loaded in the final inning to win a championship game against a team that hadn't lost a game in three seasons. What a cool way to be introduced to the sport—carried off the field in triumph. I wish I could say all my games went this way, but many did not.

I was also displaying what may be described as leadership qualities at a very young age; others might call those qualities "manipulation" not leadership, be that as it may. I wish I could tell you that I always used my gifts of persuasion to the greater good of the world, but in most cases, I just convinced my friends to do all the stupid shit I wanted to do—regardless of who got in trouble. After one scenario when her son lied to spend the night at my house, a frustrated parent told my mother, "Your son has powers over all the neighborhood children, and they do anything he says." She was almost screaming at my mom.

I think in response, my mother may have calmly offered my services to help teach the woman how to control her own child. My mother and I have a similar sense of humor.

I went to church and I had a close relationship with God as I was growing up. I loved my country and what it stands for, even at an early age. This was due to my incredibly patriotic father and a grandpa who fought in WWII. I respected soldiers as true heroes and understood that many people died in my stead. I was taught that not everyone had it as good as we do in this country and that in the world, there was real evil and poverty that we cannot even comprehend here in the U.S. I excelled in school but I could grow bored quickly. In those times I would test my teacher's long-term commitment to the profession. But I always grasped the concepts quickly and deeply when focused.

Once in the 4th grade, I took my English book home and read the entire book over the weekend. I told my teacher I was done with all the material for the rest of the year. She thought that was cute and dismissed it as me trying to be an overachiever, or teacher's pet, but I wouldn't let it rest. My dad finally requested that I be tested on the material at "year-end level." I passed and was moved up a level in English.

In kindergarten, a teacher mentioned she was concerned with the picture I drew for the infamous "What do you want to be when you grow up" project. I turned in a crayon depiction of me surrounded by bags of money. I simply wrote "RICHEST MAN ALIVE" across the bottom. When the teacher asked my father what he thought about this, he smiled and told her, "I think my son has a superiority complex." That comment became a family joke for many years.

Although confident, I certainly never thought I was better than anyone else. I never bragged or taunted people into competitions or contests. In fact, I was usually on the shy side when competition arose—I would sit in the back, content to watch. I know it sounds like a contradiction, but if my name was called, I stood up. And in standing, I could summons confidence that I could rise to any occasion. If no one called me out, I simply went on my way.

I always wanted to do great things. I wanted to do things that no one else could or would do. I wanted to do the things that scared other people or seemed impossible. After watching Terry Fox's story on the news, I dreamt of riding my bike all the way across America. I was going to call it "Bike for your Life" and I would raise money for a charity. I even bought a large map and planned all the logistics and details, but family struggles kept me from realizing the goal.

My youth was a never-ending series of times when I literally leapt without thinking, followed by considerable regret and feeling genuinely sad for the trouble I caused. I jumped off houses—literally. I jumped in pools with all my clothes on; I picked fights with three bigger kids at one time, and did many of the things that most growing boys do. If there was a difference between me and the other boys, it was my confidence in my survival instincts, even as young as 7 or 8 years old. I felt that no matter what happened, how uncomfortable the circumstance was, who came after me, or what the punishment was—in the end I could endure it and come out on the other side unscathed.

Later in life these same feelings and actions continued to dominate my behavior. I had a better understanding of how my actions affected others, so in effect, I was making better decisions, but I still tended to leap and then check out the view later. Many people go to great lengths to avoid risks in life; I always welcomed them. I didn't always look for risk, but I never shied away when it appeared. I wasn't always without fear, though. In fact, I was almost always immensely afraid of taking the leap itself—but never of the outcome. It's a contradiction inside a paradox—frightened to act, yet supremely sure I will be ok if I do, confident in my abilities and insecure in my self-worth.

On a training run just the other day, a good friend of mine commented on the way I run down steep mountain trails. She said, "Aren't you afraid you will fall? There are huge rocks all over and not a single flat spot for your feet to land."

I replied, "You have to run with complete faith that your foot will find its place on the trail if you just throw it forward."

Maybe in some ways, I was born to run—but then again, we all are.

I grew up in upstate New York and had a great and exceptionally normal life...at least at first. I was born to parents who were high school sweethearts. They were just good honest people who wanted to offer the world something of themselves, a gift to the ages to see if they could change the experience and quality of life for the human race; they had kids. My parents were very supportive and did nothing short of devote their entire lives to trying to supply happiness and love to my brothers and me. My father was a hardworking and very ambitious fellow who taught me the value in never being too afraid to take risk to capture happiness from life. Notice I didn't say capture happiness "in life" but actually "from" life. I was taught that if you want something, you better put on your ass-kicking hat and go get it.

My dad walked away from a very promising and financially secure career to chase his dreams. His willingness to risk everything he had in a commercial furniture business was based more in creating a life that would afford him time with family than it was based in dreams of becoming a captain of industry, although wealth and lavish lifestyle would have been a welcome ancillary benefit, I am sure.

My older brother Loren, my mom and I followed my father across the country as he began a lifelong quest for freedom, financial security and spiritual enlightenment. As a child I was treated to endless stories of our nation's founding leaders, entrepreneurs, and exactly what it took for them to build their visions. My father always thought that the true unspoken heroes in life were the businessmen, the guys who had the guts to go out and capture the American Dream.

My dad was in many ways my only real hero. I loved watching Don Mattingly hit a baseball or Tug McGraw pitch in the ninth, but I never wanted to be those guys. I wanted to be just like my dad. He always took the time to explain things to us; even as children, things that most adults would have never even bothered to mention to their kids. My dad treated me like an adult and told me that I had his "complete trust and confidence until I proved I didn't deserve it." I spent my life making sure I never did prove unworthy of his trust. My dad was there for us, not only in spirit but in the flesh. I have memories of him always taking the time to actually do stuff with my older brother and me. He wouldn't miss an opportunity to take us to the courts for a game of "2 on 1" full-court basketball or grab the sleds at the first sign of snow. One of my earliest memories of my father was of him taking me to work with him when I was 5 years old. I just typed gibberish on the IBM electric typewriter and wandered around the office, but it was a great day, nonetheless—we even stopped for sandwiches from the local deli on the way home.

As a father of three and busy man myself these days, I can truly appreciate how difficult it can be to give time to others, even those closest to you. We tend to beat ourselves up as parents thinking that we should buy the best shoes or ice skates or video games for our kids. We even break out the old "I wish I could afford a bigger house for my family" cliché, but in the end, all kids really want from their parents is their attention and love. In the end, I have never heard anyone say, "My mom and dad really loved me, but I really wish they would have just bought me more shit."

My father is a patriot and lover of the United States of America, and so am I. My dad made sure my brother and I were carted around to all the historical locations of our founding fathers. From George Washington's home at Mount Vernon to Jefferson's Monticello, I have seen first-hand a small glimpse into the lives of the men who so bravely fought and sacrificed for freedom and the birth of our nation. While many kids were listening to ghost stories by the campfire, I was hearing the story of General Washington taking a ragtag bunch of farmers across the Delaware under a cloak of mist at night—defying common sense to attack the greatest fighting force on the planet. I spent countless days and nights standing on the very fields of battle where men had died and fought to provide us all with a chance at happiness. I was also taught by my father the lesson of how to respond when the world decided to kick the ever-loving shit out of you over and over again. You don't ask why, you don't try to figure out whose fault it is, you get up, shake off the dust and blood, and get back in the ring.

Mainly, my father is an honest man. He is direct, he doesn't try to tell people what they want to hear, and he would never try to manipulate the facts to make himself look better. He is simply not afraid to be exactly who he is. I would describe my dad in a simple sentence, a sentence that I dedicate my life's actions to with the hope that people will use it to describe me one day: "He is a good man."

My mother is to me, as mothers are to most young men, a vision of grace, beauty and devotion. She captured my heart almost completely, and still does today. The only difference between my mother and the multitudes of the other women of the world is simple—mine is better than all those other moms—at least it seems that way to me. We had a relationship that was multifaceted and was as much of a friendship as it was anything else. When times were tough and money was tight, we both worked while my father kept collecting the proverbial bricks to assemble our family's castle. We worked together doing anything that could put money on the table. We did telemarketing (yeah, sorry about all those calls) worked at restaurants, car lots, construction—you name it. Mom and I worked endless hours and spent the night laughing until we cried, all the while my dad and older brother worked through the night at various job sites around the country.

I have never seen my mother take a selfish action. Never. I cannot recall a single time when she raised her voice in anger or frustration. Not once did she take the last soda from the fridge. Never did she choose the restaurant she wanted or even pick the movie for family movie night. I can't recall a single occasion where Mom needed "time off" from the family or walked away when we needed her. She is a saint. Maybe she was a selfish human like the rest of us and I have simply arranged my memories in a fashion that allows me to view my mother as flawless, but even if that's the case, she managed to impact me in such a way that would produce this perception—and that's something of its own. To me, my mom was a never-ending ultra runner of a parent. Never stopping to rest and never caring about anything other than moving forward until we were all happy and content. I can only I hope that in the wee hours when were all peacefully asleep that she had a few moments to herself.

She grew up in Seattle and Washington DC, and as far as I know, she had a relatively normal life as a child—if there is such a thing. She loves Elvis, cooking elaborate French meals and watching old movies. Mostly, I have seen my mother take pleasure in the form of helping others. Whether a grandchild, my dad, myself or a complete stranger—she is always reliable, always there. I will never be as close to another human as I am with my mom.

My brother Loren and I got along when we were growing up. He was four years older but because we moved around, we relied on each other a lot. We had our moments—like when he smashed my rocking chair and locked me in the wardrobe for an hour, but I made up for it by throwing him into a thorny rose bush during a kickball game. From an early age, I seemed to excel at the art of making my brother so frustrated that he would punch things and throw tantrums that would have even embarrassed legendary baseball manager Lou Piniella. But all and all, we spent hours on end playing baseball and exploring the woods and campgrounds in upstate New York and beyond. We grew apart later in life, which is very sad, but he did make his way out to Colorado and now lives close by with his own kids, and we see each other whenever possible.

My grandpa, like all the men in my family, also grew up in Rochester, NY and, in fact, took me to my first baseball game. He used to take my brother and me for soft-serve ice cream and had a way of making us feel much love. He fought in WWII and was on the beach in 1944 at Normandy during D-Day. He was wounded in action before returning home as a hero. He was an important figure in all of our lives, but he was gone before I truly got to know who he was for me.

East Rochester New York was a great town to grow up in. We had everything that was small town America, yet we still seemed to have that New York swagger and expectation. East Rochester is known as "The City of Champions" and I believe it. Whether we were playing a pickup game of pond hockey or baseball at the local park, the competition was fierce and the air was always electric. A casual passerby might think that the World Series was on the line, were he to catch us neighborhood hooligans arguing the exact trajectory of a formerly airborne baseball that landed simply "foul" or "fair." It seemed to be a matter worthy of exhausting animation and challenges from both teams to each other's not-yet-realized manhood.

I went to kindergarten and some grade school in Rochester and have very fond memories of childhood. I went sledding at Edmond Lyon Park with my father and brother and played little league nearby in Pittsford. One of my fondest childhood visions is being about 4 years old and sledding down the hill with my dad. He would purposely spill us off the sled on the way down and we would roll all the way to the bottom, laughing. Then my brother and I would fill his hat with snow and Dad would pretend he didn't notice and put the hat back on his head. I can remember laughing that all-out kid's laugh that seems to come from the bottom of the feet all the way to the top of the head before consuming your whole body. In fact, I belly-laughed so hard I may have peed myself—in fact I am sure I did.

We left Rochester when my father decided to leave the stalling economy of New York behind and take the plunge into the abyss of self-employment. We bounced around considerably during most of my childhood after that, but New York always remained "base camp" for us. As we traveled extensively for my father's business, we became increasingly closer as a family. We also became increasingly more distanced from the rest of the family. It started to feel as though we were our own self-contained unit or regiment, taking on the world in an effort to extract our own special piece of the Promised Land. I know that sounds a trifle strange, but since all the other "normal" things in our lives were temporary—addresses, schools, etc.—the only thing we really had to count on as a constant was each other.

The family business really became the nucleus of our entire existence. My brother and I were both very involved and hands-on in the business, working sometimes all night to help our parents and the crews finish a job to hit a deadline or an opening. We shared a common focus and everyone was in touch with the daily goings-on of the business and how the checkbook was balancing. In an effort to land large national and very lucrative accounts, we followed work for hotel and restaurant chains to the ends of the earth. Ok, not really the ends of earth, but at least as far south as Florida. My family was also on a quest of another sort—the quest for the truth of God. The topic of God and the Bible, and whether it was real or just fantasy, was a central part of our lives.

As we continued our journey, the calls of family and life frequently carried us back to the city of my birth. These were always my favorite times. I still can still to this day with exacting measure summons the magic and excitement of going "home" to my grandparents' house for Christmas. It was a combination of the natural childhood love for the holiday and gift-giving anticipation, all mixed with the feeling that at least for the time being, we seemed to be off "the battlefield" and at peace with the world. When we returned to Rochester for the holidays or family events, we left the struggles of our life and "quest" on the back burner for another day. I was relaxed and happy, and I felt connected to the grid for the moment. There was tremendous peace and security in all this. We all literally seemed to become different people when we went back home. I couldn't help starting to think of myself as "not normal" or somehow different from other families, including the other families within our family.

I think it is worth noting that during these periods when we were visiting family, there were many associations I was making that would come to play later in life. Being of both Irish and Belgium decent, there always seemed to be lots of booze and food around. Even as a child I took detailed note at how grown-up and sophisticated everyone looked with a glass of scotch in hand, how romantic the sound the cork made as it was wrestled out of its resting place in the neck of a bottle of wine, and how euphoric it was to eat treat after treat and then retire to the sofa and take it all in as if it were a reward for a hard time on the road. I believe this association of food and alcohol, mixed with the security and comfort I was feeling from being "off the road," planted the seed for a painful love affair with food and booze later in life.

Somewhere along the line, our fight to etch out our own life of fulfillment and success, became a battle just to survive. The nice houses and cars had become apartments and old work trucks. We seemed to be on a roller coaster of a lifestyle. When the work was good, we had money to eat out and live in nice places and buy clothes and go shopping at the mall. When the work went away, it seemed we were in a struggle just to keep a roof over our heads, and even eat.

I was becoming increasingly jealous of families who had deep roots in a community. I would look out the window as we drove by the old houses in towns and states we passed through. I fantasized in my mind of going to the same school my dad did, buying a house next door to my parents, and walking with my kids on the same sidewalks I chalked out "four square" patterns on. I could picture riding bikes with my own family to the same parks where I held court as a lad, seeing my son playing hockey on the same frozen ponds I so recklessly glided over. I always loved those television shows where the kids returned to the homes of their youth, as grown adults—you know, sitting in the same tire swing where their dad had sat when he was a 2nd grader. Now, as a grown-up, he would be talking to his own about some life lesson— probably no more important than the memory this special moment and what it represented.

I didn't hate my life, by any measure. In fact, I felt supremely lucky to have parents that cared so much about me, and I am sure many of my friends were as jealous of me as I was of them in this department. We always seem to romanticize the other side of the tracks. Even as an adult now, I recognize that there really is no "normal" in life and we all have details that we wish we could have changed.

I am glad to have had the opportunity to travel up and down the East Coast for many years of my life. I was afforded the privilege of seeing many neighborhoods, contrasting landscapes and ideologies. I spent long stretches of time in Northern Virginia, Florida and New Jersey, just to name a couple of places we dropped anchor. However, I never really felt like I had a home at all until we settled into the NYC metro area when I was in my teens.

❸
Lose Yourself

"Gas up the car and point it towards Mexico," my father said to me jokingly.

It was a line from an old *Honeymooners* episode he and I used to laugh about. Only we weren't watching TV and it wasn't meant to be funny—well, at least not completely. Are we really moving to California? I was no stranger to moving, to say the least, but this was the move of all domestic moves—coast to coast. Never being one to shy away from adventure, though, I did what I could do in my mind to make this a positive scenario. I pictured the West Coast as a bunch of little surfer girls running around in bikinis, beach parties like in *The Karate Kid*—and of course, the music scene. I had been playing guitar for many years and becoming a musician was something that I had been working on behind the scenes for a while.

We hit the coast of California in a heightened state of expectation and in a cloud of road dirt and smoke. Literally, Dad's Cadillac barely made the cross-country trip and was coughing out its final breaths in black smoke as we overtook the state line. This switching of the coasts wasn't really a strategic business move as much as it was a survival maneuver. To say business was poor and our resources were low would be so tragically understating it that we might as well say that General Custer was understaffed. There was an underlying feeling of failure in this move to the Pacific Coast. That isn't to say the move was without hope; we were all excited to be turning the page and making a fresh start—it just felt that everything that had happened up to this point was a loss. It hadn't worked. We were broke and forced to not only move, but move 3,000 miles away from home.

So we are here... what now?

My dad went about the tedious task of trying to establish a business in a completely cold market. No contacts, no local references, just balls and determination. I have come to understand that although the Clarks were not born with any privilege or pedigree to speak of, we do appear to be hardwired to keep trying against the odds; there is no quit in the standard Clark prototype. We settled into the Orange County area of Southern California. By now our family had changed. I was 18, my older brother Loren, 23 had stayed back in the NYC area to start his own family, and the immediate family had grown some, as well. I had two little brothers now: Chase and Shaun who were 8 and 6 years old. Our spirits were high as we explored our new home state. We went to some of the tourist attractions, we drove the beach communities, and we spent quality time together as a family.

Eventually, I went to work for a home products company that sold water and air filtration systems. It was a sales-based job and I was good at it. I started as an entry-level sales associate and quickly worked my way through the ranks to become one of the highest paid sales executives in the company. During this time I made lots of friends. My social network became large and I was never without things to do on the weekends. I was going into Los Angeles and to concerts, and making a bit of a name for myself at the local pub with my new friends. I was also relishing the fact that I was making a lucrative wage outside the family business. In short, I was enjoying my new life in California and I was slowly beginning to separate from my family. Although I was branching off on my own and pulling down good money, I continued to live with my parents to help support the family. My commitment and love for my family was still strong; however, after a while it was only my money that went home after work.

I never moved out of my parents place but I did stop taking up residence there. For all intents and purposes I was living a dual life. I had a room at a friend's house that was mine. Everyone there thought of me as a roommate and I was there often. At the same time, I also stayed with my parents as if I had never moved out. In fact, I think my parents would have been shocked to find out that I had a room elsewhere. I am sure they viewed my times away as me "spending a few days with friends" and it was true—sort of. The reality was that I had found two new friends in particular who were monopolizing all my thoughts and time. Their names were "Drugs" and "Alcohol" and I was falling in love. The contrast was quite striking, I would stay up partying for two days straight, playing music and abusing chemicals, only to return home and spend the next day playing with my little brothers and enjoying time with my parents. I felt comfortable now in both places and I lived between the two worlds, both figuratively and literally.

When we'd lived in the NYC area I'd never really broken out on my own. Even when my older brother and I lived in our own "bachelor pad" (which was the guesthouse behind my parents' place in New Jersey) I never stopped being my parents' son. We had parties, I had my band over to play music, and we certainly pushed the boundaries as boys will do, but I never felt disconnected from the family. I am sure that a big reason for my emancipation from my family in the sun of the Golden State was simply chronological. I was now 19 and I had spent my whole life in a very loving but extremely narrow environment. I didn't go to college and break away like many teenagers do and my developing mind and body were ready to fly. But there was another issue—I was also worn down and beat up. I wanted a different life than what I had experienced to this point and I was tired of getting kicked around the country. "Different" was better from my changing perspective. I began to deconstruct and reexamine many of the views I had come to accept as absolute. Religion, morality, and life expectation were all on the list for review, but commitment to family and love of country were not.

When I look back over the years, I recall that I always had some sort of instinct or alarm that alcohol could be a danger to me. I am not sure how this seed was planted because my parents never drank to excess and there were no alcoholics in my family that I was aware of. In fact, alcohol in general was rarely around in my parents' house. Perhaps my early warning defense system stemmed from something as simple as an enlightened sense of when I was in jeopardy. Regardless of what caused this awareness, it was there.

My first indication that my relationship with alcohol was not going to be normal was when I was about 13 years old. I went to a party with a friend on a whim. I had never been to party where alcohol was present and accessible, so I was a little nervous about what to expect. There were lots of kids there— some my age, but most were my brother's age and older. When I looked around, I tried to take it all in and there was much to see. Everyone was drinking and going crazy with laughter, the music was blasting and it seemed that the air itself was alive and breathing. I didn't want to look out of place so I went and filled my cup at the beer keg like everyone else. I didn't, however, drink the alcohol. I actually just walked around the party laughing and having a good time with my "party prop" in hand.

I never needed alcohol as a social lubricant, even at a young age. I am generally outgoing and loose in social environments, and I have even been told that I have a penchant for enjoying listening to myself talk. As the night moved along at this first party, I mixed in well the people there. I floated around some, played some drinking games (still pretending to drink), made some new friends and had a generally great night. I remember as I was leaving, I was feeling very confident that I was liked by everyone. I was both happy and disappointed to be leaving, but I wanted to allow myself enough time to walk home and still be home before my curfew.

Looking back, I realize now that my first night with alcohol was very far from what I would call a normal experience. It's not that I went to a party and didn't drink. I would say that's quite common, especially at 13 years of age. The fact that I went to a party and didn't drink... *while I was there* is what's troublesome. What I did was have a great time, throw some old wood boards on a bonfire, flirt with some girls, jam some tunes and leave for home with maybe a half a beer in my hand from my pretending to drink all night.

But as I said goodbye, I grabbed my jacket and stashed several beers in it to take with me. I am not sure exactly why I would have done that. I can't remember if I was just doing it on instinct or if I had a plan, but I left with the booze in hand, and it was comforting to know I had it. I walked home using the "back roads" and I remember feeling much more comfortable with the alcohol itself now that I was alone. I slammed the first beer, nervous about how it would make me feel—then another... and another. I was feeling awesome now. All of a sudden out of nowhere a thought hit me: "You're an alcoholic."

Where did that come from? I am not even sure I had ever used or considered the word "alcoholic" in my life until that point. But as I continued to drink, I started my very first of thousands of mental ping-pong matches to come. "I shouldn't keep drinking," I thought.

"What if I become an alcoholic?"

"Relax, it's only a couple of beers."

At this early stage of the game I was very strong, and alcohol was a weak match for my will so this battle went to me. I dumped what was left of that last beer and went home. Little did I know that alcohol had just accepted me as a worthy opponent and was now in training to kick the shit out of me for the next 20 years.

It was about two weeks after this infamous night that I jumped into the abyss without any fear of what the outcome might be—and this time without resistance from the internal voices of reason. I went to another party, only this time I wasn't pretending to drink. I drank and drank until I couldn't stand. I drank like a college student on spring break knocking back shots and getting sloppy. I laughed out loud, fell over, and got back up and drank more. I drank with a need and a purpose. I ended the night by puking all over the living room and front yard of my friend's house. No problem here.

Now that I was in California, I started to really pursue my love of music. Over the years I had picked up the guitar as an outlet and means of expressing myself. Music offered me the first real escape I had ever had from the stresses of life. I spent many hours every day trying to perfect my technique and nail down the blistering riffs of Metallica, Iron Maiden and the other boys of hair nation. Now on the West Coast, I had honed my skills, updated my image and was ready be a star.

Well, for now I started a makeshift band with some guys I met from work. Really we just jammed and drank beer, and imagined what it would be like if we could get some local gigs. My drinking at this point was taking on a different personality. Previously I never considered myself a regular drinker, believe it or not. But this was based more on frequency than it was on quantity. I was both under-aged and under-financed in my drinking aspirations to date, so it was quite common for me to go long periods of time without alcohol. However, when the stars aligned and I was able to do it, I indulged. It would be closer to the truth to say I overindulged. Now with money in my pocket and friends willing to oblige, the frequency of the drinking was on the rise.

Just before I left New York I went to see the biographical movie of the music group The Doors. I had never really listened to Jim Morrison before I saw the movie, but he certainly had my full attention now. I read everything I could find on him, and I listened to everything The Doors had recorded. I loved the idea of the genius poet, tragically drunk, yet perfect in his laser-pointed view on reality. For the first time in my life I romanticized the idea of being drunk and out of control. I saw him as a warrior against the ignorance of the establishment, but not in that "hippie-love-peace" way; he was dark. Hey, I was in a metal band. I was into bone-crunching, hard-hitting music, and lyrics about death, and fighting, and insanity. This Morrison guy single-handedly invented this macabre genre of lyrics and melody. I became a huge fan.

As I started to identify more with Jim Morrison and less with David Clark, a strange conglomeration of events began to occur in my life—almost the perfect storm of rebellion. For the very first time, I started to see myself as someone with a darker inside. I started to consider myself a musician, not a fledgling businessman and religious fanatic. I was living in the Los Angeles area. I was playing music every weekend. I was talking about demos, and getting my music (never mind that I really didn't have much music yet) to the record executives. I was going to the Whiskey A Go-Go, the Rainbow Room, places where Jim Morrison himself played. The people and parties I attached myself to changed a bit, as well. I was starting to meet other musicians and people claiming to be in the industry. I played every chance I could get, and always to mixed-reviews. The drugs were also starting to show up everywhere. Everyone was smoking dope, snorting coke or going to the bathrooms for the more hard-core drugs.

In New York I was always honest with my friends about how I felt about drugs—I don't do them, period. It's just the way I was. I had never even smoked pot. Now, in my current environment, my stance on how I felt about drugs and those who did do drugs changed. It had to—I couldn't alienate all these people. They weren't losers after all—they were just different than me.

"I like to keep control of my mind," I used to say as I refused drugs in favor of deadly quantities of alcohol.

I have heard it said that fate can change quickly in a game of cards, but I never knew how literal that could be taken. One night after jamming for some friends at a party, we all sat down and got into a serious game of Hearts and drinking. From the get-go it appeared that it was going to be an all-nighter; the cards were flying. It was something we had done a hundred times, only something was different this time—and it was me. This time when the cocaine was passed around the table, I snorted a line. My friends all stopped, looked at me in surprise and then busted up laughing. No peer pressure. No one "coached" me into it, or even tried to sell me on it, just a split-instant decision that affected my life forever. Jump baby, jump.

I rarely go into a situation without putting in my best effort, and my first experience with cocaine was no different. I was "all in." I never missed my turn when the mirror full of magic white powder came my way. I bellied up to the bar like I had done it a thousand times. We played cards and did drugs all night. How rock star is that?

I loved the taste of the coke in my throat as it drained down from my sinuses. I loved the way I felt—like me, only better—a heightened me. It felt like the drug was made just for me, a reunion of long lost lovers. After the game ended around five in the morning, I went to the couch to pretend I was asleep. I did this to insure that I would eventually end up downstairs with the cocaine alone. After everyone went upstairs to bed or had left to go home, I stayed awake. Then I sat on the couch all day, doing cocaine by myself and watching John Candy movies while everyone else slept off the evening. When the cocaine was gone, I felt heartbroken, and my heart might have actually been broken. It felt like it was beating at 200 beats a minute. Nothing to see here people, no problems—move along.

I almost felt as though I now had the rite of passage to be the shooting star I knew I could be. I was going to break everyone's heart. It was part of my new understanding of who I would become. I started dressing the role. Hat, glasses, and cowboy boots—you name it. I'm almost embarrassed for me now, looking back. I started acting the part entirely, too. I wasn't completely out of control yet, but I was in the vicinity. I was a high-functioning sales exec on the weekdays and a loud reckless ass at all other times. It didn't take long before I was using coke regularly—and meth and whatever else was available.

One Friday night a friend of mine and I went to Los Angles to catch some local bands and take in the music scene. We had it all planned out, we just had to stop by and pick up a buddy of his and then we would be on our way. We drove around the city for a little taking in "the freaks" and sights, and eventually we parked the car and went into a local bar to grab a couple of "pre-partying" cocktails before going to his friend's place.

I don't remember much of what happened after that. I know we were drinking at the bar. I know my friend kept trying to get me to leave, but I was having nothing to do with it. I was doing shots of 151-proof Bacardi like they were water. Shot after shot after shot. I was out of fucking control. I remember staggering out of the bar, shouting slurred nonsense at people walking by and pissing off my very patient friend. I had become sloppy drunk in a matter of minutes. He dragged me a couple blocks away to his friend's hotel and thought it might be a good idea if I went inside and took a nap. I wanted nothing to do with that—I was going to wait outside. Finally he agreed and went inside the hotel.

Apparently, I started walking around the city of LA, but I have no real memory of it. I remembering being lost, unable to speak, I was so drunk. I was disoriented and I even tried to stagger into the street and flag down a police car. I was mugged. I was beaten and I eventually passed out on a park bench. When I woke up the next morning, my watch was gone. I had memories of being pushed around by a couple of thugs who found an easy target, and I smelled like shit—literally. To my absolute horror, I realized I had been so drunk that I shit my pants.

Then there was another time when I went to a party and met a guitar player named Marc. I can't remember whose house I was at or even how I got there. All I knew was that I was drunk as hell and Marc had two things that had my attention: he had two guitars and he had a bag of crank. We jammed and jammed. We jammed metal music hard and fast and we jammed ridiculous amounts of crystal up our noses. When the party ended, we just went to another house—and another. We brought the drugs (and guitars) and played music everywhere.

After a while I didn't even know what day it was. I knew we had seen the sun come up at least twice, so I figured we were on day 3 of our "tour." At that point, we were out of drugs and ready to call it a night. I was driving home and I pulled off the road. I was feeling very paranoid and I felt the fabric of reality unwinding on me. I was hearing voices literally coming out of my dashboard talking to me. I was seeing "creatures" on the walls of buildings and I was seeing animals walking behind me out of the corners of my eyes.

"Get a grip, Dave," I told myself.

Somehow I made it back to my parents' place and walked in without saying a word. I dropped on the couch and slept for days.

There were many alarms bells starting to sound in my head, and it was becoming increasingly difficult to tune them out. Each bell represented some new or increased behavior or substance that was conspiring to unwind my health and sanity. As each new bell joined the others already ringing, the volume and tempo of the symphony intensified and required more and more to tune out. More drugs, more music, more booze. I had even invited some new friends to the party—I was starting to eat in a reckless manner—fast food and grease by the bucket. And I was smoking like a locked wheel at 95 mph—maybe a whole pack of Marlboro Lights in one sitting at the bar. I was going for the holy trinity of debauchery: chemical abuse, overeating and smoking.

I only needed one final step to complete my Jim Morrison crash (besides dying in a bathtub in France). I needed to take LSD. Marc (the one from the 3-night crank binge) and I decided to go camping in the California desert and party our asses off. We brought our guitars, a huge bottle of whiskey and some acid. I was nervous and crazy with energy at the same time. I was in what I would describe as a controlled panic attack of anticipation. We set up camp and started to throw back some whiskey. For this little adventure I was definitely looking for some liquid confidence. Marc handed me the LSD tab and I dropped it in my mouth before I could think twice about it.

Now we are committed, I thought—break on through. I tried to do anything I could to keep my mind clear and stop stressing about the impending perspective change that was about to manifest itself in my consciousness. We played guitar and waited. Finally I started to feel different. I was noticing things I had never noticed before. Things that were seemingly always there but now looked... different. Better, more detailed, funnier. Marc and I started to laugh hysterically. Everything was the funniest thing I had ever gazed upon.

We wrote down lyrics and streams of logic that I was convinced would change the world.

"Maybe this altered state would be just what I needed to unlock the creative genius in me and launch me into the heights of stardom and music legend?" I thought.

What really happened was I spent 10 hours stumbling around the desert like a maniac, cackling wildly, playing the lead role in a music video that would never be recorded. The whole time, I was being chased not only by the chemical-induced demons of the poison cursing through my veins, but also by the abandoned spirits and forgotten conventions of who I was at my core. A whole life's worth of hard-forged, chiseled ideals and values thrown into the fire like a discarded book that no longer holds any truth for the ages.

I was already in a battle for my very sanity before I ever realized I had been engaged by an enemy. I walked aimlessly in the desert. I stared into the ground for what seemed like days. I had a great time for 4 hours and then I spent 6 hours trying to get off this crazy train. After an eternity (which was actually only 10 hours), I lay still under the stars waiting desperately for sleep to take my body. Then it all came crashing down on me at once. The reality of my life—all the booze and debauchery, the lies, the hangovers, the hidden drugs, the dual life, it all came down on me like a thousand pounds of weight, added on a gram at a time... until it became so heavy I could no longer support it. I had been keeping that weight above my head for so long now, and I finally collapsed under its mass.

I woke up the next day to a chorus of alarms sending emergency information from every synapse in my body. I knew something was wrong, or more succinctly, I knew nothing was right. I wasn't me anymore. I didn't feel like me, I didn't feel like anything other than a huge black hole where David Clark once occupied a space in the universe.

When I arrived back at my parents' place I didn't even look at anyone; I went right to the bed, dropped down and slept. I slept the sleep of the potentially dead. I had crazy dreams while I was asleep. I had crazy thoughts while I was awake. I was in fear for my sanity; I was a cracked human shell. I am sure that must sound overly dramatic, but I could never over-dramatize how scared I was and how insane I felt. I was trying to just bide my time and let the drugs slowly work their way out of my system and bring me back to reality. (Well, at least my old paradigm of what "reality" was.) I no longer felt like I wanted the life of anyone other than exactly who I was one year earlier. No rock bands. No poet warriors. One thing I was sure of—Jim Morrison is dead—the actual Jim Morrison and the one I was impersonating.

I remembered a line from one of my favorite movies, *Wall Street*. It's the scene where the young broker confronts his mentor after a tumultuous rise and fall in the glamorous world of stock trading. He says, "I thought I was

Gordon Gekko, but it turns out, I am just Bud Fox."

That's exactly how I felt, only I wasn't even sure I would ever be Bud Fox again. I had spent over 6 months with hardly a sober day. I had humiliated myself and I had lost myself for the effort. I just wanted to heal. I wanted to get to the other side of whatever river I had crossed and reclaim myself and my serenity. But with my body in a state of absolute depletion and wreckage wrought by months of abuse, wouldn't you know it... I got sick.

I had hardly slept more than a day or two a week in months. My body was breaking apart and I barely had enough energy to stand. The flu worked its ways through my body, gaining momentum and aggression as it tried to reach its full potential of destruction. I was experiencing panic attacks, anxiety, racing heartbeat, confusion—you name it. I spent a couple weeks going to doctors and sleeping, barely conscious at all. Every waking moment I had was spent taking inventory of my mental and physical body—every second, every minute, waiting for normalcy to set in, and it appeared it wasn't coming. My panic was increasing. Would I ever feel normal again? I couldn't shut off the constant stream of voices and mental pictures so resolved to make me relive every bad thing I had ever done.

As time passed, the weeks became a month, and a month became two. I felt more and more desperate and discouraged. I had done permanent damage, that was it. I was doomed to spend the rest of my days in a battle for peace of mind. At any moment I could be lying in bed watching TV feeling somewhat natural, and out of nowhere, the floor would drop. The blood would rush from my head, my heart would hit my feet, and then it would return to my chest, pounding at 1,000 mph. My thoughts would race and I just wanted to die.

"What's wrong with me?" I would agonize.

I turned my head into my pillow and cried. I cried like a child does—with no shame, completely vulnerable to everyone and everything around me. I cried like a child in his father's arms. I looked up and saw my dad's face. I was actually in my father's arms now, somehow. He looked at me with a pain in his eyes that can never be accurately transcribed into written or verbal language... without diluting the depth of the anguish there.

"Tell me, son. Tell me what's going on."

He knew. There was comfort in the fact that he knew. He had absolutely no idea what I had been up to, but he knew I was dangling from a very thin string. I talked. No, actually I released. In an emotional and angelically pure stream of incoherent thought, I confessed all the events of the last several months. I knew he wouldn't judge me. I was never even concerned with that for a second. I was in a bad place, and I needed help to get out. I didn't even know exactly how I got where was, I only knew that I was in trouble and the person I trusted most in the world was there. It was just a coincidence that he was also my dad.

I went to the emergency room with my father that night, and we had a long talk with a nurse about panic attacks and stress. She recommended a therapist I could talk to about what was going on in my head, and they also addressed my more immediate condition, bronchial pneumonia. It appears I was also very sick. Lying in the hospital bed, I prayed and I felt something for the first time in many months. Peace. I knew that I was going to get thought this. I didn't know how yet, but I knew.

Everything that I had been through would only make me a stronger and better person if I put it in perspective—that was my guiding thought. I went to a couple of therapy sessions and I got a chance to dig into what was going on in my brain. I learned about how to manage stress, what causes panic, and how to manage my thoughts. I decided that I was going to capture the highest form of existence I could seek. I spent the next month-and-a half getting over the pneumonia and trying to make sense of what happened. I turned over a new leaf. I decided I was going to make health and wellness my priority. I was going to start working out again, I was going to lose weight (I was now about 50 pounds overweight), and I was going to quit smoking too.

Although many of my experiences during this period were some of the darkest times of my life, I have learned to see the events through a prism of experience and hindsight. Much of what happened there, and the rise from the ashes afterward, set the stages for what turned out to be a much bigger fall and a resulting climb from the depths that would launch me to heights I never imagined possible. I'm not sure if that's good or bad, but it was part of what needed to happen, I suppose. Unfortunately for me, I had it all wrong. It wasn't using drugs and alcohol that caused me to break away from reality. It wasn't a half year spent abusing my body and spirit that resulted in my unwinding. The unwinding was happening from the inside out. There was something deeply disturbed inside me. Something that was causing me to drink, causing me to destroy myself.

Yes, I was going to make some changes. And some of those changes resulted in an increased quality of life in the interim. But I never addressed the nature of how I really saw myself. I simply walked out of that room and shut the door. Later in life, I walked back into that room and locked the door behind me. It took me over 15 years to clean the room out and walk away—but that's another story.

As I was physically mending, the family was experiencing more hardship. My dad's business was not doing well on the West Coast either. Our problems had followed us across the country. Go figure. At the same time all this was playing out, the company I worked for went out of business—literally overnight—and we were left standing in the smoke and rumble again, wondering what was coming next. I was unemployed. My family was at rock bottom—again. Then my dad had an epiphany of his own. He had put to bed his seemingly lifelong religious quest. We spent two long years trying to get things together in the

Golden State. We had ups, we had downs, but when all the smoke settled we were two years older and none the richer. Were we wiser? Yes, for sure. We also had a newfound respect for the simplicities of life, as well as a clinical aversion to earthquakes, smog, big city hustle and the grind. California never felt like home, not once, not for an instant. I always fancied myself a smart guy, but for the first time in my life I was getting sick of swishing around like a turd in life's toilet bowl. We decided to make one last move, and I was ready to put California behind me, I couldn't get to the U-Haul dealer fast enough.

"How much does it cost for a one-way rental to Denver, Colorado?"

❹
Rocky Mountain Highs and Lows

The move to Colorado was an emotional, as well as physical, relocation. I was now older, wiser and ready to find out what my path on earth was meant to be. I had put my experience with drugs and the rock and roll lifestyle behind me. I had a new life and perspective. I felt alert, aware and enlightened. I was also sporting a slimmer body. I had lost about 50 pounds and managed to quit smoking too. I was working out, and I recaptured my love of playing sports. All you needed to say was "jump" and I was out the door to the tennis court, basketball court or golf course. I still felt a tremendous amount of love and commitment to my family, but I was also bursting at the seams to break out on my own and see if I could fly. I knew my parents needed me to help contribute to the family getting settled, so I needed to be patient for a bit longer. This, naturally, created quite a bit of inner conflict for me.

I had always had a deep-seated desire to help others. Not in the do good-er "let me interfere in your life" kind of way, but a burning in my soul that wanted to believe that the world would someday be a better place because I was here. I had many possibilities running through my mind. I was considering joining the military, I was thinking of starting my own business, and I was thinking of going to college—and, of course, many various combinations of the three.

We settled into a large family style apartment in Thornton, Colorado, a suburb of Denver that was located about 15 miles north of the city. It was my mom and dad, my two brothers and me all trying to make a fresh start. We moved our meager possessions into the apartment and decided to get down to the business of finding jobs and starting over. We figured we had six months (the length of the lease) to figure out where the best place was to look for a house. After being on the road and living in and out of hotels and temporary housing for the last two years, I was ready to be in a house—an actual house, with a fireplace and a mailbox out front. A place that would be "ours," a place where I could rest assured that my parents could settle down while I went off into the wild to stake my own claim.

I finally decided going to college was my next step. I really wanted to join the Air Force Reserves, but they wanted a 10-year commitment from me. That was half my life at that point in time, and it seemed unimaginably long and impossible to digest. I liked the idea of serving my country and contributing to the greater good. I wanted to do something more than just go to college for the sake of hanging a degree on the wall. I wanted to do something big, something worthy of respect and something that afforded me the opportunity to change lives. Thus, I became determined to go to medical school. I enrolled at Front Range Community College to get some prerequisites satisfied and then eventually transferred to the University of Colorado Denver (UCD).

I had never graduated from high school. In fact, I had never really gone to school on a regular basis at all since the 5th grade. I was in a school for a month or two at a time until I was pulled out and on the road again. But even on the road, I read like crazy: novels, business books, texts and my mom home schooled me, as well. So when I say I "satisfied some prerequisites," I mean I squeezed in years of missed school in a couple of semesters. I filled in the gaps and ended up with a GED at age 22, and with a 4.0 GPA, I was accepted as a transfer student to UCD.

After 6 months in the apartment, my parents had found a nice house in nearby Northglenn. It had everything I had hoped for: a fireplace, a mailbox, and even a swimming pool. I loved to sit out in the backyard working on my tan and listening to the Knicks's game on the radio, all while watching my brothers Chase and Shaun play with the kids next door. It seemed like home. The kids would play basketball, hide and seek, and sometimes I would even go over and offer the three kids a "fourth" player for an even two-on-two game of hoops. I had become quite a gym rat since I moved to Colorado and I loved to be outside. My body was strong and lean and I had lost all the weight I had put on in California.

I was also enjoying my newfound life as a college student. Going to class, exploring Colorado and just soaking in the environment was a paradise unimagined just a few months earlier. Then one day a miraculous thing happened; I saw a girl go into the house next door. She was tall and lean and absolutely stunning. She looked like a supermodel. She was about my age, maybe younger, she had beautiful almond-shaped eyes, and I could tell even from a distance that she was gentle and kind. It was just something about the way she carried herself.

One day while the neighbor kid was over, I asked her about the girl I had seen. "Is that your sister?"

"Yes, she is home from college for the weekend."

Sometimes I still think of my sister-in-law as that little girl in a red ball cap who spoke my future wife's name to me for the very first time. "Her name is Heather. "

Heather and I had a faced-paced and thrilling ride on the dating roller coaster. We spent every moment we could together. I would drive all the way to Boulder (20 miles) just to pick her up at her dorm, and drive her to my house so we could spend a couple of hours together. We would watch a movie at my parents' house or just talk for hours, and then I would drive her all the way back so she could make class in the morning. Sometimes I would leave Denver and drive all the way to Boulder just to pop into one of her classes and sit with her for an hour. I was falling in love and in a big way.

One day after we had been seeing each other about three months, we drove up into the Boulder foothills to just sit and look out at the lights. I told her casually that I was probably going to ask her to marry me one day. What neither of us knew was that day was today. As we sat and soaked up the cool night air, I became increasingly aware of how much I wanted—nope, scratch that—how much I *needed* her in my life forever. Before I knew it, I asked her if she would marry me—just like that, totally unplanned. And she said yes! We drove down the hill and had cheesecake at a small diner. It wasn't the grand spectacle I imagined that moment would be. I don't think it was what Heather dreamed of either, but it was uniquely ours—and from then on, everything was "ours."

Heather and I moved into a two-bedroom apartment in Northglenn and set about starting our adult lives together. She was working part-time in the childcare field and I was selling mattresses, of all things. We bought a little Ford Festiva and commuted our asses off between school and work, all the while still getting to know each other. We were engaged at that point and planning on taking our time before setting the date.

I started drinking again. I say that like it meant something, but it really didn't. I never *quit* drinking. I never really thought of booze as a problem. The problems I experienced in California, I wrote off to an identity crisis mixed with hardcore drug use. I was done with drugs; that was non-negotiable. But it felt so grown up to come home from a long day at work and relax in my own living room with a cold beer. My wife-to-be would cook us a nice meal or I'd prepare one on my days off. Booze just seemed to fit in nicely. I was working full-time 45 hours a week and going to school all day on my two days off. Hell, I deserve to reward myself, right?

I kept on working and going to school, and Heather kept working to help support our common cause. She had decided she needed a break from college and now seemed like as good a time as any. I can honestly say at this point in my life, that although I was drinking to excess on occasion, I didn't feel as though it was a problem. The only problem was that I stopped working out; I just couldn't find the time anymore. I was also eating more than I should. It was just so romantic to come home and put on some music, open up a bottle of wine (or two) and cook up every imaginable dish I could think of. I had never cooked before and I found I liked it. In my mind's eye I would picture my grandparents' house and feel the soft and subtle peace that came from the smell of the food simmering, I could almost hear the ice cubes rattling in my step-grandfather's glass as he would sit in his comfortable chair and talk politics and sports.

I became quite attached to the whole process of drinking, as well as the good feelings it created inside me. I would go to the liquor store, buy some alcohol, and then proceed next door to the grocery store and buy groceries to prepare before Heather arrived home from work. I was being a great future husband, cooking for my wife and trying on my grown-up slippers. All week long I looked forward to my days off so I could repeat this ritual. The dinners got more and more extravagant and the booze became more and more plentiful.

I was starting to put on some weight again, but still everything appeared to be moving forward perfectly. I was maintaining a 4.0 grade average and excelling at work. I was developing a reputation as the big boy on the playground when it came to the sales staff. I loved to talk to people. I had a way of making a connection with people that seemed to supersede any preconceived notion the customer may have had before they entered the store. Month after month I worked hard and broke many sales records.

I was offered promotion after promotion, but I refused. I was in school for a purpose; I wanted to be a doctor. Eventually, I had to switch my schedule. I had to go from part-time school and full-time work, to full-time student. It was the only way I could schedule my classes. This opened the door for me to experience something truly life changing. My reputation as a sales producer was about to explode and launch me to national awareness in the industry. My company told me they couldn't afford to pay me full-time salary and benefits for part-time work so they switched me to a 100% commissioned position. I was nervous at first because I didn't want to experience a large drop in pay, but it really forced me to become a student of the sales process and refine my communication skills.

I was only working a couple of hours on Friday evenings, plus Saturdays and Sundays, but my income nearly doubled over what I had been making full-time—and in the year to come, I set the national sales record for the 300-store chain. The national sales trainer came to Colorado to meet me and was completely shocked when she learned that I was attending school full-time and only working 18 hours a week. I felt like I had the world by the balls. In reality, it had me by the balls and I didn't even feel a pinch.

I would come home from work each day riding a high from life in general as well as the day's sales victories. I was in love with my girl, I was making a great living, and I was working my way through college. I had finally pulled myself out of whatever cycle I was in as a youth and connected myself to a community. My weight continued to bounce up and down dramatically, however. It seemed like I would lose and gain 50 pounds with an alarming regularity. The main culprit, I noticed, was alcohol. When I was drinking heavily, I didn't want to work out—and I ate recklessly.

Heather and I got married and moved into a small house in Louisville, a suburb of Boulder. We were renting the place, but it was a huge upgrade from the apartment. Home ownership, once a fantasy of monumental proportion, seemed as though it might actually be possible one day soon. I could absolutely see spending my whole life here in Colorado. We continued to work trying to make true that vision I once had of having a house where the grown kids could come home for the holidays as adults. I was still doing well at work, Heather was in a new position in the radiology department at the hospital in Louisville, and we were pulling down two decent incomes, all while I was still in school. Two years came and went in that little house in Louisville, and we were very happy. But just when you feel indestructible, and you let your hands drop just an inch, the world has a way of coming along and handing you a real sucker punch.

My good friend Dan and I had decided to take a weekend trip to Fort Collins to have some fun and blow off some steam. We had known each other for a couple years, and were as close as any two friends could ever be—and still are today. We were going to play golf, smoke some fine cigars, go out to a steakhouse and frequent all the local bars. Times were good, we were both making a lot of money and we liked to flash it around every so often. My sales numbers were now becoming secondary to the legendary amounts of alcohol I would drink on the weekends, and Dan was no slouch in the booze department either. When we went out, we did it grand style.

We checked into a fine hotel and I started to call the restaurant for a reservation, but before we dropped our suitcases, both of our lives changed instantly when Dan's phone rang.

"Cancer?" I heard Dan say. "Are they sure? He's only 36 years old, for God's sake."

Dan got off the phone and looked at me for a while before speaking. He sat down on the edge of the hotel bed and told me that a couple of weeks ago his brother Dave had started to complain that he was having difficulty swallowing. He had done some internet research on his own and convinced himself he had cancer; turned out he was right. Of course, we all thought Dave was just psyching himself out. He would go in for a couple of routine tests and we would find out everything was ok; he just needed to change his diet or get more exercise. That's what happens in the real world, right?

I didn't even have a clue what to say to my friend. We checked out of the hotel and drove back to Denver. To say that Dan and I had become close friends would not be accurate—we were practically family. We worked together, we played golf together, and we always seemed to be on the exact same page. At work he would be in one store location across town while I was at another, and we could actually talk on the phone every day for hours and never run out of stupid shit to say. On the weekends we worked together at the store he managed. For the entire hour-long drive home we hardly said a word, we just sat in our own thoughts, staring ahead in silence. I think we were stunned into silence.

"Should I say something," I wondered. "What would I to say?" I knew his brother very well, and considered him a friend, although not a close one. Everyone's lives had changed forever; I knew that. Hospitals, treatment, stress, struggle were all on the horizon. And David Lynn was in a battle for his very life.

"It's nothing. It will all turn out to be a big scare for nothing." I did say something to that affect as Dan pulled up to my house and I got out. "Keep me posted, man. It's going to be fine, we'll figure this out."

"I will. I'm scared," Dan said. He didn't turn to look at me. He just looked straight ahead over the steering wheel.

"Me too," I croaked out.

Dan backed out the driveway and headed home to be with his brother. He was gearing up for an all-out fight, a battle that would carry the Lynn family from hospital to hospital and as far away as Mexico, trying to exhaust every available treatment known.

I met David Lynn for the first time when Dan and I met him for a beer in Denver. Dan's brother was a large guy with a huge a smile that seemed to say, "I know something you don't." He looked me right square in the eyes like he was trying to see through me, but not in a way that made me uncomfortable. Even at over 6 feet tall and 300 pounds, he was still a warm soul. His hands were as large as cinderblocks, and he appeared as if he could throw you through the wall if he wanted to. He looked intimidating; however, it didn't take long before we were chatting like we'd known each other since childhood. As the night went on, the conversations seemed to shift topic without notice or warning. Our voices raised and lowered, and laughter reigned supreme. Regardless of the details, we figured out we could all debate either side of an issue.

I started to get a clearer picture of who this large man in the Coke-bottle thick glasses was. He was actually a kind spirit hiding somewhere underneath his abrasive surface. He and Dan had a tough life as kids; they lost their dad to a horrible car accident before they ever got to know him. They had each other, and they had their mom. There were some similarities between how they grew up and my own experiences—at least from the perspective of bouncing around a lot and building a wall around themselves from the world. I can't say that I ever really got to know "the true" Dave Lynn, but I liked what I did know. He came to my house for a Super Bowl party and I saw him many times over the course of a year or so. There were parties, and family get-togethers where we always shot the shit and jousted a little verbally. It was always out of respect and fun, though, and I considered him a friend.

I was meeting Dan at the hospital to hear the latest results of Dave's surgery. The doctors were going to open Dave up and see what they could do with the tumor that was growing out of control on his esophagus. The entire family and many friends were gathered about, awaiting the doctors' report. While we waited, Dan and I went for a walk around the hospital and talked.

I told Dan, "I am here for you, brother. Dave is in great hands, everyone is supporting him, the doctors are doing what they can, so my question is, how are *you* doing?" He smiled and told me he wasn't well. I pulled a bottle of 90-proof schnapps out of my pocket and asked if he wanted a snort of stress relief. We sat and talked about what was going on at work. Dan had taken a leave of absence to be there for his brother and hadn't heard any of the juicy details of the company soap opera, but he didn't appear in the least bit interested. As a matter of fact, Dan had just gotten back from Mexico where they took Dave for an experimental procedure. As we sat and drank, Dan relayed to me the obvious: the laetrile treatment had failed to shrink the tumor.

We took turns sipping out of the bottle and catching up on exactly what was going on with Dave and the options moving forward. There was one thing for sure—no one was quitting or giving up hope yet. Dan and I walked back into the hospital to get the results. The doctors came in to share their findings with the family. We were all thinking best possible scenario—they got the tumor the hell outta there and we are done. Have fun; see you at your 89th birthday. Instead, we stood and listened as they explained that when the surgeon opened Dave up, he saw that the cancer had spread everywhere. It had moved throughout his entire body and wasn't slowing down. They closed him back up and came out to talk with the family. Game over.

Six months had passed since the night Dan and I drove to Fort Collins for a weekend of golf and partying. Dave's battle with cancer had taken him all over the state, to several hospitals and many doctors. The family sought healing through conventional means, from alternate therapies, natural herbs, and even an Indian Shaman—not to mention the experimental treatment in the Mexican clinic. In the end, the cancer had destroyed David's body. It never touched his spirit or his will to fight, though.

I was there with my friend Dan as his brother passed. I hugged him and told him I would be there for him forever. This experience may have taken one brother away from Dan, but another was added. Not a replacement by any means, but someone to count on for sure. I told Dan that I had read many amazing stories of the human will to survive and endure, but I have never been so inspired and touched by a single individual's depth of strength. David's battle with cancer was the bravest and most courageous act I have ever witnessed.

We always tend to think of death as something that happens to old people or other people. We all know we are going to die, yet somehow we are able to avoid thinking about our own mortality. We are, in fact, willing to avoid thinking about our own deaths at almost all cost. My conceptions of what death was and how fragile life can be were rocked to the core of my being when I saw Dave pass so suddenly. What happened to him was an act of violence—not in the actual action which caused him to draw his last breath, but in the way he was ripped so suddenly from a normal life. He was jerked out of his place just as he was just finding his rhythm; he was in his early 30's, recently married and talking about having kids. His was not the funeral anyone ever expected to attend. Observing this heart-wrenching and tragic unfolding of events changed me forever. I no longer felt safe and warm. I didn't feel bulletproof like I previously had. I felt venerable. There were, however, many positive things that came into my life through this experience. Dan and I, once "golf pals" and drinking buddies, became profoundly more important to each other. You hear people describe close friends as "brothers" or even "part of the family," but that didn't come close to depicting our friendship.

Life went on, at least for the rest of us, as we tried to make sense of who it was that we were now and how exactly we had changed—and of course, what we would become going forward. I started to rethink my life's goals. I started to examine very closely where my career and college goals were taking me. I started to look at specifics of the life of being a doctor. Not the big picture of "helping others" or other such platitudes, but what would be my daily ritual and how would that affect my happiness and ability to nurture and provide a healthy environment for a family. Being in the hospital and watching Dave's fight from a dual "outside and inside" perspective gave me a unique picture of the medical world. I watched the battle from the perspective of my friend, who was hopelessly losing his brother no matter what he did. I watched Dan's mom have her son ripped from her arms after losing her own husband so early on in their own marriage, and I watched the doctors and nurses all try to do anything they could to battle the disease and comfort all of us. I watched this through the eyes of a friend, the eyes of a brother, and the eyes of a medical student.

I came to realize the obvious—that nothing is written in stone. No one is guaranteed any specific amount of time on earth; certainly no one is guaranteed happiness itself. I further came to realize that it wasn't written in stone that I go to medical school. Suddenly the prospect of finishing my undergrad degree, going to 4 years of medical school, then residency and internship, didn't seem so inviting. I had opportunity knocking at my door every day to advance at the company where I was working. The owners of the company were even starting to talk about backing me in a franchise, should I decide I wanted to jump into the fire of business ownership. I decided to take the summer away from school and do some soul searching.

Speed Bump

I decided to chase the dream. Not the dream of being a doctor, but the dream of making a life for myself in Colorado—the dream of buying a house, raising a family and jumping in the game. After a summer of playing golf, drinking a lot of beer, and making some money at my part-time job, I decided to take a full-time position with the company. The timing was right. A management position within the company had opened up and they really wanted me aboard. In fact, they were offering to take me all the way up the chain in a single swoop—to store manager. I took the job with the understanding that I wanted to learn everything there was to know about the retail furniture business in the event that I wanted to go into business for myself one day. The company had talked to me about possibly franchising, so I put all that on the stove and let it simmer.

In the ensuing time, I went about the merge from salesperson to manager. I had a tough task ahead of me. The guy I was taking over for was very successful and a tremendous salesman in his own right. He vacated his position to oversee a chain of stores for the company in another state. Furthermore, there was very little room for improvement because the store I was taking over was already the number one store in the state and was doing quite well. My task was simple—don't mess it up.

My first month in my new position of store manager was a good one. Well, it was a *great* one, to be precise. The first month's sales were actually the third largest total in the store's history. Compounding the accomplishment was the fact that my first month as manager was historically the slowest month of the year. And honestly, I was just getting started. I smashed the all-time sales record for the store in my third month as manager. Then I went on to beat that month three out of the next four months. What was more incredible was the profit margin went through the roof at the same time. I learned that treating customers well, taking care of them as people, worked as a model to not just feel really good about what you were doing—but it really set you apart from your competitors. And if you would ever like to experience a pleasant and nurturing relationship with your boss, just increase sales by 40% across the board while raising the profit margin 8%.

I was paid based on how well I did as a manager, and I was blessed with a great staff and a great economy too. The money was rolling in like it was building up in a dam and someone had opened the gate. I bought a new car and a house in the same month. Heather and I picked out a lovely home in a new community and started socking away money while also enjoying the rewards of success. Everything was great on the surface and, in fact, it seemed much better than that. I thought I was completely happy. Everything seemed great down to the core—everything, that is, except for my drinking. My relationship with my wife was solid, I was excelling at work, and I was becoming more and more the person I had hoped to be. So why was I drinking so much? What was going on below the surface? The weekend drinking had now become quite regular, and like the Pringles Potato Chip commercial, "I couldn't have just one."

Also troubling was that late at night, when I was alone, the drinking was getting dark. In the light of day it was easy to just blow off my drinking as nothing worrisome, just a little extra partying with the guys. And I did write it off as just that, but there were times when I was sitting in my den late at night after drinking an entire of bottle of scotch by myself that it didn't seem like much of a party. I did what I could do to make my drinking appear "polished" on the surface—I drank scotch. I drank brandy. I drank in fine restaurants. I drank while driving my brand new car (well, at least the car was polished). I drank when I took my mom out for lunch at the finest places in town. I drank with my golf buddies and I drank with my bosses in their season seats for the Colorado Avalanche. I pretty much just drank all the damn time. I didn't really need an excuse to drink but I was sure good at finding them:

"I'm Irish."

"It's the playoffs."

"It's Memorial Day."

"I'm in a sales business."

One of the ways I enjoyed my newfound success was to buy expensive booze. I became a connoisseur of fine wines and an aficionado of cigars. I romanticized my drinking with music, candles, food, and movies showcasing affluence and indulgence. Alcohol was becoming my most cherished piece of jewelry. I also had acquired an entire network of people to share my newfound status symbol with. It seemed like every single person I hung out with drank. Most of the new salespeople were hired right out of college and came to us direct from the frat house. The vendors from the company drank heavily; even the owners of the company drank to excess and didn't seem to mind if we all did the same. The most difficult time to identify that you have a problem is when everyone else around you has the same problem. And that's how it was, or at least that's how it seemed. We would have raging company parties with open bars and open arms.

"Come drink with us!" (It should have been on the company logo.)

It got to be where going out and drinking until 2 am, even when you had to open the store the next morning, was not only acceptable, it was bragged about. Every single weekend was a party. There was no question what we were going to be doing, it was only a matter of where—maybe downtown, maybe a football game or just at a BBQ at the owner's house—but we were going to drink and we were going to drink a lot. Most of the time I didn't have to go very far to find the party and, in fact, many times it was delivered directly to me in the form of a phone call circulated through the company:

"You are meeting us at Bennigans, right, Dave?"

"Hell yeah."

Or sometimes my invitation to drink would simply come spitting out the fax machine:

"COMPANY FUNCTION AT THE BOWLING ALLEY THIS SATURDAY"

We worked hard and we played hard. At company functions we played even harder than usual because the booze was "on the house." This created an interesting atmosphere of drinking, to say the least. The temptation to drink was amplified simply by the availability and fact that the alcohol was complimentary. We also had many "big ego" salespeople (me included) who liked to drink and throw their money around at the same time. Invariably this would lead to many rounds of top-shelf alcohol purchased and shared with everyone as a means of flexing the "paycheck muscle." It seemed every 15-20 minutes a waitress came by with a tray of some exotic shot of alcohol purchased by one of the crew. I would look around the room and find a co-worker looking at me while raising a shot glass in the air to acknowledge, "Hey, I bought you a drink."

Everyone at these functions drank, but we all didn't drink with the same reckless abandon. At the time, I was convinced that everyone was drinking the same as I was, or at least at their own pace that would produce a similar level of intoxication as my own. I later found I was wrong. Some people actually enjoyed a few cocktails and went home with some of their wits still about them—how crazy. It's interesting how we filter information to support a preconceived idea; I tended to notice the people drinking excessively and completely dismissed those who didn't indulge as if they weren't even there. I also did this with members of my own family.

Years after I had quit drinking I realized that whether it was a co-worker at a company function or my father-in-law at the Christmas party, most folks really didn't drink that much at all. Certainly not anything close to what I was drinking. What happened was I remembered I was always having a drink with someone. I may hang with my cousin for two drinks and then my father-in-law for three drinks, etc. But the only constant was me. By the end of the evening I had my twenty drinks; they in return, had their three or four each. Little did my friends and family know that the real drinking came later in the night when I got home.

I was amassing a reputation as being the guy that could drink insane amounts of alcohol without getting drunk. Of course I was drunk, I just didn't seem drunk. Even those closest to me, such as my wife or mother, couldn't tell how much I had to drink—or sometimes even if I had been drinking at all. I could drink to the point of total blackout; yet even in this state, apparently I was under some sort of control. I could go to bed so drunk that I didn't remember an entire late night conversation with my wife, yet when I explained to her that I was "pretty popped last night" she would say, "Really? You didn't seem like it." Maybe she was being kind. I'll never know for sure.

But the negative consequences were piling up, too. All of these small little issues that would arise, such as blacking out entire conversations or drinking to the late hours alone, would somehow become justification for continuing to drink instead of causing me to quit like most sane people. "Hey, I am still making it work. I am not having issues with the wife. How bad could it be?" I thought.

The embarrassing truth is I was almost proud of my drinking prowess. I liked it when people would gather around me and listen intently to my wild animated drinking stories. I liked being able to drink more than everyone else. I enjoyed being constantly prodded to regale the group with tales of previous drinking endeavors. "This is a part of who I am," I thought. Drinking was just another thing that I was really good at. Not my fault if you couldn't handle your booze... but the truth is I was losing control and I was using every skill I had as a sales person to convince myself it was ok.

Let's talk more about my drinking.

Months went by, as they have a way of doing, and everything aside from my alcohol consumption seemed to be on the uptick. I was drinking to excess almost every time I drank now, yet it was still very difficult to think of what I was doing as anything other than "heavy drinking" or just "enjoying myself." And if all I was doing was drinking a little too much on the weekends that might have been all right. The problem was I wasn't only drinking more than my friends; I was drinking differently than my friends. Even after a night of drinking for 4-5 hours until the bar closed, it was normal practice for me to go home and continue to drink. In fact, I enjoyed this time alone as much as I did being around others in a social atmosphere. The two parts of the evening just seemed to go together—almost a logical extension of the night. By myself late at night I could drink a large amount of alcohol in a short period of time without having to worry about getting home or passing out in public.

I remember I would come home after a night of partying and put in a movie. It didn't matter what movie as long as there was drinking in it. I would pour the alcohol into the glass, and even in this highly inebriated state, I was keenly aware of the booze. The alcohol was like a secret lover with whom I was separated from during the party. She was there and I was there, but we had to keep up appearances. We may have danced a couple times and run into each other during the evening, but I couldn't really be with her as much as I wanted until we were alone.

I would take in the smell of the scotch, the sound of the ice clinking in the glass, and the burning touch of the alcohol to my lips. It was both cold and warm at the same time, cold as it hit my mouth and warm and comforting on the way down. I would close my eyes and sway on the couch, back and forth as I drank myself farther from the world. The sound of the television would bring me back to reality on occasion as Dudley Moore's Arthur made a sharp one-liner delivered in slurring eloquence. He made it seem a perfectly honorable thing to be drunk and sloppy. Or on a different evening I might intently watch Doc Holiday drink himself into a stupor, only to still be able to out-shoot and outwit everyone in the bar. I simply loved the drunken hero.

These late-night solo drinking sessions were now a normal part of my drinking. I would go out on the weekends, come back home to unwind myself further into the alcohol abyss, and seemingly return to normal the next day. On the days I drank, I worked everything I enjoyed into my drinking. I would sit with my wife for hours and talk while drinking. I would cook for hours while drinking. I would sit with my guitar or listen to music or read books, all while drinking. I didn't need to drink to enjoy theses thing, but I enjoyed them more under the umbrella of a sweet warm alcohol-induced glow.

I continued to justify my drinking by comparing myself to clichés of the tired old pathetic alcoholic. I was doing well at work, I wasn't a mess (well, not in public anyway) and I didn't miss work. Fuck it—I'm ok—deny, deny, deny. There were glimpses, however, of the hardcore abuses to come. The frequency of my drinking wasn't the only thing building; the severity was, as well. More and more it seemed like I was depriving myself of something when I wasn't drinking. It was uncomfortable to "not drink." When I did get to the weekend, I would jump completely into the bottle. I had developed a very effective on-off switch for my drinking, but the side effect was intense pressure. As the pressure of not drinking every day would build, it would surge into a runaway current of compulsion when the switch was finally flipped on.

I flipped the drinking switch to the "on" position one particular evening after I had been away for a couple days. I wasn't planning on going out to get hammered; in fact, I was going over to my buddy Dan's house with my guitar. I had been giving him free guitar lessons and we were planning on just jamming and sipping on a few really fine glasses of scotch whiskey. Dan and I had recently bested our boss in a head-to-head sales contest. On the line was a $250 bottle of scotch that I was eager to sample. I had become very appreciative of fine scotches and I had never tried the Johnny Walker Blue Label—hadn't even heard of it, in fact, until a week or two earlier. I made our bet with one of the owners of the company when I asserted that we could outsell him over the course of a busy holiday weekend.

I received our 25-year-old aged-to-perfection prize earlier that morning at the sales meeting, and I was looking forward to sharing it with Dan over cigars and guitar chords. After work I changed my clothes, grabbed my acoustic, and made my way to Denver. Dan and his wife Monica had just moved into a three-story townhouse near the Cherry Creek section of Denver and were still in the unpacking process. Monica was out for the evening so it was just us guys to fend for ourselves and entertain each other. We moved around some boxes and cleared off a couch and some chairs to relax on. We put some meat on the grill and wasted no time opening our bottle of scotch, as well as our guitar cases. The scotch was indescribably smooth and nothing short of perfect. It was as smooth as spring water wrapped in silk, and it left the mouth with zero aftertaste. It seemed to cleanse your pallet as it went down like a houseguest that cleans up after himself so well you never knew he was there. This was a scotch that deserved to be savored and I was looking forward to sampling a little bit here with Dan and then saving the rest for future special occasions.

I started to feel a nice warm glow from the booze and my fingers were dancing around the fret board. We sipped the regal alcohol and played some Eagles songs as well as other classic rock favorites. Dan and I always had a great time whether we were on a fishing boat in Mexico or just strumming a couple of guitars in a living room. As we finished song after song, we finished glass after glass of scotch. Dan upped the ante by offering some painkillers and I was in without a thought. The only thing better than being drunk was being drunk with narcotics... at least I wasn't doing coke or meth, I thought.

I was in mid-lyric when I glanced at the bottle on the table and saw it was about half empty already. I was very disappointed to see the supply of the good stuff dissipating so rapidly. I had every intention of having a snort or two of this fine whiskey and that's it. I envisioned this bottle of scotch hanging out above my refrigerator for months as I shared a single taste with friends and family as the holidays came and went. Now I stared in disbelief at the half-empty bottle. I was half snapped by now and playing music with $125 worth of Blue Label in me. Oh well, good times, good friends, right?

We played a few more tunes and continued to drink (about ¾ of the bottle gone) before finally deciding we should save the last of the scotch for another night. But this night was young, so we decided we should head out to a bar for a couple of Johnny Walker Blacks—you know, "just to compare the difference while the Blue was still fresh in our minds." We went to a hole-in-the-wall bar and ordered a couple of drinks. The conversation and booze started to flow rapidly and I don't recall how it happened exactly, but we ended up getting talked into shooting some pool with some other guys. I was on the absolute edge of being out of control. I drank at least 6-7 double scotches within the first hour we were there and I felt my composure slipping away at times. Add to that the effects of the Vicodin, and I was a time bomb. I was ok for now, but walking a fine line.

One of the fellows we were shooting pool with liked to talk a lot of trash. It didn't seem to matter to him whether he was losing or winning, making shots or missing shots, he just ran his mouth constantly. After another 3-4 doubles of whiskey in me, I had had enough. Growing up in New York had made it difficult for me to listen to what I perceived to be disrespectful talk for too long without ending or escalating the situation. I got right in his face and placed my hands on either of his cheeks like I was his grandmother. But instead of telling him how much I missed him like his grandmother might, I slapped him hard—first with one hand, then the other. He took inventory of my 250-pound frame as I told him to keep his fucking mouth shut if he didn't want to be dragged out of the bar and stuffed in a can. He didn't have much to say at that moment and, in fact, complied with the request for a while.

I am very embarrassed to say that I didn't leave him alone, though. In fact, from what I can remember, I bullied him for the rest of the evening every time he said anything. I was approaching the 25+ drink tally (plus earlier drinking) and this was usually blackout territory for me. We continued to play pool for a while as I continued to slap the ever-loving shit out of this guy and humiliate him in front of his friends every time I felt the urge. All he did to deserve my "special attention" was to get a little cocky during a game of pool—at least that's all I can remember. Way to go, tough guy. There were several times in my drinking career when I felt unable to stop myself from whatever it was I was doing even though I was keenly aware that I was going to regret my actions the next day. This was certainly one of those nights.

We arrived back at Dan's house after making a 2 am pit stop at Taco Bell. The credit card receipt showed we spent $24.54, and if you have ever been to Taco Bell, you know that $25 buys a truckload of food for two people. As we smashed and banged our way into the house in the middle of the night, I was surprised Dan's wife didn't call the police and report us as intruders. The house was completely dark and quiet but Monica's car out front alerted us that she had returned from her trip and must be sleeping upstairs. We bumped into furniture, laughed loudly despite trying to be quiet. You know, those really loud "whisper laughs" that drunks employ thinking they are keeping the noise down, when in fact they are almost screaming. We decided to go down into the basement to eat and thus try to get some distance between Dan's sleeping wife and us.

As we made our descent into the basement, me in the lead and Dan right behind, I was carrying three bags of Taco Bell and the remaining ¾ empty bottle of Johnny Walker Blue Label I'd grabbed from the table as we walked by. The stairs down to the basement were steep. I had taken two stairs on my descent into the basement when I stepped on something soft and squishy. Dan and Monica had six cats and my first thought was, "Damn, I just killed Piper."

In an amazing effort to save Dan's cat from being squashed, I tried to pick up my foot before I did any further damage. This resulted in me somehow catapulting myself over the entire flight of stairs. Now, I am sure many people have fallen down stairs due to intoxication. I, however, may be the only person to fall "over" stairs. I say this because I didn't touch a single piece of stair or floor until I landed on the basement floor. The only thing that saved me was the three bags of Taco Bell and the only piece of furniture that had been unpacked and carried to the basement, a folding metal chair that I completely mangled by landing perfectly on top of it and crushing it in the same instant.

The resulting aftermath of the free-fall was me lying on the floor in a mess

OUT THERE · 41

of tacos and burritos with a twisted metal chair woven around my limbs like a full-length scarf. I was laughing before I hit the ground and so was Dan. My pants were torn up and my knees were bloody. I felt cheated that I hadn't had Dan's view of the tragedy as it unfolded and I fell over his stairs right in front of him. As we were laughing, we heard more hysterical cackling coming from the third floor. It appeared that Monica was awakened by the sounds of the event, which evidentially were equally as funny when simply heard secondhand. The cat, which was not a cat at all but a box of chocolates, was unharmed. Miraculously, the bottle of scotch also made it through my freestyle plummet unscathed. After the laughter finally subsided, Dan gave up and went upstairs to bed after he saw our food had been pounded into what he considered to be an inedible blob of beans and sauce. I was not so easily discouraged, however.

The rest of the night involved me sorting through that mess and tangle of Mexican fast food, eating what I could pull out of the globs and wrappers smeared together as a result of my impact. There was absolutely nothing funny going on now in the basement by myself. I didn't feel sophisticated or refined while I was enjoying these "spoils of success." In fact, I was so drunk I had to consciously focus on my hand and direct it to the item I was trying to pick up. I could barely keep my eyes open, much less enjoy anything that I was trying to eat. I had been reduced to a slobbering fraction of a functioning human. I wanted to eat and I was too drunk to get it right. I am sure the remainder of that $250 bottle of scotch was a wonderful selection perfectly suited for my fine dining choice of the evening. I am not sure exactly how much food I managed to get into my body, but make no damn mistake—I finished off that exquisite bottle of scotch just in time to pass out covered in food, blood, and cat hair from lying on the basement floor.

There are times, even in the depths of addiction and self-delusion, when it becomes clear that all systems are not go. "Houston we may have a serious chemical problem" was being broadcast into the consciousness. Alcoholics refer to these as moments of clarity. If that's true, what follows should have been the clearest moment of my life.

It was a Saturday night and I was driving down the highway when all of a sudden I knew it, I was way too fucking drunk to be driving. I looked at the speedometer and it read 95 mph. Crap. The music was cranking at full volume and just a few seconds ago I felt fine. I was singing at the top of my lungs and beating out the rhythm of the song on the steering wheel. Suddenly I started to feel disoriented and nauseas. Now I was starting to swerve all over the place and I couldn't summons the coordination to just stay in my goddamn lane. I closed one eye to see if that would help me to focus on the road that was dancing and shifting around in front of me as if I was seeing it through a curtain of fog and liquid. "Holy crap, I am going wreck this thing," I thought.

Strangely, none of these impending issues compelled me to take my foot off the accelerator or pull off to the side of the road, I just kept trucking. I was heading up 1-25 North, bouncing around between the painted stripes thinking that if I could just get home I may never drink again. I was starting to think I may be a touch out of control with my alcohol consumption. (Ya think?) I was also feeling an increasing amount of pressure to get off the road—or at least get somewhere where I was less likely to encounter a police car. I took the next exit without thinking and almost went right off the ramp and into the ditch—if it weren't for a last minute course correction.

I tried to remember how much I had to drink. That was going to prove to be difficult because I couldn't even remember where I was coming from. Hell, I couldn't remember when I left or how I even got into my truck. I seemed to just "come to consciousness" driving down the road. Just then, I did remember something—I remembered something that had happened only about 15 minutes earlier that I had somehow lost to my inebriation until now. I was on the phone talking to Dan and I had asked him if he had "taken the pill." What the hell did that mean?

"Come on, man. I took mine, you should take yours... Take the pill, take it, man!"

I was trying to make sense of this fragmented memory of conversation from just a few minutes earlier, all the while still trying to navigate my vehicle (using one open eye) through the streets of Denver. Suddenly I remembered another little piece of the puzzle. One of the guys from our warehouse had received some painkillers for an injury he recently endured, and earlier that day, he gave Dan and me each one of the narcotic painkillers. At some point in the evening, and I think it may have been just as I got into my vehicle to drive home, I had added the mystery pill to the contents of my already overloaded blood chemistry. With the narcotics working through my drunken body, I decided to call my friend and see if he had also taken his pill, or if I was alone and crazy to do such a thing.

I honestly have no idea why I even decided to accept the painkiller so nonchalantly in the first place; why I actually swallowed the pill after an entire evening of drinking was another question altogether. The hard truth of the matter was I was so drunk by the time I took the pill that I could barely remember doing it. Now I was driving down the road at 95 mph, weaving around like blind drunk moron. Other parts of the evening flashed through my mind as well—a game of pool at Jose O'Shea's. A tray full of whiskey shots purchased at some other random bar, a drunken argument over sports. I vaguely remembered stopping at a friend's house around midnight on my way to the next bar. I was disoriented and growing more alarmed by the minute. This confused state happened to me sometimes after heavy drinking. It was almost a panicky feeling like I was forgetting everything while it was happening, which only increased the discomfort I was already having.

I got off the freeway and onto the side streets, trying to stealth my way home. I really don't recall much of the journey once I got off the freeway but I do remember the speed bumps. The section of road I was on went through a residential neighborhood where the city installed long, brightly painted speed bumps to deter motorists from speeding through while children were at play. I took the first bump doing what must have been about 40 mph because it shook me so hard my hands flew off the steering wheel and I went flying over into the passenger seat. In a scrambling effort, I somehow managed to get back up and into the driver's side before the vehicle struck a parked car or curb. I tried to gather myself and just as I regained control of the car, I hit the next speed bump. This time I was a little more prepared, although I was still moving at the same speed so, again, I was thrown around but managed to stay put in the driver's seat.

Then I started to vomit—the actual act of vomiting, not a figurative expression of how disgusted I was. I was physically throwing up in my car, while driving. I frantically tried to hit the button to lower the window next to me. In my inebriated reckless state, I didn't even consider hitting the brake; I just hung my head out the window and vomited as I sped through the night. I remember the cold air hitting my face as I was trying to take inventory of how much I had vomited inside the car before I got the window down... I think I may have been laughing.

I have heard it said that "God watches out for drunks," and this is most certainly true in my experience. Unexplainably, I made it back to my place without hurting myself or anyone else. I parked and just sat there for several minutes. I think even in my obtuse state I realized something very significant had occurred. But I was so drunk that I couldn't concentrate on anything for very long, and I felt almost helpless to even make it into my house. I looked over and saw that my gym bag was on the floor of the passenger side of my truck. I had gone to the gym after work before I went out on this crazy bender.

I grabbed my dress shirt out of the bag and started to try to clean up the vomit from the inside of the door of the vehicle. After a few passes with my new "cleaning rag" I summoned the strength to get out of the truck. Apparently, I had exited with my gym bag because it was around my shoulder now. I started to walk away and I noticed that there was also a mess on the outside of the vehicle. I had left a trail of my stomach contents covering the outside of the window and all along the entire length of the vehicle. Even with my limited comprehension of the situation, I figured it would be bad to leave the truck in this state. I made a couple of half-hearted swipes at the mess with some other article of clothing from my bag, put the dirty rag back in my gym bag and threw it back in the truck. There, problem solved. I staggered up the stairs and went inside.

I didn't shower; I didn't do anything that I can remember other than walk into the bedroom, drop my clothes at the foot of the bed and climb in bed with my sleeping wife. I can't imagine how horrible I must have smelled and how horrifying I must have looked, but she never said anything to me the next day. Not out of fear of starting a fight or certainly not because she wasn't concerned, she just knew I was going to have to figure this stuff out on my own. She was an angel; she had the patience of Job and she was right.

Complete horror doesn't come close to describing the feeling I had when I woke up the next day. For one, I had to be at work in less than an hour. And two, I felt like death in a microwave. I jumped out of bed and into the shower in one motion and then flew out the door without even thinking what was going on. I had the sinking feeling that something really bad had happened but I didn't remember anything—until I took a look at my truck.

The aftermath of the evening came back to me in the form of partial memories and physical stimuli at the same moment. I visually remembered vomiting out the window as I opened the door and "re-experienced it" in full Technicolor. I didn't want to touch the inside of this vehicle, much less get in it and drive it 20 miles to work. But I did. I drove to work and pulled up to the front of the store without so much as whimper or hesitation. I was working alone at the store that day, thank God, and Sundays were usually slow in the morning. I got out of the car, walked into the grocery store next door, and purchased some cleaning products and paper towels. I sat in my truck in front of my store for an hour and attempted to wash away the shame and loathing—out of my car and my head.

"This is it. Who am I kidding? I obviously have a problem here. This isn't normal." I sat and stared into space as these thoughts echoed inside my throbbing head. "I'm out. No more booze, I quit"...and I meant it—I did quit this time. The scar was deep from this wound. This was inextricably different from any other hangover or "tough morning." I was so ashamed and mortified by my actions, I could barely stop the panic waves. This hurt, deep.

In the days and weeks that followed, I immersed myself in work and my home life. I fell back into a somewhat normal pattern. I watched movies with my wife, I stayed home and just tried to relax and slow things down. The cliché is "time heals all wounds," and it turned out that the healing time for this wound was about a month. After 30 days of not consuming any alcohol at all, the severity of my actions seemed almost a distant memory. I was able to shrug it off as a moment of temporary insanity. I just drank too much, and I threw drugs on the fire to boot. No wonder I was so out of control.

"Lesson learned," I said. I wish I could say I never drank again. I can't. I wish I could say I never got heavily intoxicated after this debacle. I would be lying if I did. I was correct, however, in describing what resulted from this binge as a deep wound that scarred me, because it still hurts me today. The fact that I could have killed myself—or much worse, someone else—does not escape my consciousness. The reality was that I was in love with drinking, and I wasn't ready to say goodbye. The grip of my lover and the intoxicating effect of her spell on me left me almost powerless to abstain for very long. I was willing to forgive alcohol for all the horrible things "she" was doing to me.

When you apply yourself completely to a business goal and expect great results, you must have a large picture of what success is. I feel you must truly have a greater vision than simply amassing wealth or driving sales numbers. Although on the surface we were selling high quality furniture to clients at low prices, it really had very little to do with my real commitment. Without giving a sales meeting here in the middle of my story, I will simply say that I committed to providing my customers the best experience a person would ever have in any retail environment—ever. Now or in the future.

I gave free furniture to people if I messed up their delivery. I made people laugh and I gave myself completely away to those around me. I made friends, I laughed with folks, we putted golf balls in stores with customers, grilled burgers for families and hoped the business of making money would take care of itself. It turns out it did. Don't get me wrong, I was a fierce competitor in the industry with a firm grasp on the bottom line. I wanted all my customers— and yours, too—but I looked out for the customer's best interest in order to achieve this.

Eventually, I was asked to take over the responsibility of training all new sales employees in my unique style of sales and management. This added training aspect was another part of the business world that I truly enjoyed. I loved to teach and speak in front of groups. I have heard it said that public speaking ranks high on the "list of greatest fears," second only to death itself. I personally couldn't get enough of speaking at meetings. I loved the thrill of connecting with people; I enjoyed the looks exchanged by the audience when I said something really crazy. I savored the instant I made someone laugh at me or themselves, because I knew that immediately after that laughter response, I had created a narrow window to impact their thoughts directly.

The new employees were getting better and better, and the impact I was having on the company outside of my one store was growing. Some of it was luck; some was hard work, but my career was moving along without a hitch and I felt on-task. Mine was a difficult marriage of management and sales theories to communicate to others, but when seen in practice, it was hard to argue against the result. I was aggressive in my policies toward the competition and altruistic in my practice towards customers, and business was good.

The highest award that anyone could be awarded at my company was "Manager of the Year." This was a very sought-after milestone and a difficult one to obtain. Part of the reason for this was the incredible amount of competition in a very competitive business, but the trickiest part lay in the fact that politics were involved. In fact, the largest part of the selection process was a vote left up to all the salespeople, as well as the other managers who were competing against each other for votes.

You had to have amazing numbers, you had to be well liked, and you had to be respected by your peers. If you knocked it out of the park in sales but everyone hated you, you were probably not going to get the cash and plaque that came with the prize. I was up for the manager of the year award with my numbers being unchallenged for sales improvement, but I had a reputation for telling it like it was. I didn't sugarcoat much, but I did treat people with respect and directness. If your numbers were down, I let you know about it, but I took the time to show people how to fix problems instead of just yelling. I was curious to see how it would all pan out. In the previous year I had won "Salesperson of the Year," which was an accolade in itself, only one more to complete the two-year sweep.

The awards were always given out at the company Christmas party, and this year was to be a special party indeed. This year we had reserved an entire restaurant in downtown Denver, and I rented a limo to carry my wife and me to the gala. I truly enjoyed the company of my bosses and fellow employees and I was looking forward to a great celebration. These events were always special for everyone because the owners took the time to acknowledge each person and what they meant to the company. Each person received the affirmation of all their hard work and effort, while their peers and spouses sat and took it all in. There was a very distinct feeling of being a part of a team and this was our night to be together. We were a chain of many individual stores spread out over the entire state of Colorado. We saw each other occasionally at company training sessions and talked on the phone frequently, but this was the only time we were all under the same roof at one time.

I was sitting with eight people, all of whom I had a tremendous amount of respect for. As the owners worked the crowd and thanked the guests, we shared our own memories of the years past and poked fun at each other, as those who are comfortable around each other tend to do. We had a great meal and several cocktails and truly savored the night. As the plates and glasses were taken away, the owners took the stage to announce the winner of the awards. I sit and watched the "Salesperson of the Year" award be given out and recalled my own trip to the stage to receive that honor a year earlier. As the clapping ended and the recipient took his seat, my table, as well as the entire room, grew deathly quiet as the owner started to speak again.

"This final award for Manager of the Year is the highest honor this company has to offer any employee. If you receive this award, you have truly accomplished something in the industry. This year's winner is..."

I stood up in mid-sentence, before I realized I had, and the owner finished with "...David Clark."

The owner gave me a sly look as I walked up to the front of the room. I shook his hand and took the microphone. I thanked everyone who helped me get to this place, and there were many to thank. I was handed a stack of 100-dollar bills and a nice plaque that still hangs in my office at home today. I would love to tell you how the rest of the evening played out but I can't. I drank myself into the oblivion of blackout. I didn't do anything stupid or crazy, so I was told, but I drank an entire bottle of scotch. My wife said I had a great time; I had to take her word for it.

❻
Ground Zero

I came home from work one night to find my wife Heather lying in bed reading, she looked very cute in her slippers and T-shirt, so I walked over to her and kissed her forehead. She smiled and handed me a tiny sweater. I thought what a strange thing it was to give to me. It looked like something you would put on a teddy bear or a small stuffed animal. I turned it over in my hands and looked at it more closely; I noticed it wasn't a sweater at all but a tiny Yankees jersey. I realized this was my wife's way of telling me that I was going to be a dad. I was in shock—and I was glowing. We just lay in bed next to each other and smiled and talked. It was a fantastic night. I was drunk.

I cannot describe the amount of pure energy and total contentment I felt as I drove to work. The music sounded better, the sun felt warmer and I was bursting at the seams. I thought I might jump out of the car and skip all the way to work. I was going to be a father! Wow, the real deal. I have created another human for the world. My mind danced around all the possibilities. Was it going to be a boy? Will he play professional baseball? Was it a girl? Will she be a Supreme Court Justice? One thing I knew; this child would be loved and given every possible advantage that was in my power to supply.

Looking back now, it's amazing to me that my drinking wasn't causing me more alarm. I was considering every tiny detail of my life and how it could impact my unborn child—money, education, health care. How is it that my drinking was off my radar? It was a cosmic joke of epic stature. I felt that there wasn't anything going on that I didn't have complete control over. And yet at the same time, alcohol was sinking its death grip into me, one drink at a time. I was lost and out of control and I couldn't see it. I think the booze liked that I was so distracted by the other areas of my life; it caused me to lower my guard and set me up for seemingly fatal blows, one after another.

My wife and I went to the work of preparing our home for our newest family member. There was much to be done, and much to be decided. Would we be buying Yankees curtains or Princess drapes? Am I getting ready to go stock up on tiny baseball gloves and balls or am I going to be studying up on fairy tales and dance studios? I know that probably sounds stereotyped or sexist to some, but we had a traditional sense of family and there was nothing wrong with that as far as my wife or I was concerned.

Of course in the end, the kid would be however he or she wanted—but until then, we were planning on raising our kids in a traditional environment. Anyway, before we picked out colors or got too far ahead of ourselves we needed to find out who was coming. We debated for some time on whether we should find out the sex of the baby or if we should wait and be surprised at the grand entrance. We decided that if I tried to wait 9 months before we even settled on a name, my head might actually explode. We made a deal. For this first child we would find out the sex in advance, but then all bets were off for any future additions. With that, we headed to the doctor's office to end the suspense.

I was sitting next to my wife trying to make sense of what I was seeing on the ultrasound screen. My wife and the doctor seemed to be able to identify the entire spectrum of human anatomy on what appeared to me as a black and white depiction of a satellite photo of the ocean.

"Do you see what I see?" the doctor said.

"Oh my, yes I do!" my wife smiled and said.

I was staring at the screen lost. "What? Boy? Girl? Come on! "I asked impatiently.

My wife looked over at me and said, "Twins."

My heart dropped and my mind raced in the same moment. I looked up. I actually looked up to the sky and thanked God; I didn't know what else to do.

I didn't think I could love my wife any more, it just didn't seem possible. But somehow my heart must have grown right there in the office. My soul and capacity to protect and appreciate my life increased in size and depth, and my love for Heather and our unborn children blossomed instantly. We were going to be a family—and a big family all in one fell swoop. We knew we were having twins. We knew that things were getting ready to get all kinds of crazy at the Clark house over the next few months, but we still didn't know if we were painting rooms blue or pink. We returned to the doctor's office a couple of weeks later to uncover the final mystery. I didn't care too much about what the doctor said about boys or girls as long as "two very healthy babies" was somewhere in the sentence.

We eagerly sat and waited to hear the verdict. The doctor came to us and said that the jury was in. It was a girl! That made me happy. Even though I was one of four boys and never had a sister, I had always heard that the bond of a daughter and her father is special. The doctor was still talking and I snapped back to reality for a second.

"...and a boy," I heard him repeat to me, seeing that I missed the second part. Holy perfect scenario, Batman. We were going to have boy and girl twins.

I went to work each day and so did Heather, at least for the first 7 months of the pregnancy. She said she wanted to keep busy and it was nice to hold onto the two incomes for a little while longer. The entire family was abuzz with expectant chat and activity as we drew closer to the date. Our twins were going to give Heather's folks their very first grandchildren, and my mom was chomping at the bit to have a baby around again—well she was getting two at once! Heather was amazing as she worked, took care of herself, and the babies, as well as all the household chores. I was working around the clock and I was home very little during this time, so to say she held it all together would be perfectly correct.

Heather stopped working as we approached the due date and all I could do was think of how our lives were getting ready to change. Not only would we have a baby around the house to care for, we were going to have two. I had many procedural questions about exactly how this was going to work. Will they sleep at the same time? How about feeding? How exactly do you breast-feed two babies? I was in the dark on all this stuff, and in fact, I felt a little overwhelmed.

The arrival horn sounded late one night as I was just getting ready to go bed. I had been up into the wee hours of the morning doing some accounting for work and I had just shut off my laptop to go to bed when Heather came into the room. She had a beautiful smile on her face that was equal parts anguish and anticipation. She was stunning.

We arrived at the hospital and were taken right up to a private room. Heather worked in the hospital and we were given the royal treatment. From the window in the hospital room I could see the golf course below. It was a course I had played many times over the years. Little did I know that I would one day look out over the course as I waited for my daughter and son to come into the world.

Heather made it through the labor and delivery like she had done it a thousand times. She did everything that she was asked to do by the doctors and nurses. She worked hard, and believe it or not, never complained—not once. She never even took any pain medication despite the staff asking her to do so. She had her reasons and wanted to have a 100% natural delivery. Her strength and determination impressed me and I still draw from her example today. In many ways my life started on that morning. It not only changed, that would be stating the obvious, but it was almost as if everything that had happened in my life until then didn't count. It was just an appetizer, or a dress rehearsal. This was the real world and it was here to stay. David Brent and Emily Lynn came into the world, and in doing so, made it a better place to live—not just for Heather and me, but for everyone.

Emily Lynn Clark captured my heart before she captured a single breath on earth. No sooner than she was in the world did she have my every thought and focus. She was my daughter, she was in my arms and there was no need for concern anymore. I knew that whatever knowledge I lacked, whatever wisdom I had yet to acquire, my love for her alone would suffice for now. I knew my bond with her would guide me and insure that I always acted in her best interest as her father. I held her in my arms and stared into her face in utter disbelief and complete vulnerability. She wasn't the fragile one; I was. I knew that from this moment on, my very space on earth would be occupied not only by my physical presence, but my connection to her as well. We were inextricably bound together for the ages. She smiled at me; she knew too.

As Emily got older our connection only increased with time. When she was just a couple of months old I used to come home from work and dance her around the kitchen in my arms while Frankie sang to us from the CD player.

She would look directly into my eyes and smile like she knew this moment was important to me. She could break my heart in an instant and was as safe from harm as any human would ever be in someone's arms.

Now at 9 years old, she is like me in a way that can't be seen in hobbies or similar tastes, but is palpable nonetheless. We don't watch the same movies or like the same music but I always know what she is thinking. She views the world as I did at her age. She has a kind heart and a loving soul that will continue to grow and will steer the ship for her as she gets older. I know that Emily will be fine, and that is very comforting as a parent. She may have to learn things for herself and do things the hard way, but she has a spirit and intuition for the world that is intrinsically priceless. She will always be my Irish princess.

My son David Brent Clark has my exact name. He also has my heart and my drive. I held him in my arms on the day he was born, and in some ways, he has carried me ever since. I stared directly into Davey's eyes after the doctor handed him to me. I was trying to get a little bit of a read on him. Did he look like me? What type of man is this I hold? Will he be an athlete? A businessman? What is he thinking right now?

If I took every friendship, every teammate, and every feeling of camaraderie I have felt in life up to that moment of time and combined them together, they wouldn't equal half of what I felt for my son. I was proud, and I was humbled to be in his presence. I suppose it was a fitting start of life for my son. I have always seen Davey through the eyes of the world, as well as my own. I have great anticipation of his potential to climb high, but I never project on him any expectation other than that he be happy and confident in his life.

He was born with an uncommon sense of his surroundings and seems to be very deliberate in all his actions. Davey is as determined as any adult I have ever met—and that is not an embellishment. I see so much of myself in his every action, that it simply overwhelms me at times and sends me into a kind of mental vertigo. I put him in ice hockey when he was just five, and he fell in love with the sport. He works harder than every kid on the ice— every practice and every game, without exception. He is both immensely talented and humble at the same time. He has become a great teammate and a great friend. He makes me laugh out loud on occasion—and not only when he launches himself into a high-energy no-fear mission of comedy, but in his actual wit and view of the world. He has a casual way of shrugging off the superficial things that people do or say that indicates an understanding of human nature that eludes half the population, it seems. We play catch, we sit on the couch, and just being around him eases my soul.

If I were to take a blank sheet of paper and go to the work of constructing the perfect son, I would end up with an exact representation of my own. He displays every characteristic that I admire in men. He is honest. He is strong and confident, yet he is sensitive to those he cares for. He works hard at school and in sports. He sets goals and will not be distracted. And incredibly, he looks to himself when things go wrong. I cannot account for why this is, or how he could manifest these traits at just 9 years old, but I am humbly thankful to be afforded this great gift of such a young man for me to call mine. I know I would like him if we ever met in a different life. I am privileged to be his father and mentor for now, but I suspect he will teach me much in the years to come.

Right after the twins were born and Heather was cleared medically, we all retired from the delivery room to the private hospital room. The families wanted to take a moment to share in the celebration of the newly arrived twins, and also to just be in each other's company. It was my proudest moment on earth and I was glowing; my very soul was on fire. I never missed an opportunity to celebrate, and there had never been a better occasion to do so. My entire family, my dear friend Dan, and my wife's family were all present at the hospital while the kids were being born, so we had three generations all assembled under the same roof at the same time for this monumental day.

My father brought in a $250 bottle of Johnny Walker Blue scotch and my friend Dan brought in a bottle of Dom Perignon for all to enjoy. The family celebration had a certain sense of luxury and indulgence, and I didn't mind that one bit. I hadn't thought much about alcohol during the delivery but I was glad to see it now. We all indulged in a glass of champagne, and I added a few cocktails onto my tally, as well. My parents suggested I go back to my house to grab some clothes and some comforts from home to bring back for Heather, and I thought this was a grand idea. I, thank God, didn't soil the memory of my kids' birth by staying and getting drunk at the hospital. It was perhaps one of the only special occasions I didn't desecrate with excessive drinking during the months and years to follow.

Heather was amazing at home. I have no idea how she made it all work. Somehow she managed to go from never being a mom to flawlessly taking care of two newborn babies alone. And she really was doing it by herself. I was being pulled in a thousand directions at work and I was rarely home before the house was dark and silent. I offered to bring in a maid to help Heather with the housework, and she looked at me like I was crazy. Heather cooked, cleaned, did the laundry, and mothered two babies all at once. It was the Super Bowl of homemaking, and she was kicking the shit out of it.

Months ticked by and everything was great at home. At work I was growing increasingly ambitious in my desire to secure a better future for my new family. I was content in my position and making a good living, but retail is a long, hard grind no matter how many zeros are on your check. I worked long hours on the weekends, extra hours on holidays, and it was a dusk-until-dawn commitment. I was burning the midnight oil to get ahead—plus, I had also been weighing the possibility of starting my own business for some time.

Of all the commodities in life, there are none so precious as time. This was one of the great lessons I learned when my friend Dave Lynn passed away so suddenly. It does no good to amass a fortune if doing so prohibits you from having a life. I can't imagine there is any man who on his deathbed wouldn't give away every possession he had for just one more day with his family.

I had a good thing going right now in my career; I was liked and well respected at work and I was making a great living. And for the most part I did enjoy what I was doing. The only problem was I seemed to be doing it all the time. Every holiday weekend I not only worked, I worked extra hours. I was the manager of the store, I was doing sales training and talking about what the next "bump up" in the chain would be as far as a promotion. But the truth was, I was in a dead end of sorts. The store manager in my business reported directly to the owners; no place to move up. I could leave the company for a job with a manufacturer or try to get on with a bigger company, but that all seemed sideways to me. I started to get serious about the idea of working for myself.

With a new family in the picture, it's not surprising that I was spending a considerable amount of time looking ahead to the future or that I was doing some calculus on what my time was worth and how much time I was willing to give up in exchange for financial security. I was always trying to balance the equation in my mind. Do I quit my job and work part-time so that I can spend every waking moment with the kids? No, that didn't seem like a realistic option, but neither did working 60 hours a week, including every weekend, for the rest of my life.

Without a transition my conversations and thoughts took a sharp turn from "considering working for myself" to "what business should I start?" I always thought that the true magic in a retail business was the people, not the operation itself. I was blessed with great employers to work for, but so far I was the magic ingredient in the sauce. I knew how to turn a store into a cash machine. Why should I do all the lifting for a small percentage of the take? In the last few months I had started drawing out business plans on scratch paper and cocktail napkins without even realizing what I was doing. I figured if I worked hard for the next five years at building my own business, I could create a life for my family that would give me the financial and personal freedom to enjoy life. It only took the balls and commitment to change.

I started to research ways to borrow against my home, ways I could put together a plan to make this idea a reality, not just a lofty goal. The burgeoning spark was starting to become a roaring fire. I conceived of opening my own store. Hell, maybe a whole chain of stores by the time it's all said and done. If I was going to be a bear, I wanted to be a grizzly. I wanted to run the greatest retail furniture store that had ever been. I wanted my store to be so unique and earth shattering that no one would even consider going into business against me.

My friend Dan was also looking to break away from his position, and we had been talking about being business partners over cocktails since we first met—only now it was no longer talk. We were doing it. We were a good partnership, the two of us together in one room resulted in an infectious chemistry that spread to others. Dan was also a leader in the industry and our combined enthusiasm was a tool and weapon we could use effectively to acquire capital and investors, as well as market share once the store was established.

We met with bankers, we asked people we knew if they were interested in investing, and we met with an advisor from the Small Business Administration. We had done the homework—we had the business concept and we had a business plan. So that was that, I was "all in." I was going to break away from my current employer and jump into the market. The only obstacle remaining was money. I had just bought a new house and, despite having a great income and at just 29 years old, I didn't have much collateral or a long credit history. Dan was in a similar financial situation so we were basically starting at zero. We had some operating capital but not nearly enough to launch an entire retail operation. In approaching a few friends and family members to borrow start-up money, I was usually treated to some version of, "You aren't going to walk away from a 6-figure job while you are just getting established... are you?" And, "Does Heather know about this? Are you nuts?"

We needed financial support to make this happen. I didn't have enough equity in my house to fund the start-up but I did have a reputation in the industry that I could leverage, so my resume was going to be the starting capital. Dan and I both had been besting the competition for years and I wondered if some competing furniture manufacturers were interested in helping us break away from our current employer and set up shop selling for them. We called and set up an appointment with the CEO and CFO of our biggest competitor at their corporate offices in Chicago. These guys weren't our direct competition but they were the main supplier for the competition in the Denver market. I was betting that they would be interested in a double whammy of a business proposal:

"Help us break away from our current employer and two things happen: One, we won't be selling against you any longer. Two, we will be selling your products against our former employer."

On the trip out to Chicago I was going over my presentation in my mind as Dan drove. I realized that in reality, as much as I wanted this to happen for me, my family, and for Dan, it was a much bigger deal for the manufacturer. On the table for them were millions of dollars in potential orders. Taking control of the meeting in my mind, I thought as long as they believed in our ability to deliver, we had a shot at getting what we were asking for. And what exactly was I asking for? Really I was just seeking a little help to start a new furniture store.

I was going to ask them to front $40,000 to $50,000 worth of product and extend a credit line to us. If I was feeling strong, I might even suggest they kick in some advertising dollars to get us up and running—no big deal for a multi-million dollar company. I tried to put myself in their shoes; what would I be thinking if I were them? What would I expect from this deal? What is the best scenario for them in all this? And a thought hit me like a ton of bricks: I wonder if they will ask us to buy out the Denver stores that we had been competing against? Is that possible? If I were them, I would want me to do precisely that. I gazed out the window and let that simmer for a while. As a few miles ticked by and the thought gained some momentum in my head, I looked over at Dan and said, "I think they are going to offer to sell us the Denver market."

He looked at me and thought about it. He blinked like he didn't know what the hell I was talking about, but he heard my conviction in the statement. "Really?" he asked rhetorically.

"Wouldn't surprise me a bit," I said coyly.

Once in Chicago, I could barely sleep that night in the hotel room. I lay in bed and thought of all that was on the line. Flashes like photographs from paparazzi kept exploding in my mind. The possibility of a new lucrative business, the risk involved in the venture, the fact that I had all but put in my notice at my current job. The reality was if I didn't make this happen, I was going to be unemployed. I'd go from becoming a business owner to looking for a job in the span of a single meeting—that's how it felt. I didn't know what else to do, so I smiled at the thought of the stress and the pressure building up, and like when I was a kid, I just jumped. No thoughts of the consequences, just leap and do the best you can to land gracefully.

The next morning I walked into the meeting as if it were something I had done a thousand times. I was not only sure of myself, I was enjoying myself. My deliberate step and knowing smile may have seemed misplaced in another world, but not today, not here. I was 29 years old and I was walking into a room with the CEO and CFO of a 100 million dollar-a-year international conglomerate—but it was our day, not theirs. I looked over at Dan as we walked down the hall and said, "These are the moments that define men's lives."

In a very uncharacteristic move, I threw out my formal presentation the night before in place of feeling the big boys out and seeing if there really was possibly a bigger deal to be had. As much as it made sense for me to imagine how they would want us to take over the existing chain of Denver stores, there was still the glaring fact that we didn't have any real world experience in the day-to-day operation of a business, much less a large multi-store operation, and honestly we were without the capital to purchase an existing business. Hell I didn't even have the money to open just one store; that's why I was here in the first place.

But my confidence came from a very deep and pure well that never runs dry. I believed I was the best at what I did and the record supported it, at least in my mind it did. I had my great good friend by my side and we were going to go stake our claim. There were no tricks, no luck involved, we had both proven ourselves over and over again. I know it sounds cocky, and it was, but the brashness of youth was in our favor that day.

I started to speak about our plans and reasons for wanting to break off from our current employer. I asked questions and listened intently to what these very intelligent men had to say. These guys were the very top of the food chain in our industry and that didn't happen by accident. After some time and some back and forth, I felt that we had successfully positioned ourselves on the stronger side of the bargaining table. I told them we needed help to start our own store and that we were in a position to really make a splash in the Colorado market. I told them in exchange for selecting them as the premier vendor for our store and signing an exclusivity deal, we would want some credit and other concessions.

As I watched them react, I knew my suspicions might be right. These guys wanted us selling their products—they wanted a change in the Denver market and we just walked through the door at the exact right place and time. I was about to find out that they had also done their homework before this meeting and were very familiar with both Dan and me.

We were sitting in a beautiful conference room in the worldwide headquarters of a company I had spent the last 5 years competing against. I noted the textured carpet, the wood grain on the table I was resting my hands on, and the art so perfectly hung on the walls. I looked at my shoes under the table and then met their eyes with a direct gaze as they started to speak. I knew this was going to be moment I would remember for some time.

"We would definitely be interested in helping you start a store…" the CFO said. There was a moment of silence as that statement hung out there. I knew by the inflection that there was more to come. "But we have a different proposal, if you are interested." Now it was our turn to listen. I listened as they explained that they weren't happy with the current ownership of the Denver stores. They were under-performing and the owner himself was living out-of-state and had no time to put into this market.

"How would you feel about taking over 13 stores instead of opening one?" they asked.

I didn't even hesitate in speaking the truth directly. "I don't have the money," I said matter-of-factly.

"We would consider becoming the bank to finance the purchase…"

My life was never the same—and that night we celebrated. We laughed about my "psychic vision" about the end result of our meeting. I obviously wasn't a medium but I did trust my gut. It was because of this intuition that we named the legal entity "Instincts, Inc." We had some large issues to address to make this acquisition work, but once we agreed in principal, we proceeded to move forward.

I was in a scramble to secure as much seed money as I could. Dan and I put up our houses and all our cash and the manufacturer agreed to loan us the lion's share of the purchase price of the company, around a half million dollars. In essence, we acquired the chain for the value of the in stock merchandise alone. Over all, the company had been losing money for years so the only value was in the inventory. I was betting everything I had that I could take this struggling chain of stores and turn it around, and Dan was doing the same. If I failed I would lose my house, my savings—and since I was getting ready to go into direct competition with my old employer, I didn't think I would be getting my old job back any time soon.

"There is something really wrong with owning 13 stores that sell mattresses and not being able to sleep at night." I remember saying this every time someone would ask me how the new business was going. I knew I was going to be in for a roller coaster ride, taking over such a large operation, but I had no idea just how crazy it would be. The transition from the old ownership group to us literally happened in one single day. We signed the paperwork, got the keys, and we called a company-wide sales meeting for the next day. Nobody knew what had happened. The employees were going to meet their new boss without ever knowing the old one was gone. Talk about stress. The fate of 30-some employees were in my hands now. They all had families and mortgages and dreams, and they were relying on me to provide them with a job.

When word spread through my former employers that Dan and I had broken off on our own, I started to get calls from ex co-workers looking to come to work with us. I had resisted the urge to actively recruit the salespeople I had trained in my previous position, but now that they were calling, I wasn't going to say no. I really didn't know what to do with everyone at first. I had all the salespeople that were employed when I took over and I had 10 or so "new hires" that I was bringing with me. I wasn't sure how many people I was going to need; I wasn't even sure which of the existing employees were worth saving. I had heard customer-service nightmares from people about the company that I now owned, so I was going to be fighting a culture of negativity and laziness. One thing I was sure of—everything that the company was doing before was going to change.

We didn't want to keep one single procedure or practice from the former management, not one. If they were using blue ink, we wanted black. If they answered the phone with their left hand, we were going to use the right. Everything was going to change. I knew everyone would think I was crazy, but I needed everyone to rethink even the smallest detail. We knew with such sweeping changes that people were going to be upset. People fear change and some would just go away in the wash, and perhaps the employee overload would balance itself out to a degree. What we decided on was a 30-day free-for-all: "Everyone here lost their job yesterday when the old owner gave up, sold the company, and walked away from this business," I said to a room of troubled faces. "The good news is we are hiring," I said.

I could almost tell just by looking around who was going to stay and who was leaving by the look on their individual faces. Some people are inherently so afraid of change that they give up when confronted by it. Others respond to the challenge of change even if it makes them uncomfortable at first; it was the latter type of person I was looking for. I kept everyone who was game employed for a "30-day interview period." Permanent positions would be offered at the month's end, based on attitude, ethic, and performance. Before I sent everyone on their way to ponder what the hell had just happened to them, I told them they will make more money and have more fun than they ever imagined they could—if they make it through this month. I also said, "I suggest you put aside the gossip and rumor mill, show up with a smile and an open mind, and see what is going to happen here for you. Squash your fear and embrace the change."

So for 30 days we had no managers, no accountants, no set work schedule, just a mass of 30 salespeople traipsing all over the city working a new store each day. Dan and I went to the stores and worked with people first-hand and we tried to get to know everyone personally. I was also trying to gain control over advertising, accounting, warehousing, and distribution—all at the same time we were attempting to do something that eluded our predecessors—sell some furniture.

I worked around the clock. I watched the numbers and, more importantly, the attitudes very closely. I wasn't alone in this process. In fact, I had surrounded myself with some great people, such as my business partner Dan, my father whom I brought aboard in a temporary role, and several other people that I had gone to war with in the past. After this ridiculous and grueling experiment came to a close and we tried to make sense of our first month in business, we noticed a completely unexpected thing—the company posted its largest sales numbers in history, a history that spanned over 60 years and several different ownership groups. The boys in Chicago called to congratulate us and express their gratitude. They also told me that the entire nation was awake and watching.

Everything was happening so fast it seemed like a dream at times. We took that first month in stride, hit the ground running and never looked back. We assigned managers for each store, changed the entire product line and even updated the look of the stores. Sales were through the roof and we were posting a healthy profit. However, I still didn't have the cash reserves yet to implement my vision of what the chain was to become. I had a precise picture of what the stores should be and I was aware of where we were now, and the two didn't match yet. We still had some major league growing pains to endure. We were trying to better understand how the whole machine worked within its parts, but we were climbing high and showed no signs of slowing down.

In the coming months we continued to knock down huge numbers month-after-month. Every month was an increase from any month previous to our ownership. As the money came in we continued to put it back into the operation. We moved into a new warehouse. We purchased computers for all the stores and networked the entire operation together. We purchased new delivery vehicles, paid our employees very well and even invested in opening new locations, as well as closing a couple that weren't performing.

My plan was simple: create a large well-oiled machine with sufficient structure in place that will allow me to step back in a few years and enjoy life on my terms. I never drew a salary close to what I was making before and I was content to reinvest every cent the business was making. Years later I would sometimes lie in bed and wish I had written myself a $250,000 bonus instead of buying a new warehouse—or maybe a nice new V12 Mercedes instead of the computer system? Oh well, hindsight is sharp as a damn razor.

Nine months into our first year, we had posted an increase in sales of close to 2 million dollars. We had the best year in the company's history by the first 6 months we were in business and we were showing no signs of slowing. I had been burning the candle at both ends for months, non-stop, so Dan and I decided it was time to take a few days to recharge. We settled on sneaking away to Mexico for a golf-fishing trip. We arranged to leave right after the big Labor Day weekend and, if all went as planned, no one would even know we were gone until we already back in town.

I made first class travel arrangements and we both cleared our calendars for 3 days in Cabo San Lucas. We touched down in Mexico and even though we landed on the ground I was still floating high above the earth. I felt that everything was going very well with the company and at home and I was ready to unplug and enjoy some relaxation in the sun. We only had a couple of days away, but we planned to jam in a bunch of stuff: deep sea fishing, golf—and, of course, the booze was on my mind even more than soaking up the sun. We checked into the hotel and dropped our bags in the room. I booked us a spectacular 2-bedroom luxury condo and the views were simply amazing. The place had huge open living areas, two ridiculously large master bedroom suites, a full kitchen and every possible luxury. The place was wide open so the ocean air could glide through and the 15-foot ceilings and imported tile floor made us feel like kings.

I stood out on the balcony overlooking the many swimming pools of our hotel. I could see cruise ships docked just off the shore and hundreds of people lying on the golden sand, seemingly without a care in the world. You would think that I might have felt a touch of pride or accomplishment, and even though it did it seem like it was my hard work that was paying off, actually I felt just plain lucky—lucky to be born into a country like the United States where a dumb kid from upstate New York could walk into such a great opportunity without any pedigree or privilege. Hell, I didn't have any resources to speak of at all when I started. Nine months ago I was just a glorified mattress salesman. I also felt lucky to have a supportive and loving family, all of whom were healthy and vital. But I think the most humbling thought of all was that I was blessed to somehow be in a position where I could provide so many others with a means of employment to care for their own families. I felt like I was making a difference in the world.

Late that night I left my room and went for a walk. I walked down to the poolside bar and grabbed a scotch. I lit my Don Carlos cigar and walked over to the beach where I could see some kids playing in the sand. I wanted to sit down with my toes in the sand and take a moment to myself and try to take in all that had happened in the last year or so. It was close to midnight by then and many of the guests were in for the night, so I was growing increasingly curious as to why there were kids out on the beach so late.

As I made it to the sand, I saw two boys running up and down the length of the beach, laughing hysterically and taunting each other to run faster and faster. They would kick sand at each other or trip each other as they passed by but it was obvious they were having the time of their lives. Upon further inspection, I realized these were not guests from the hotel, but local boys. It didn't take much to put that together, they were really dirty, the shorts they were wearing were old and tattered, and they had a harder look to their exterior than most 9-10 year old boys do.

They continued to run back and forth along the sand and I realized that they were pulling something along behind them; it appeared to be a large 10-foot section of chain link fence or other such metal grill. It hit me then that these boys actually worked for the hotel. What they were doing was dragging the sand to make sure it looked nice and perfect for the morning when the guests came out to sunbathe on the shore. The contrast of this scenario hit me hard. All these guests here spending lavish amounts of money to have a little fun, yet all the while most of them will never experience the true joy of life that these lads are having while performing a menial task. And their wage for the task was what, five dollars? Ten? Two dollars? Of course I will never know how much they were paid by the hotel, but I was pretty sure it was less than most guests pay for lunch. In my mind I imagined that they would go home and take whatever money they made to their families and that money would, in turn, go a long way.

I called them over to me.

They stopped what they were doing and looked very skeptical, and perhaps worried that they were in trouble. They walked over to me, not sure what to make of me—at 270 pounds, a shaved head, straw hat, gold jewelry and a big cigar. I must have looked like a silly character from a movie. I tried to make chit chat in my limited Spanish as I told them that their hard work impressed me and I suggested if they kept it up, maybe good things would come their way. They just smiled at me and looked at each other, trying to make sense of this encounter. I reached into my pocket and pulled out a wad of cash. I gave them each $50 and I thought they were going to fall over as they slowly took the fifty-dollar bills from me. It wasn't charity. It wasn't an act designed to make me feel good. It just seemed like the right thing to do; after all, being in the right place at the right time and working hard should pay off every once in a while. I told them goodnight and exited quickly to leave them to their work.

The next day Dan and I had an early morning and a full day planned. We chartered a private boat and planned to go fishing in the Sea of Cortez all day. I have always had a love affair with the water and, in fact, I come from a long line of Irish sailors who have competed in international sailing races going back hundreds of years. Something about being out at sea has always comforted me and I was looking forward to the new experience today, as it was going to be my first attempt to catch a fish large enough to be worthy of stuffing for my den wall.

We headed out to sea for hours on end, looking for the perfect location to find the best fish. The waves were beating against the front of the boat as we crossed the tides and we were slamming up and down in our chairs as we went from laughing out loud to silently gazing into the pre-dawn darkness without even noticing the roughness anymore. As we continued to head farther and farther into the black of the ocean, we started to see the sun rising up and peeking at us from the horizon. The heat felt good and I closed my eyes and drifted off to sleep.

Finally we arrived at our destination and immediately went to the work of dropping our lines and trolling about for fish. Although I have been on the water many times in my life, this was my first experience fishing for Dorado. I was excited and relived to get a bite on my line almost immediately. The seal was broken and the day had officially started. The hours flew by as we pulled one fish after another into the boat. As the fish came, in the booze went down and I was just soaking it all in—literally. Hours of fishing and fun culminated in an epic battle of man and fish as I found myself in an hour-long fight with a 90-pound fish that took every ounce of strength to finally reel in. What a day! Sunshine, time with my best buddy—and now I was going home with a huge fish story. I remember vividly telling Dan as we started back towards the shore that, other than my wedding day and the day my kids were born, this was my best day ever.

The captain of the boat turned the controls over to his first mate and joined us on deck for beers during the return back to land. We chatted like old friends, the three of us, and began to drink like old pros. As the conversation started to flow faster and easier, the drinks were following suit. I started to panic a little. Why was I anxious? I had to stop and think about it. It didn't take long to find the source of my stress—I did some calculus in my head and figured that we were going to run out of alcohol at the rate we were going. That's the thing with alcoholics, it's not enough to just drink to excess—we need to possess the booze, need to know it's there even if we choose not to drink it. We find comfort, not in just consuming, but in the revelation that we won't run out.

I tried to act like I wasn't concerned, but I was. I asked if there was any more alcohol on the boat and everyone replied, "No, but we'll be back to shore in an hour and we can get more drinks then." Not good enough, I thought. I went into the lower deck to grab us all one of the last few beers remaining. I slammed two beers really fast before anyone could notice and then I drank the last two little "airplane" bottles of tequila that were in the cooler. I did this out of sight from everyone else before I went back up to the main deck. Feeling a little better now, I returned to the main deck with a beer for everyone and reported the bad news that we were in fact all out of alcohol. Oh well, we'll be back soon enough...

It is embarrassing to report little stories like the boat and the beers, but I think it's important to understand the nature of alcohol dependence. I was very protective of my alcohol, and I was even jealous of it. I loved to share in conversation and good times with friends, but let's just make sure you brought your own supply; mine was for me. We eventually arrived safely back at shore, and I was ready to continue drinking. The captain sent the fish we caught to the hotel and soon it was in the kitchen being prepared for us. I was told dinner would be sent up to our suite immediately. I thought that was pretty cool.

I made sure we stopped for alcohol on the way back to the hotel, so we were stocked up as far as booze went and, in fact, I was halfway down the road to complete inebriation by the time the food arrived at the room. The meal itself was perhaps the most amazing I had ever eaten—a fresh piece of fish that I had myself wrestled from the ocean just a few hours earlier, consumed while sitting in my luxury suite after a couple days of golf and relaxation in the sun. Wow.

My thoughts drifted a few thousand miles to my family back home, and I wondered what they were up to at that moment. The twins were too small to travel, and Heather didn't want to make the trip to Mexico—and I missed them. I thought of the company I was building, hopefully into a small little empire someday, a company that would insure a life of many vacations and family moments such as this one, only better. I was feeling so grand, I thought I might just float away. I knew there would most likely be turmoil waiting for me when I got back to work but I didn't even mind; in fact, I was looking forward to it—after all this is who I was—David Clark, Father, Husband,

Businessman... right?

I arrived back in Colorado from Mexico on Monday, September 10, 2001. I was feeling supremely relaxed and restored and I had the deep suntan to prove it. As I made my way off the plane and through the airport, I was stumbling a bit. I was already half in the bag at just 2 pm in the afternoon. Actually, I had been drinking since I hit the airport in Cabo early that morning. I was drinking scotch on the plane and beer in the airports between flights and I was already looking for my next drink when we landed. I gathered my luggage and went out to look for the car.

We had a private Cadillac limousine that dropped us and picked us up these days (helps to have a friend that owns a limo service) and it was a welcome sight to see it already waiting for us at the curb. The AC was cranked up and our driver had Bloody Marys already mixed for us; he was a good man. I just sat and looked out the window as I relived some of the highlights from the trip and the last several years since I'd moved to Colorado. A huge smile spread across my face as we drove through Denver. I felt that the opportunity I had in life came to me through hard work, but I still couldn't shake the feeling that luck or fate had a hand in things, as well. The car dropped Dan at his place first and we hugged and exchanged big smiles and warm laughs as we said something about seeing each other at the office the next day.

When the car dropped me at my house, I couldn't wait to get in and see Heather and the kids. I tipped the driver and walked into the house. I was greeted immediately by my beautiful wife and my twins; somebody pinch me because this all must be some sort of dream. We had dinner together and enjoyed an evening that included a couple more bottles of wine, some scotch and, of course, brandy afterwards. Oh, my wife wasn't drinking if you're curious—the alcohol was all consumed by me, and it was in addition to all that I had over the last 12 hours or so. I was hammered drunk. We still managed to get caught up on Denver, Mexico, fish stories, and kisses—and then spent the remainder of the night, just the four of us, playing like kids on the living room floor.

My wife went to bed early with the twins and I stayed up late, as was the ritual. I opened my laptop and started to piece together what my day would look like tomorrow. I went to the kitchen and grabbed the bottle of Johnny Walker Black that had been unopened earlier that day, but was now about half-empty. As I sat and worked, I finished the remainder of the bottle of scotch and went to bed. I closed my eyes and said goodbye to the night. It was after midnight when I went to bed, so that meant it was just a couple of hours into September 11, 2001. Little did I know that the world I lived in, along with my entire life was about to change forever.

I opened my eyes and my vision was still a little cloudy. "How much did I drink last night?" I thought as I sat up in bed and listened to the drummer in my head.

I must be a little jet-lagged, I decided as I looked over to the television. Heather was ironing my shirt for the day and the local news was on the bedroom TV. I saw smoke billowing out from one of the World Trade Center Towers. Having grown up in the NYC area, I recognized much of the background, as well as the street view, in the footage the cameras were showing. I felt like I was dreaming because it appeared that a plane had crashed into one of the towers. I tried to imagine exactly how something like that could happen. I was very familiar with Newark and JFK airports and I was just dumbfounded. I was still sitting there on the edge of the bed with my mouth open, looking like mental patient, when I met my wife's gaze. "Is this for real?" I asked.

I sat there helpless like everyone else in the world at that exact moment, and waited for more information to come in. I looked at my watch and I realized that I was going to be late for work. Just as I stood to leave, I saw a large object come flying into the screen of the television. I think I actually felt the impact that the second plane made as it struck Tower Two. My knees buckled at the instant the plane violently collided in an orange and black explosion of flame and smoke. I stared in horror as the destruction made its way through the building and out the rear of the structure in a tornado of debris and death. I dropped down onto the foot of the bed and looked at my wife.

There were so many things running through my mind at one time, I felt as though I might actually go insane. I literally felt incapable of managing the information that was streaming through my mind in the form of actual images from the television, as well as the thousands of pictures and scenarios I was conjuring on my own. My brother was still in the New York area—was he there? What kind of malfunction in air traffic could cause this to happen? Shit, I was going to be late to the office. I jumped up, kissed my wife and ran to my car. I told her to keep in touch today.

I knew something bad was happening, but I still couldn't process it. I tore out of my driveway like a bat out of hell. I got on the highway and I put the pedal down. The Mustang responded by jumping forward and the speed felt good. It was something I was in control of, the car. It felt good to be in control of something, even if it was only the speed of the vehicle I was driving, because I felt like instantly I had lost control over every other thing in my world. I was helpless and I still couldn't make sense of what was happening back home in New York.

As the sound of the engine started to ease into the background, I started to place the pictures and sounds of the morning's events into a more coherent picture. I felt a shimmy start to settle in and I wondered if the car was out of alignment. The shimmy became a full shake and soon both my arms were shaking so badly I could barely keep my hands on the steering wheel. As I took my hands of the wheel I realized it wasn't the car at all, but me that was shaking. I was shaking so violently that I felt I was being electrocuted. I pulled off to the side of the road before I crashed the car. I put my hands to my face and I could feel my legs and torso joining in the convulsions; my entire body now almost thrashing. I looked up from my hands and started to sob out loud.

"They are flying our own planes into our own buildings," I screamed at the top of my lungs to the empty car. I punched blindly at the dash and steering wheel with both hands—anger, grief, sorrow, all boiling in my blood like a poisonous concoction of rage and retribution as I tried to tear the steering wheel off the column without realizing what I was doing. I stopped all at once and just sat in the car. I was breathing heavy and tears were streaming down my face. I felt humiliated, angry and incredulous. Someone picked a fight with us—and those motherfuckers had better be ready to answer the call when we responded.

As I made it into the office, everyone was gathered around the television on the conference table. As more information came in, it became clear that this was no accident. We were under attack. I remember vividly tuning into the reality of the television coverage as the reality of the actual world was slipping away. The entire consciousness of the world was focused on New York.

I heard strange noises from the TV speaker. (THUD) (SLAM)

"What are those sounds?" I asked. The cameras were showing some of the footage of the firefighters entering the towers. "Those are the sounds of people hitting the roof of the mezzanine," one of the office girls said. My stomach turned. I didn't say anything. As I turned that thought over in my mind, I realized that whatever was happening on the upper floors of the Trade Center in lower Manhattan was worse than the option of jumping out the window to a certain death.

I closed the stores and sent everyone home to be with their families.

Most Americans were profoundly and irrevocably changed by the events of September 11th, and I am no different. Twelve years later I still find it hard to talk about that day. Our country, our civilians and our very peace of mind were all causalities that day. In the coming days, months and years I was in mourning for all the men who so bravely gave themselves to help others in peril. I was grieving for the families and all the children who would never see their mothers or fathers again. We expect that our soldiers—and even our police and firefighters—may lay down their lives to protect the innocent; that is precisely what makes them heroes, but what do you say when the innocent are targeted in such a cowardly and pathetic manner? You say nothing; you cope. You persevere, and you keep moving forward. You watch baseball, you mow your grass and you put up the biggest American flag you can find. Then if you can, you go find a soldier who is packing up and leaving his kids to insure that the battle goes elsewhere, and you thank him from the bottom of your soul.

As a company and as individuals we did just that. We tried to get back to the business of being Americans. We went home to return to being fathers and husbands, wives and mothers, and we decided collectively that no terrorist group could take our way of life from us unless we let them. On September 12th, we also returned to the business of being an actual business. We discovered very quickly, however, that our business had changed entirely. People just weren't shopping anymore. People were still, rightfully so, very much in turmoil and unsure of what the future would bring.

Bad news was everywhere. You couldn't go into a liquor store or restaurant without seeing 24-hour coverage of ground zero. The entire world was different and the cameras were on. We all watched as the stock market tumbled. We all saw the retail shopping center parking lots empty and the airports closed. We as Americans all just wanted to stay home and be with our families. I certainly couldn't blame anyone for their reluctance to go shopping, but I was panicking, my business may as well been closed. And I was losing money... fast.

We went from three quarters of a million dollars a month in sales to averaging less than four hundred thousand—literally, overnight. Our sales dropped into the basement and we were ringing up debt fast. We had positioned ourselves in such a way as to out-compete and out-sell our competition in the long term; however, we accomplished this by putting all the money we had made to this point back into the company. I wasn't sitting on any cash reserves at all and I was about to find out that this was, in fact, a potentially fatal error.

I was paying $90,000 in rent alone for the stores, so it didn't take an accounting degree to figure we were in the red each month and racking up triple-digit debt like it was a simple bar tab. I was losing close to $150,000 a month and we needed to make some serious changes if we were to survive. I cut my personal salary to almost zero, we liquidated our large inventory into a much smaller and leaner version, we closed a couple stores, and we settled in for a long fight. The question was, could we last long enough to make it to the other side? Eventually things would get better and people would start buying furniture again if I could just weather the storm.

The final accounting figures for 2001 presented an amusing chart to behold; the numbers graphed themselves as a perfect angle—straight up for the first three fiscal quarters, then straight down for the last of the year. It turns out that despite the huge increase in sales and profit margin, we lost over a half a million dollars from September through December. We still had the capital improvements and stores to show for the rise in sales, but we were cash poor and in big trouble. I owed money to almost all my vendors and it was becoming difficult to stay above water. But as the year came to a close, I was hopeful and excited to move on and start a New Year fresh. It was an immensely stressful time for my family, to say the least. We went from thinking our future was mapped out for us, to wondering if we would lose everything we had. I had put my personal credit, my savings, and even my house on the line to start the business, and now it was all in jeopardy.

We weren't the only company struggling in our market; in fact, one of our competitors, a large national chain, closed up shop locally and left town. My other competitors were also struggling as far as sales went, but they had been around for a while and had the cash to ride this out unharmed. Our competition was hoping and praying we would go under. We had been causing quite a stink and everyone would rest a little easier if we closed. In fact, a couple of phone calls came in with offers to purchase the business (for pennies on the dollar) and I slammed the phone down without so much as a thought to selling. It seemed the other places did have much deeper pockets and they were looking to steal what we had built.

We kept our wits about us, though, and went on. Within a couple of months into 2002 we finally got our heads above water again. We had made enough changes, cut enough expenses that we could at least break even on a hold-pattern for the immediate future. Sales nationwide in our industry were still down 30-40% but at least now our expenses and income were in equilibrium. The problem was our debt. We had accumulated a massive amount of debt over the last 6 months and it was becoming a challenge to keep the creditors at bay. I owed almost $200,000 to the local newspapers and television stations, and I was going to lose my ability to advertise any day.

As the months went by, we kept afloat until finally a new offer to sell came in—this time from out of state. It really wasn't so much an offer as it was a lifeline. We simply couldn't go forward anymore; it was obvious. I was tapped out. The manufacturer that had helped launch us into our orbit had found a buyer that wanted to step in and continue the work we started. They loved the company and they were committed to growing it. We talked on the phone and met with the bank and it became clear for everyone involved this was the best option. Honestly, I was tired of fighting by this point, too. I hadn't had a decent night's sleep in years and I wasn't feeling so warm and fuzzy about owning a large operation anymore.

The details of the deal were kind of simple. They take everything I have for free—the entire business—and I walk away with no money. Doesn't sound very good does it? But they agreed to take all our debts too, and that was good. This meant I could walk away free and clear—no bankruptcy, no lawsuits, and I would be unencumbered entirely in my next venture. It also meant I kept my house, my good credit and all my possessions.

Fuck it. I need a drink. Where do I sign?

No Guarantees

After I walked away from the company, I just kind of simmered for a while in a strange bowl of emotional soup. I was happy to be done with all the stress that the company brought, but I was also very sad and conflicted to be forced to sell. I felt like I had failed. And I was right, I had failed. The bottom line was that I got chewed up and spit out of the business world in one fell swoop. It didn't really matter what caused it or what the justifications were, I was out. So much for the hotshot kid that was going to show everyone how it was done.

I was out of my old company but I wasn't without options. I received a couple of lucrative offers from within the industry, and I was happy to spend some time at home and weigh the options. Although I was pleased to walk away from the business unscathed, I was broke nonetheless. I hadn't drawn a real salary to speak of in some time, and my wife had quit her job long ago to stay at home and care for the twins. I was forced to borrow some money from my in-laws just to float the next couple months of expenses while I figured out my next step. This was probably the most humbling and horrible experience I have ever had. A couple of months ago my father-in-law had been clipping my newspaper ads out of the paper (I was always featured in the ads) and bragging to his friends about me. Now I stood, hat in hand, asking for a hand-out.

One of the options I was considering was buying a restaurant with a couple of other partners. I also interviewed for a few executive positions and I spent a month trying to piece together a plan. I went on business meetings in the morning, played golf in the afternoon, and then went home and drank all night. For the first time in years, I was home on the weekends. I was home every night for dinner and I was able to just sit and watch television without my laptop opened in front of me and my cell phone ringing every 10 minutes. I couldn't decide if I liked this new free time or hated it with all my heart. One side effect of the lifestyle changes was that drinking was moving up higher on my priority list at an alarming rate.

It seemed that my whole life I had had some major direction in which to direct all of my energy and focus. Whether it was supporting my family, making music, going to college, working my career or building a business—I had always had a specific focus before. Whenever I was trying to distract myself from whatever that was and just enjoy some leisure time, I played golf and drank, then went to work. Or maybe I sat at a bar and drank, then returned to work. Perhaps I went camping on the weekend and drank... (you guessed it)... before returning to work. Whatever it was I was doing in my life, there was always a theme—work hard, then go play, drink, repeat as needed. Now for the first time in my life I didn't have that guiding light. I had my wife and my beautiful kids—important, to say the least—but no career. Just drinking and then returning home to drink more.

A very tiny, yet life-changing adjustment, was made during this time—and it was made on a very subconscious level. One day I woke up and my only priority was to drink. I had other things to take of, but drinking was on the top. It was a subtle change, but it changed my whole focus without my even being aware of it. I now spent all my time planning my drinking and how I could make it a bigger part of my life. My goals and plans started to take the shape of businesses and lifestyles that would allow me to "enjoy the finer things" or live "the life of leisure."

I thought of starting restaurants and bars (where I could drink) I conceived of starting vacation and touring services where I could just enjoy the outdoors (and drink) I thought I might even move my family to the coast of Florida and start a small furniture company without all the hassles of multiple locations. Then I could just work a few hours a day (and drink on the beach) and enjoy my family. The switch was flipped—I was no longer a businessman who drank heavily—I was now a drinker who was trying to start a business in his spare time.

Meanwhile, back at my old company, the new owners were struggling to get any momentum going. Despite my own ringing endorsement to my previous employees and my admonishment to give the new guys a chance, people were unhappy with the current management. Sales were dropping again and people were quitting. The new owners were in a complete panic now and making rash decisions as a result. They changed the pay scale, opened up a couple of terrible new locations and dug themselves into a deep hole before they even started. They could barely manage the Denver metro stores, much less the satellite locations we had opened. In a desperate attempt to save money and consolidate the operation, they closed a brand new store that I had opened just before they took over. This was in direct violation of our agreement. The store in question was in Summit County, in a ski resort area that was about a couple of hours' drive from Denver. Dan and I both had put a personal guarantee on that lease and would be sued by the property management company to the tune of three hundred thousand dollars in the case of default.

The Summit County location was to be the crown jewel of all my stores. When I first conceived of opening it a year earlier, I had no idea that I wouldn't own the company when it opened its doors for business. Everyone thought it was a loser, but I was quite sure it would be a home run if given the right chance to grow. The new ownership opened the store and closed it shortly thereafter, citing not being able to get any traction in the local tourism-based economy. After lots of thinking (and drinking) I called the landlord in Summit County and explained what was going on with the current owners of my old company. I told them they (the new owners) had defaulted on the lease, not me. Since technically it was my credit still on the line and my name on the lease, the store was mine to do as I wished. The options were do nothing and go bankrupt, or go back into business in this location and give it another ride.

I remembered a classic line from *The Godfather III*, "Just when I think I am out, they pull me back in..."

Dan was also on the hook for the lease, so it appeared for the time that the old partnership was back together. We contacted a colleague whom we thought would be interested in helping us get started again and within two days, we were literally moving product into the store. The store was already painted, finished and ready for business, so it was going to be a very simple transition. It was a half-assed attempt the previous owners made here before leaving. They did a dismal $20,000 in sales in one month before turning off the phones and closing the doors. I sure hoped I knew something they didn't, and not the other way around.

I was relieved to find that the magic was still there. Amazingly, we were selling beds before the "Open" sign was even installed. In fact, we did almost $130,000 in the very first month—almost twice as much as any of my old stores were currently doing under the new management in Denver. Within 30 days I had one of the best stores of its kind in the entire state of Colorado and I was completely under the radar for the time—no one even knew I was back in business. I barely had time to consider why or how this all happened.

The store was cruising along and I was making money again. It was easy to believe that in many ways this was a better situation than I had before--fewer headaches, less hassles, and there was lots of black ink on the balance sheet. Everything was back on track... well, maybe every *thing* was, but I wasn't. Drinking was still my priority number one, though I would have called you a lair if you had told me that at the time. It was simply very easy to fit drinking into my new business model. This was a small operation with just me, a single business partner, and one other employee. So I could do whatever I wanted, when I wanted, in terms of drinking. My partner Dan, also a heavy drinker in his own right, would never say anything if I showed up a little hung over, or even if I decided to start drinking a little early in the day. It was easy as hell to just keep drinking the same way I had been. In fact, in my new business I broke a rule that was for the most part sacred in the past—I started drinking at work.

Dan and I rented a mountain condo in the company name to cut down on the commuting back and forth from Denver. The move to Summit County was, on the surface, a very good lifestyle change. We could both take multiple off days at a time without concern for the store going into the dumps. My wife and kids came up to the mountains for a few days at a time and we would enjoy the high country; then I could leave the store in my partner's watch and return to our house in Denver for a few days of regular family life. It was a sharp contrast to the multiple locations, unending hours, deadlines, and all the headaches that went with having a large staff and thousands of details to worry about. But my drinking continued its journey to a darker and darker place. It was another noticeable turn in my personality. It was almost as if I walked through a door and into another world. I turned around to see if I could go back, but the door was gone. One door after another, I drank myself farther away from the world. I remember actually saying the words out loud to Dan, "I feel I have crossed a line with my drinking, and it's going to be very hard to go back."

I noted how need and desire sort of rearranged themselves. It seemed that now I drank all the time, whether I wanted to or not. In fact, sometimes what I really wanted more than anything was to *want* to drink. I would leave the store after closing, feeling like crap, thinking I should probably just go home to sleep, yet I couldn't possibly conceive of an evening when I wouldn't drink. A normal night would be for me to go to the liquor store and buy a 6-pack of Heineken and a liter of Johnny Walker and head to the condo. I would sit at the table, looking at the beer and liquor in front of me and think, "The idea of drinking this seems repulsive, yet if I just slug down a half a glass of that scotch and one of those beers, I will be ready to drink more."

So I did. I would choke down about three inches of scotch from a glass and chase it with an entire beer, get up, go to the bathroom, and by the time I returned to my chair, the magic had happened—I wanted to drink again. This would usually begin a long night of loud music that included me swaying back and forth and singing out loud my favorite songs of tragedy and sorrow (sad songs are awesome when you're drunk). I would cry and play the same song over and over and over again. I would drink until I could barely stand up. I would come to consciousness in rooms with no recollection of how I got there. I would also get angry for no reason. I would vow to the mirror that I would make a million dollars and buy out all my former competitors. I was sad and I was lonely, despite having many friends and a large family. I was a hollow soul, a cavernous chamber of echoes and promises of what could have been. Each drink took me farther away from a perfect life that I knew I had—if I could only make myself put down the bottle.

"Maybe tomorrow... Maybe I should call and get some help tomorrow..."

The next day would be an exact duplicate of the previous one, with perhaps a few modifications. As the months went on, I started to go to the liquor store by mid-afternoon. I would sit and drink in the store between helping customers. I would drink at my desk, I would drink in my car, and I would drink while out on deliveries. It just didn't matter anymore, I drank. Perhaps the most amazing feat of all during this time isn't that I didn't die, wreck my car, or go insane—it's that I still maintained a decent family life. I never stopped loving my wife or trying to be there for my kids. When the family was around I would lower my drinking to "maintenance" level and return to the "actual" drinking when they were asleep or out at the park—at least in my mind, that's what I did. To those on the far outside, there really wasn't a problem with my drinking at all. I had become proficient at hiding and distributing my drinking so that it was inaccurately interpreted. However, if you drank with me, or saw me actually drink, you knew "normal" simply did not apply.

My weight was also out of control. Breakfast was usually two or three McDonald's sandwiches and hash browns. Lunch was some other fast food that I would purchase by the bag-full. Usually I would stop eating by the time mid-day rolled around and switch to alcohol. I would drink until late in the night and make a midnight run to McDonalds for my final nourishment. Usually, this would be a Double Quarter Pounder, a Filet-O-Fish, and large fries. I was on some run-away train. I was eating in the same reckless manner as I was drinking. Some days I would go to McDonalds three times in a row. I knew it was killing me; for some reason, I stopped caring about that too. I was up to 320 pounds now and the burden I was carrying was even larger. I began to hate the world and everyone in it.

The store continued to do reasonably well despite my drinking, but it was having an effect. My heart wasn't 100% in building the store anymore, and with drinking being number one and business being number two on the list, I was only doing a decent job of keeping the sales up, the bills paid and the customers happy. Early on in this new venture, we had made a strategic move and decided to become a franchisee of another existing chain store. Our thought was that being able to use their name and advertising dollars would help us to increase our penetration into all the Colorado mountain communities. We had also discussed expanding with the franchisor into a small chain of stores servicing the resort areas.

The reasoning for the franchise agreement was sound; both Dan and I agreed it was mutually beneficial to both parties. What really happened was that we let down our guard and invited in a shark to swim in the water with us. We were doing all the lifting and working to keep the store growing, but all the promises of advertising and investment dollars, along with promises to help the expansion into the other communities, never happened. We were giving up 20% of our earnings to the franchisor and we were getting zero in return. We began a back-and-forth exchange involving lawyers and screaming matches that seemed to go on for months. We tried every possible way to break, change or renegotiate, but no one was budging. The bottom line was we were in business with these guys now and had to figure it out.

One day I was sitting in the store and a gentleman walked in. I knew right away he wasn't a customer by the way he carried himself. He walked right up to me and asked, "Are you David Clark?"

"Yes," I replied.

"You are served," he said casually and walked out.

I can't say that I was totally shocked to be sued, but I must admit I almost fell off my chair when I saw who this lawsuit was from. I assumed it was from the franchisor we signed our new agreement with or maybe one of his associates; it wasn't. It seems that things were going really bad for the new owners of my old business. I called my lawyer and a few people in the industry to try to figure out exactly what was going on. The lawsuit named me personally for over $600,000 on a defaulted lease.

In our purchase agreement, it was written that the new owners would not abandon or close any existing stores without notice to all parties. Further, it was written that in the event of default, the manufacturer would make sure that the leases were honored and didn't fall back on the selling party, namely me. This was the same agreement I made when I purchased the stores years earlier. Basically, it meant it didn't matter how bad it got, there was no defaulting on the leases and leaving the seller in the breach—you had to find a way.

The new owners had run my old stores straight into the ground before the ink had barely dried on our agreement. Not only couldn't they keep up what we were doing in sales, they couldn't even do what the company was doing *before* I bought the operation. They had run through all their considerable cash reserves, chased away all my former employees, and were getting ready to duck and run out of town. The manufacturer, in a despicable move, gave the new owners the green light to break our agreement and abandon the slower stores to cut expenses. When they defaulted on the leases, they simply gave the angry landlords my phone number and said, "Yeah, that's not our lease it belongs to this guy."

The lawsuit that I was recently served named me personally for 5 years' worth of rent at about $10,000 a month—and that was just one store. Dan and I both got served with three others over the next few days.

At this point in my life I wasn't surprised about anything—except maybe how much I was able to drink each night and still function the next day. I spent the next month or so trying to figure out exactly how this pending legal action was going to affect my current situation—more specifically, my current business, my personal credit, and my assets. They were all in jeopardy now... *again*. These leases were all personal guarantees, not just signed by a corporation. Worse still, we found out the "new owners" were filing bankruptcy, both personal and corporate. They were closing their doors for good and that meant there was only one party left for the lawyers to go after—me and my partner Dan.

"Goddamn it!" I yelled and kicked the desk in the showroom. "This is exactly what we were trying to avoid when we sold the damn company!"

"If we had known this I would happen, we would have kept the chain of stores and fought until the bitter end," Dan added. He was pissed too.

To compound matters further, I was getting a ton of pressure from the franchisor we had brought aboard in our current store. It seems he was no longer happy with his 20% and was willing to pull the franchise unless I renegotiated to 50% for him! It was almost funny, it was so outrageous. Not only hadn't he done anything to earn the 20% he was getting; now he wanted more. I was simply beside myself. This was nothing more than a cowardly act of taking advantage of the current situation. They knew if they pulled the franchise and I was forced to reopen as a new business, no one would give me credit or even sell me product in the middle of a lawsuit. He had me defenseless and he knew it. Some might call it shrewd business; I called it extortion and theft. We resisted at first but eventually we had to cave in. We signed a new agreement giving him 50% of the store—the store we opened, the store we alone built and envisioned to be the powerhouse it was now. We gave him the 50% he demanded on the day he had trucks scheduled to come take the signs down and get the product. I waited until the very end before I called him and begged him not to leave me on the street. I sat in the dark at the store behind my desk and stared into space.

"How could it come to this?" I wondered. I sat and drank at my desk for hours and then I went home and drank more.

The next morning I opened up the store that I was now a small ownership partner in; 50% for the shark, 25% for me and 25% for Dan. I was now getting twenty-five cents of every dollar that I made while a guy in an office somewhere who hadn't even been inside my store was getting fifty cents. Who is the dumb-shit in this picture? I wondered. I smiled as I turned on the lights and got ready for the day. Needless to say, I no longer felt like I was on top of the world looking down. Actually, I felt if I looked up I would see everything and everyone. I was on the bottom of the bowl.

If I needed an excuse to drink more, I had it now—but I never really needed an excuse anyway. Most of the time I drank now, it was to feel better—not in the sense of having a better outlook, but to not be physically sick. I would feel like crap most of the time until I had three or four drinks. Then it was ok for a while—some belly laughs, some suicidal humor—depends on when you caught me. In my late-night solo drinking efforts, I was starting to get angrier. I wanted to stop this freefall I seemed to be in. All the momentum in my life was negative now; every new piece of news was bad news. Every time I found something to be positive about, it seemed the carpet was jerked out from under me again. With the financial and business struggle looming, and with my drinking and weight spiraling out of control, I had to take some desperate action to get back on top. I felt that if I could change my body, I might be able to change my circumstances too.

The months ticked off at lightning speed and I continued to get drunker and fatter. I thought I needed do something before I died. Maybe at least go on a diet and start to work out again. This thought came to me after I saw a picture of me and two of my brothers standing in front of my house. It was taken on Thanksgiving Day and I had a huge smile on my face. As I gazed at the photo I thought, if I knew what I looked like as that photo was being taken, I would not have been smiling. I was wider than the two of my brothers put together. I was wearing waist-size 50 pants and my face was tired, with old-looking broken blood vessels riddling my nose—more signs of drinking.

The first step was trying to ease back on the drinking (amazing revelation) so I decided to drink only on the weekends. I went on an all-protein Atkins-type diet and I lost about 30 pounds in a month's time. During this period that I was managing to only drink on the weekends, I was drinking even more than usual—but it was limited in frequency, at least. I was still struggling to keep the booze at bay so I thought maybe if I cut out the hard alcohol I would be ok. This experiment ended after an evening where my mother came over to the house for a "Movie Marathon." While watching movies all night with my mom, I drank perhaps 40 beers or more. Hey, at least I wasn't drinking hard alcohol. I barely remember the evening with my mom, other than literally going to the restroom every 5 or 10 minutes. I fell into the wall going up the stairs into my bedroom and passed out. I was embarrassed, to say the least, so when I mentioned to my mom that I was a "little drunk" she said something about how it didn't seem like it, although I know the reality was I was passing out, slurring my words and talking over the DVD all night.

Of course, it didn't take too long before my motivation to diet and work out wore off. Despite feeling better and looking better, I just lost interest. It was almost as if all I wanted was to prove to myself once again that I could lose weight, like it was a "systems check." Ok, good news—we can lose weight, store that information for the future when I decide to get serious—now give me my Big Mac. I also lost interest in "drinking only on the weekends," and this whole "only drink beer" thing? That sucked too. I was right back into a bottle of scotch a day with some beers to throw in for good measure.

In my personal life, things were getting worse too. I had already started the process of my own personal bankruptcy and now it was only a question of how much I included in the filing—specifically, if I had to include the current business and its obligations. The store was still doing well overall, but the spring months were always slow for mountain retail shops. Now, with the larger franchise fees to absorb and two partners left to struggle with the leftover crumbs, it seemed more and more ridiculous as time went by. There was also an unspoken 900-pound gorilla in the room between Dan and me.

We had both considered the possibility of what would happen should one of us leave the company. With only one owner, the whole thing would be a much more appealing scenario. Initially I was hopeful that Dan would actually leave, since he had been talking of walking away for some time. In the end I think both of us knew it was just a matter of time before the shark made another move and pushed us both out completely and tried to take it all. So, after long consideration and debate, we both decided to get out— on our terms. Neither of us could stand being in business with someone we didn't trust, someone who had actually proven he couldn't be trusted. And it actually made me feel dirty to make someone else rich, riding on my back while I was just barely getting by. I had some offers of employment elsewhere, and I was starting to think that maybe working for someone else wasn't that bad a choice. After all, how could 225 million Americans be wrong? I included the lease and the store in my bankruptcy and walked away.

As I left the store for the final time, I stopped at the door and took a look around the empty showroom. With my hand still on the light switch, I just stood for a while and took it all in. Images started to fly through my mind as all the memories of the last few years and all the different stores I had owned fired randomly through my synapses. What the hell happened? It didn't make any sense and it really didn't matter anyway; I was out of this business for good and everyone else got the last laugh. It turned out they were the smarter and better men this time around. I wasn't sure exactly what would happen or how I would find my way out of this hole, but I had never given up on myself in my entire life and I wasn't about to now. I actually managed a smile as I flipped the switch off. I thought of Lee Greenwood's song *God Bless the USA*.

"If tomorrow everything were gone that I worked for all my life,
And I had to start again, with just my children and my wife.
I would thank my lucky stars to be living here today,
Because the flag still stands for freedom and they can't take that away."

I still felt lucky as I locked the door and drove back to my house to see my family. I drank almost 2 liters of alcohol on the one-and-a-half-hour drive home.

Bottoms Up

It felt as if I'd been hit by a bomb and left to sift though the rumble to try to find meaning in the aftermath. Once again I tried to adjust to a new life, and once again my drinking seemed to pick up momentum and carry me farther down into the fire and hell of addiction. If I had any lingering doubt that I was, in fact, addicted to alcohol, the delusion was nothing more than thin smoke. Although I did maintain a surface-level of motivation as far as my career or professional life was concerned, I was so beaten down and so firmly in the grasp of my addictions that I couldn't remain focused enough to make anything happen. My confidence was shattered and drinking made me feel better—better right up until it made things worse.

My current life didn't much resemble any life I had ever envisioned or even ever heard of, with perhaps the exception of some millionaire trust fund baby lost in the world drinking his way through life. Of course, I was broke, had no trust fund and if I didn't find a way to start making money again, I was going to be on the street. The bills were starting to pile up, and for the first time I was missing payments—car payments, house payments, credit cards— everything. It really didn't matter, did it? I was being sued for over a million dollars, what the hell did it matter if I paid my $2,000 credit card bill? Why not just go play golf and get drunk?

So, that's what I did. I played golf, I went on job interviews, and I drank... every day. Period. I went to the bar every afternoon—and sometimes I went to several bars. I would wake up each morning with a plan for that particular day's events, but really everyday was the same: take care of errands (as early as possible) so that I could get to the local bar to meet my friends. I would drink there until early evening and then go home for dinner and the real drinking. The real drinking I did at night was usually a large bottle of booze and several beers on top of the 10-12 drinks I would have in me before making it home. I was up until two or three in the morning, drinking myself into a stupor. If I had to guess, I was probably near 2 liters of alcohol per day.

The plans and schemes to try to reinvent myself post-business ownership took on many different and conflicting faces. There were times when I conceived of starting a company in my garage with the intent of growing it into a multi-million dollar enterprise. Then I would spend a week or two investigating and meeting with people to try to put my vision into a plan— before losing interest and moving on. Other times I would just throw in the towel entirely and think maybe the secret to happiness for me would be to surrender all this big-shot and overachieving stuff and just settle into a blue-collar working class life.

During this time, I took several jobs and started many new ventures only to quit on the spot without a reason or any notice. Many times I accepted a position after days of interviews, only to never show up for my first day of employment. I went to real estate school and sold a few houses. I was hired as a security guard. I sold lamps and lighting. I was hired as a general manager for a mattress manufacturer. I applied for bartending jobs, executive positions, you name it. Can you say confusion? I would vacillate between wanting a simple basic life to wanting to make a huge name for myself to prove to the world that I was no fluke. There was only one certainty—I was going to drink.

My typical morning now looked something like this: I would come to consciousness around noon or 1 pm. I would try to pry my red, blood-shot eyes open against the sun glaring into my empty bedroom. Heather had long since left the house to cart the kids around to various activities or to her part-time job, so I was left to myself in the quiet house. I would force myself to get out of bed and stagger to the bathroom where I knew the vomiting would begin—hell, I needed the vomiting to begin so that I could start to feel better and get to the pub. Normally my head would throb without mercy to the point where I could feel my heartbeat in my temples as I climbed into the shower. The dry heaving would usually start by the time I turned off the water. As the retching would take control of my body, I was constantly taking inventory of how I felt... more precisely, "if I felt like drinking yet." That's really what it was all about. I wanted to go to the bar to drink, but in this condition I couldn't make that happen. I would jump out of the shower and grab my spot, kneeling in front of the toilet, the heaving becoming more urgent and more violent.

As I jumped into my car, typically only minutes removed from the episode on the bathroom floor, I usually started to feel ok. I was not ok, nor did I feel ok, but I did feel better. Years later, I told friends that if I woke up this way now and felt "ok" like I did when I was leaving the house on those days, I would drive to the nearest emergency room and check myself in.

Next in my daily progression, though, I would arrive at my local bar, usually still drunk from the previous night. I would quickly grab a barstool and try not to seem too anxious, even though I needed the alcohol badly. I would order a cold beer and at the last minute, add a double shot of whiskey. I always ordered the whiskey as if it were an afterthought. "I'll take a cold draft... oh, why don't you pour me a shot too."

It must have been comical for the bartenders to see me relive this day after day. I can still see the frosty glass of beer and the shot glass parked right next to it on the bar. It looked wonderful and horrible at the same time. The thought of actually pouring that stuff into my head caused me great pain, made my stomach wretch and my skin crawl. Yet I knew once I got that booze past my lips and into my body, I would slowly start to feel good. No, that's not right. Actually, I would start to feel great—and I was right.

A few minutes later I was laughing out loud with the staff, poking fun with the other patrons and feeling like I was living the high life. Others in the place may have thought, "He sure seems like a happy guy." I would have my 9 or

10 drinks in me by the time I hoped off the barstool. And I was only getting started.

My best drinking was done when I was by myself. And by "best," I mean the drinking I enjoyed the most, and it was also the time when I did the most damage. Each afternoon after leaving that local watering hole, I would stop at the liquor store and buy my supplies for round two. There were usually three rounds in each heavyweight drinking night during this time of my life. Round one was always getting out of bed, making it through my vomiting practice and safely to the local bar to drink the afternoon away. Round two was the liquor store on the way home and the drinking I would do between dinner and when Heather and the kids went to bed.

This second-round drinking was the lesser of the three evils. I usually would drink some wine, sip some scotch and slow things down a little bit while the kids were around. I would focus temporarily on playing with the rascals and trying to make Heather laugh. Round three consisted of the serious drinking that would occur after the house went silent. This was (as always) the dark place, but the dark place was now darker than it had ever been—in fact, it was pitch black. Many times round three included a last minute midnight run to the liquor store before they closed. I made this run out of fear of running out of alcohol in the middle of the night. It usually didn't matter how much alcohol was in the house; the thought of being out of booze with no way of buying more would push me out the door and running to the liquor store. And of course I usually would take advantage of this trip to stop into McDonalds for a huge helping of "going-to-die-really-soon."

After my night run for greasy food and booze, I sat and drank alone in the sleeping house. I would turn out all the lights except for the TV. I routinely refused offers of going to concerts, out to movies, or to visit with old friends—all in favor of drinking by myself. Sure, I could drink out at a concert, or at a restaurant, but I couldn't drink the way I wanted to, or in the quantities I wanted to. I wanted to keep the alcohol for me. It was mine, my lover, my confidant; I didn't want anyone to even look at my booze. I even started to turn the TV off and just drink in the complete darkness.

We had a guest bedroom upstairs that I was spending considerable time in. The room was a very frequently used guest room; however, I relished the times it was unoccupied. I cannot tell you exactly why, but I was drawn to drinking in this room. I felt at perfect peace when I was there, all alone. I felt safe and I felt like I could drink the way I wanted to. I would buy two or three liters of alcohol and bring it up to the room and hide it. I wasn't hiding it so that my wife wouldn't know I was drinking; she knew I was drinking my ass off—it just made me comfortable to do this.

To know that no one else in the world knew about that particular bottle of booze was calming. I would usually start off in the dark with the TV on. I specifically remember watching *Lord of the Rings* or some other dark movie and just drinking down gulp after gulp of scotch. The warm alcohol felt like a thick wave of pure pleasure spreading through my body; I felt as if I were not dying by drinking, but the alcohol was actually making me come to life. Each swallow made me feel more alive and more like the person I truly was. It is a strange thing to feel like the poison is keeping you alive, while in reality I was in a car speeding out of control, directly towards death.

Like most abusive love affairs, mine with alcohol inevitably took me to places that I didn't want to go to. It would start out with a little light petting (or a sip or two) until the passion and need grew to the point of obsession; the booze tearing me up and beating me down, all the while I asked for more. More love, more pleasure—and more and more sweet numbness. I didn't care that booze didn't love me back; I still wanted her. The months and years slipped away and so did I. Over and over, I made my morning trip to the toilet, and every day now I was telling myself that I needed to get help.

"I know my life would be better if I didn't drink."

I said this almost every day now, even to my closest drinking friends. They would smile and look at me as if saying, "No shit, Sherlock." But they always played it off, because in their own words, they knew I was as hopeless a drunk as they had ever seen. I was starting to think they were right. How was this going to play out for me? Was I going to die in a car crash? Go to jail for a third DUI? Forced rehab, intervention? I couldn't even think straight anymore. Alcohol was causing everything in my life to fall apart, including my confidence, and now my body itself. I felt bad all the time. I was concerned that every ache and pain in my body was some form of cancer, cirrhosis, kidney failure or some other ailment that would kill me before I ever had a chance to see my kids grow up. My heart was beating irregularly now and sometimes I passed out just from laughing really hard—no warning, just lights out. None of these things stopped me from drinking.

After a few really scary episodes, I finally went to see the doctor. I was put under a 24-hour emergency observation to monitor my heart for an irregular heartbeat. They did test after test to determine what was causing my heartbeat to skyrocket out of control. I knew, even if they didn't. The doctor asked me, "How much alcohol would you say you consume in a week?"

I wanted to tell him right there and come clean with the entire unwashed truth, and I started to do just that, but I chickened out at the last second. I said something about how I had been drinking way too much lately and it was starting to be a problem. Then, when prompted again as to what amounts I was consuming, I said I was drinking five or six beers a day. It's funny, because even with the watered down drink count, the doctor thought my drinking was cause for alarm. I wonder what his response would have been if I had told him, "12 beers and a liter or two of 90-proof is usually enough for one day of drinking." I think mine might not have been the only potential heart attack in the room.

The doctor told me to cut down the drinking and adopt a better stress-relief system—and in fact, a whole new lifestyle if I wanted to live much longer. He knew I was also smoking cigars like crazy and eating like I would never see food again. Before he was done, he dropped a couple more bombs on me too. He said I was going to have a stroke. He didn't say it as if it were a possibility, but rather a certainty.

I looked down at the floor as he told me I needed to be on blood pressure medication immediately, within the hour. My blood pressure wasn't high; it was so dangerously high that it was a medical emergency. He told me my liver function was also dangerously low, but needed to be tested again after an alcohol fasting period. I was also just a hair from being a full diabetic, my skin was yellow and splotchy and I was 150 pounds overweight. He wrote me a prescription for the blood pressure medicine, ordered more blood work, and scheduled me for a follow-up appointment.

I never showed up. I continued to drink.

The holidays arrived again, as they do, and I was still managing to present what I would have described at the time as a "relatively normal family life" despite killing myself every day. The denial was massive enough to be its own planet. There was nothing "normal" at all. Sure, I still spent time with my kids, I still had dinner with the wife, and I still had a fully functioning role as the patriarch of my household, but I was nevertheless falling farther and farther into the abyss. I remember taking a test from Johns Hopkins Institute about diagnosing if you were an alcoholic. If you scored over 10, you were definitely an alcoholic and if you hit 15, you were in the advanced stages. I scored a 20 out of a possible 22.

I went to an AA meeting and after one session I quickly ruled that out as an option for me—in fact, I chose to see that I had things under control. Those AA guys were the ones with the problems; drinking mouthwash? Beating up your wife? I didn't do either of those two things, so I dismissed the 100 things that I did have in common with the other people at the meeting, and I went home and got drunk.

The day arrived that I was to put up the Christmas lights on our house; it was a chore that I enjoyed immensely. The holidays have always been something I looked forward to all year long, and I counted down to the next Christmas, starting on December 26th. I invited my brother Chase over to my house to help me with the lights, as was our tradition, and I remember feeling absolutely at peace when he arrived at the house. My brother and I were, in addition to family, lifelong friends and drinking buddies—and in fact, he is one of the only people I knew who could drink with me for hours and not get sick. Of course, we had planned on drinking while decorating, that was a given. But we went right for the hard stuff this time.

We started with a bottle of 100-proof peppermint schnapps mixed with some hot chocolate. It's amazing to me that we ever got the lights up on the house—or didn't at least kill ourselves trying. We drank the first bottle within the first hour. For the second bottle, we dispensed with the hot chocolate mixer and just dumped the coco powder directly into the schnapps. The second bottle was gone in another hour and we switched to Irish whiskey and beer. I can't tell you what happened the rest of the evening because I don't know. That night was like many others previous to it; the evening played out as normal, I didn't do anything crazy or nuts, but I was so drunk that my mind lost the ability to record the evening for review at a later date. It's like turning on an old VCR for the evening, but there is no tape in the machine. Nothing, just blackout. I went out to the front yard the next day to admire and see what the lights looked like. I was happy to see that the house looked nice so I collected the various empty liquor bottles from the garage floor and yard and went back inside to drink.

On Christmas Eve a few days later, I had been drinking (no shock there), but I was really doing it in grand style. I spent several hundred dollars on top-shelf booze and I had the people closest to me coming to help celebrate the season. Every December 24th we had people over to our house for our traditional Christmas Eve crab and lobster feast, and this year I made sure there was enough alcohol there for an entire army platoon. I bought bottles and bottles of wine, cases of beer, and so much hard alcohol that even if everyone there drank as much as I did, I would still have plenty left over. Just knowing that the arsenal of alcohol was there was enough to put a big festive smile on my face. I drank an entire bottle of scotch just preparing dinner before anyone showed up. I then switched to wine and beer as our guests arrived and we had a spectacular evening of laughter, warmth and connection. I made sure everyone, including myself, never ran dry and always had an alcoholic beverage in front of them. Occasionally I would leave the room and turn around to watch everyone unaware they were being observed; I took in the laughter and ease that alcohol allowed everyone to slip into and the way the conversation flowed, just as the alcohol itself did. "What better a thing is there besides alcohol?" I thought.

Eventually the evening ended and everyone went home. Heather and I spent a little family time together with the kids before sending them up to their rooms in anticipation of Santa's arrival. Heather eventually went to bed, as well, and I was left to myself to do my final gift-wrapping and preparation. I had already consumed God knows how much alcohol over the course of the day, but I was still at least functioning at a level that would allow me to do basic actions such as cut wrapping paper, open a bottle, put ice in a glass, etc.

But something happened. I opened another bottle of scotch and the deep need took over. I turned on the Christmas music and sat back and drank. I forgot about the gifts and I drank freely and uninhibitedly. By the time I knew what happened it was 3 am and the bottle was empty. I looked at all the gifts I had spread across the living room floor and panic hit me hard—there was no way I could wrap these gifts. I didn't have the faculties to operate a toaster in my current super-inebriated state; I couldn't even process what I needed to do to get started. I just stared at the wrapping paper and boxes and started to cry. Yes, I started to cry. I am ashamed to write it, but I was too drunk to wrap my wife's gifts and I didn't know what to do.

Being a drunk makes it almost impossible to control your emotions, and my tears quickly gave way to frustration and then to irrational anger. I tried to stand up and fell off the couch face-first onto the floor and received a nice carpet burn on my face (I wouldn't know about that until the next day). I attempted to wrap the gifts but it wasn't working. I kept forgetting what I was doing in mid-wrap; I was dropping things and getting more and more confused as the booze in my stomach continued to make its way into my blood. My blood alcohol level was rapidly raising and, at the same time, lowering my ability to do anything that required thought. I dropped the scotch tape and couldn't find it. I was too drunk to search the living room floor and find it, though it must have been within three feet from my hand to the floor.

I was starting to get angrier now. I stood up, fell down, stood up again and went into the garage. I grabbed some electrical tape, which was the first thing I saw, and I went back into the living room and grabbed the first gift. I slammed the gift into what was probably a sheet of wrapping paper large enough to wrap a grandfather clock in, and I folded the paper around the box like I was wrapping a deli sandwich. Then I grabbed the electrical tape and wound the tape around the paper and box like I was wrapping a mummy or rolling up an extension cord. I used maybe an entire roll of wrapping paper and a quarter of the roll of electrical tape on one gift. "One down!" I said triumphantly. I wrapped the remainder of the gifts this same way and threw them under the tree, feeling angry, sad and embarrassed all at the same time. I walked to my bedroom and passed out.

Christmas morning came and I woke up to a feeling of absolute hollowness; my soul was gone. I felt guilty and I didn't know why yet. I could vaguely remember what happened the night before, but as I rose to go vomit, the details came crashing back in. I turned on the shower to cover the sound of my retching. I finished and came downstairs and into the living room to watch the kids open their gifts with the excitement and magic that only kids can bring to Christmas morning. As I sat and felt my head throb, I watched my wife as she handed out the gifts. "Yours are the ones with the electrical tape," I said, trying to make a joke out of what I saw under the tree.

I was horrified. The gifts looked like a mess of black tape and torn paper that had been thrown into a paper shredder and then set afire. My wife didn't even notice how horrified I was. She laughed it off as me getting frustrated with trying to wrap gifts, something I have always been poor at. She smiled as it took her several minutes to try to unwind and cut through all the tape to get to each gift. She remarked that she would never forget what she got that year because of all the work needed to uncover each prize. This is one of the memories that still haunt me today. Heather, I am sorry—you deserved better.

My parents called later that day to see when we were coming over for dinner. The plan was to go over to my mother's house for Christmas afternoon. Christmas is very big to our family and this was planned months in advance. I told my mother I had a toothache and would not be able to make it. "Sorry, I love you," was about all I could manage to say. I was lost. She was heartbroken, but really, she was more concerned for the pain she thought I was in. Moms are special, to say the least. Of course the only pain I was experiencing was the black and dirty sorrow of regret, self-loathing, and the throbbing headache from my hangover. I was never more out of control and now I had let it ruin Christmas. What the fuck was wrong with me? The final kick in the balls came when my father showed up at my house later that afternoon to see how I was doing. He brought me some pain medication the dentist had given him last time he went in for a root canal. He told me not to worry and we would get together as a family after my tooth stopped hurting. He left the house to go back to their Christmas dinner, and I went to go pour a big glass of booze. I looked at the Vicodin bottle my dad gave me, opened it up, ate a few of the pills without thinking, and then slammed an entire glass of straight alcohol. Merry Christmas.

There was no longer even a hope of drinking normally. In fact, there wasn't even any hope of stopping. The booze had me completely. I surrendered to it; it was going to run its course even if it took me all the way to death. And honestly, I didn't even care much if I died, either. I didn't want my kids to grow up and see me like this, I didn't want to live like this anymore, and I was pretty sure everyone would be better off if I just drank myself to death or stepped in front of a bus. I wish I could say that this was rock bottom for me, but I went on like this for years and it got worse, in fact. It's hard to imagine that I made it days, much less months and years, in that state. There were hundreds more stories like the gift-wrapping incident or the Christmas lights. Those are merely examples in a collection of a hundred, or perhaps thousands, of times that I drank myself completely out of reality and into a world that was lonely, dark and confusing.

I drank a gallon of Jagermeister one night and was so drunk I couldn't sleep, so I just lay in bed next to my sleeping wife, crying in alcoholic confusion.

I fell down the stairs in front of Bennigans Restaurant after sitting on a bar stool for 6 hours even though I only went inside for "a quick drink before heading home."

I ate an entire bottle of pain pills after having my wisdom teeth removed; I used a bottle of Irish whiskey to wash down the Vicodin.

Over and over, each week brought a new humiliation and a new low. I kept drinking anyway. I drank every day, all day, and into complete oblivion. I would chose to be alone in the dark and cry for no reason, sitting on a chair in the dark, sobbing to God asking, "Why do I do this?" I was literally praying for death, asking God to take mercy on me—not by saving me from drinking, but to just let me die. I started smoking cigarettes again. I felt so lost that it didn't matter what I did to myself. I bought a pack of cigarettes on the way home one day, sat down, got piss-stinking drunk and smoked the entire pack—a ritual I repeated for months. I sat in the driveway in front of my house drinking until 3 am without saying anything. I would stare into the neighborhood and drink until I could barely stand up. All the while I was thinking that everyone in all those sleeping houses knew some secret of life that I was just too dumb to see. "Why is everyone so happy, and I am so miserable inside?"

Adding fuel to the fire was the fact that the pending financial devastation I had been running from had finally arrived. I was a million dollars in the red and I had no real income to speak of. I had burned through all the money I had stashed away and I didn't work long enough in any one job to ever get ahead of the bills. I was now pawning my own personal items just to keep the lights on. It was more honest to say I was drinking away all the money I was earning and pawning my possessions to cover the deficit. I gave up my $2,000 gold watch—sold for $60. My jewelry, music equipment, you name it—all gone. The foreclosure notices had been piling up for months and bankruptcy was inevitable. I knew it was coming, but I had been putting it off in hopes I would find some miracle way out. I received a final notice from my bank saying they were going to auction off my house if I didn't get the mortgage caught up in 10 days. I filed the bankruptcy paperwork, and then I went and got drunk.

"This is it—I am going to die," I whispered. And oddly, although the thought seemed heavy, it seemed ok. At the same time, though, I summoned one final plea. "Please," I said so softly I barely heard it myself..."please, help me."

The jig was up. I didn't need any more proof; I didn't need any more mornings like this one. In fact, I'd had way too many already. I finally accepted in that instant that I was powerless to fight this addiction by myself. I was in over my head, I was in deep shit and I was scared. Somehow I picked myself up from the floor, showered and left the house for work. A couple of years earlier I had filed bankruptcy just in time to save my house; now I had a regular job to make payments to the trustee, three years' worth of a monthly reminder of my failure in the business world. I was drinking at work every day now and I was worried that despite my current acceptance of rock bottom, I might drink again when my hangover wore off. I knew this was my moment, this was it. The time had come for me to die or fight.

I had spent literally thousands of hours over the last several years relentlessly debating myself on whether I was truly an alcoholic or just a problem drinker of some sort. I played every angle possible and I tried every way to moderate my drinking. I tried to modify my drinking. I tried hundreds of times to quit, and I always went back to the bottle worse for the wear. I wanted to quit drinking forever, I wanted to get better; but how? The only thing I knew at this point was how not to quit.

It is very difficult to describe to someone who hasn't battled the demons of addiction, the power and hold that dependency has over the addict. It seems so obvious to me now that I was out of control, but in the moment, I was very invested in any justification that would allow me to continue to use alcohol excessively. I could never in all those years past bring myself to admit I was an alcoholic, and it was a huge roadblock to my seeking help with my addiction. I could joke about it; I could say it out loud, even with tears in my eyes, while I was drunk. But I could never accept its reality. I was incapable of understanding the true meaning of it.

It's like the difference between memorizing a fact or the definition of a word, and possessing the true understanding of how something actually works—two very different things. At this point of the game, I was very close to finally making the connection on a real and meaningful level. A thought in the form of a question hit me hard from nowhere—did I display any behaviors that would suggest I was chemically addicted to alcohol? Forget the labels of "alcoholic" or "problem drinker." Do I treat alcohol the same way a heroin addict treats their drug? Do I obsess over alcohol? Do I keep going back to it no matter how much pain it brings? Am I willing to go to great lengths to hide or protect my drinking? Yes. The answer was yes, yes and yes. So if I display all the characteristics of addictive behavior, isn't it safe to say that I am addicted to the chemical of alcohol?

As I said before, the concept of being an alcoholic wasn't new. In the past I would use the word "alcoholic" to describe myself to friends. I would laugh about it and even consider it internally, but never in my heart-of-hearts was I ever able to make the leap to acceptance of the label "addict." I just assumed I drank way too much—I was probably depressed and maybe even a shallow human being, but alcoholic? No way. That's for people who have no control over themselves. Alcoholics are weak, they have no power; that wasn't me... was it? When I considered the question of whether I was just "addicted to alcohol" as opposed to being alcoholic, I could see a small window of clarity opening. It was hard to argue that I wasn't addicted to alcohol when every single behavior and practice of my daily life seemed to confirm the hypothesis.

As humans, we can become very obsessed with compartmentalizing and labeling ourselves into small bite-sized, easy-to-digest pieces. I was so concerned about how the moniker of "alcoholic" would change my life that I couldn't see I had an alcohol problem. As the truth started to worm its way into the frozen ground of my head, I started to become aware of the looming shadow of my past behind me. I was growing uncomfortable at the prospect of truly seeing my own reflection—for the first time in years—as it truly was: blurry, blistered and at the bottom of a bottle.

I realized I didn't care anymore. I surrendered to the concept that I was beaten. I wasn't up to the challenge. I lost the battle. It was over. I conceded. I gave in without another thought. I knew the longer I waited or the more I thought about it, the greater the chances were that I would find a creative way to justify my actions and keep drinking. I didn't know what it meant to my future drinking or what was going to happen in 5 minutes, much less 5 days into the future, but I jumped through the rabbit hole. I decided to accept that I WAS addicted to alcohol. I could buy that for now and worry about the labels later. In the light of this particular day and hour it seemed obvious; if I display all these characteristics of addiction, I must in fact be addicted. Period. Who the fuck cares if that makes me an alcoholic or not? Maybe I would never be sure if I was an alcoholic, but I did know that alcohol had control of me, not the other way around. In fact, it would sure explain some of the stupid shit I seemed to do if I was blinded by the power of a chemical dependency—and not driven by a hidden unknown compulsion to destroy myself.

As fate would have it, on this very first day of my enlightenment, a good friend called me and told me he was quitting drinking. He said he had enough of the bottle and he needed to start living a better life before it turned ugly. I know for a fact, that my friend knew I was farther along the road of alcoholism than he was, but I don't think he had any idea as to the true depth of my struggle with alcohol. I told him I would join him in quitting and he was surprised and very pleased. "Let's quit together," he said. "We can find all kinds of cool shit to do without getting drunk." I agreed. We talked about going camping and hiking and all manner of fun "non-drinking" adventures. I told myself that this time would be different; I was going to stay sober this time.

I went to work that day and managed to work an entire day without getting drunk. I even stopped at the bookstore on the way home (instead of the bar) and purchased a book on alcohol and addiction. I read the entire book that night and cried several times. My mind was moving at a thousand miles a second, and I was uncomfortable just sitting in my own skin. I was horrified as to what the next day would bring and to what would happen as my head hit the pillow that night without alcohol in my body for the first time in years. The truth is I was more afraid of *me* than anything else. I knew I was a gifted debater and speaker, and I knew I could talk myself into or out of anything I wanted. So the question was, "Who is going to win this battle for control—the good me or the bad me?"

My friend called me the next day as I left work. It had been two days since we made our "quit drinking" pact and he was calling it quits on calling it quits. He told me he had drunk that afternoon and, in his words, "I didn't feel bad about it at all." He told me he just needed to slow down his drinking a bit, but he saw no need to deny himself something he enjoyed so much. "Life is too short, man," he said.

I agreed.

Not only did I agree, I thought my friend was right. Why live a life where you have to fight yourself all the time? I decided to stop at my regular bar on the way home and get drunk. It was a huge relief. I could put away all this nonsense about addiction and sobriety and just go be me again. I didn't have it that bad, I was just being melodramatic. "Of course you do some stupid stuff when you drink, but that's just because you drink so much," I told myself. "You just need to find out why you are so unhappy, and then you won't drink so much."

That actually made sense to me. I could taste the ice cold beer already and a shot of whisky (or ten) sounded absolutely heavenly. As I drove down the road I turned up the stereo. I got on the highway headed towards my local pub. As I tapped out the beat to the music on my steering wheel, I felt happy and light. What a fucked up thing to feel in that circumstance. Happy? I just threw away a shot at having a life, on a whim no less, without so much as a struggle. How could I be happy? However, as I got closer to the bar, I started to feel uneasy. I was sensing a crucial moment slipping away. What was I doing? Where was all my resolve? Where was this going to end? I suddenly remembered my hopeless plea from the bathroom floor, "Please, help," I had said. "What if...?" I started to ask. "What if I just didn't drink tonight?"

I started to get very anxious as the tension between my addiction and my thin grasp on reality battled. I looked straight ahead as I drove and wondered out loud, "What the fuck is this? What is going on in my head?" I pondered what the stakes were in this mental ping-pong game. It occurred to me that if I drove to that bar, I might never see my son or daughter grow up. I might never see that look of respect and admiration that a good father deserves to see in his grown children's eyes. If I go to the bar—even just one more time—maybe I'll never get another chance at a new life. Or worse, maybe my children will grow up to pity me. And if I died from my alcoholic activities, would I become a painful memory for them? Would I be just the memory of the dad that drank himself to death before his kids ever really knew him?

I made a split-second decision—I wasn't going to the bar tonight. I cannot explain how or why, but I was certain that if I didn't decide to *not* drink right then, right at that very second, I NEVER would. This was it. Get up and fight or lie down and die. I looked into the rearview mirror and said with as much conviction as I could, "I'm not a bitch—I'm not going to lie down and die like one either." I was going to fight with everything I had. I drove home in silence.

The relentless internal chatter that goes on in an addict's mind is nothing short of pure insanity. There really is no other way to accurately categorize it. The monologue follows no logic, so we produce romantic evidence to justify chemical abuse, and we present the evidence as if it were fact. The voice inside is willing to make emotional pleas to convince the body that it is ok to go back to using, even when doing so will cause greater depression, pain and perhaps death. There were times where I was actually afraid I was going to win the argument and be forced to never drink again. I was worried about talking myself into sobriety... how fucked up is that? Other times, I was horrified of the opposite. I was scared I would quit and find happiness, only to unwind it all in a moment of weakness when I talked myself into "just a quick beer."

I was simply all over the map. I would wrestle around every possibility that my drinking could be somehow managed and done responsibly. I would find a place where I was comfortable in quitting and then end up pulling a complete 180 in a matter of seconds. I needed an epiphany of some kind, one piece of actual leverage or wisdom that would override everything else. That wisdom came to me in one simple thought, "People who aren't alcoholics don't sit up at night and wonder if they are alcoholics."

I went to an AA meeting on my third day of sobriety. I think I went to AA if for no other reason than to prove to myself that I was taking the life change seriously this time around. I made a pact with myself before I arrived, I decided that I was going to trust that I didn't know everything in the world, and maybe I could learn something if I opened up and listened without defense. I had been here before, but I had never really been here to *be* here.

With a firm resolve, I found the nearest meeting place and I left my preconceptions at home; I was going to go make a couple friends and see if I could glean a few nuggets of wisdom from those that had been where I was. What I found at the AA meeting this time around was real people; people that work and live and die on the same ground that I did. I saw some folks I would call winners and I saw some I might have described earlier in life as losers. I saw a couple people that I had some common ground with and many others with whom I did not. But whether I liked it or not, I did have a common bond with all these people. Alcohol was wrecking our lives. It didn't matter if I drank the same exact way that this person did, or had the same consequences that person did; we were all being devastated by booze. I remember vividly in exact detail the first time I introduced myself...

"Hi, my name is David... [excruciatingly long pause] I have come to realize recently, or maybe I always knew, that I am an alcoholic."

I felt the final piece of weight I had been carrying fall off as I finished the introduction. In an instant I saw the last few years in front of my eyes—luxury boxes at the Pepsi Center and $1,000 dinner tabs. I saw rooms at the Ritz and limo rides to the airport. I saw my kids being born and the first time they smiled. I saw the day I bought my house and the day Heather and I brought the kids home from the hospital. Then I saw all the horrible places I let myself go—the drunken nonsense, slurred sentences, and humiliation. Although I slumped forward with the realization that I had fallen so far, I felt strong to know I was finally done descending. I was at the bottom, and I was going to start to climb out, God help me. I didn't say much during the meeting but I listened and watched. As I left the meeting, I wasn't sure if I had really listened to anyone before in my life. It seemed as though my previous idea of listening was simply hearing what the other person was saying before I dismissed it or extracted a useful experience.

I was about a week into sobriety when I was finally able to sleep. In fact, it was the first time I actually slept in several years. Previously, my evenings ended, not with a restful slumber, but with me passing out and/or blacking out on top of my bed covers—or many times out like a light on the couch. It may have resembled sleep to the outside observer, but it was the rest of the walking dead. Over those first few nights without alcohol in my system I tossed and turned and jerked awake in a nervous sweat every few minutes. I had crazy dreams of drinking again and I even had nightmares haunted by bottles of booze chasing me through the woods. I couldn't stand still for more than 10 seconds during the day and my mind was bouncing around like a pinball. My hands were shaking so bad that I was embarrassed to take them out of my pockets, and as the night approached, I was anxious as to what would happen when I closed my eyes to attempt sleep. Would I talk myself into drinking again as I laid on the bed listening to the chitchat of my withdrawing brain? Would I go crazy and run out of the house naked into the night? Anything seemed possible.

After 7 days of not being comfortable in my own skin, sleep finally did come—and it was a true deep, rejuvenating and restful sleep. I didn't pass out, I didn't black out; I was at peace. That night I simply walked into my bedroom, stood at the window looking out into my neighborhood, and then climbed into bed and drifted off to sleep—not because I was in bad shape, but because I decided I wanted to sleep. It was a victory. It was a small one, but I was in the game and I was doing ok for now.

It was obvious that I had lost who I was somewhere along my plunge into chemical addiction. "Who am I now?" I thought. Was I an entrepreneur? A father? An alcoholic? Am I even a "good person"? Was I a man that I would like to know? The only thing I was sure of anymore is that I wasn't sure of anything. I was tired of battling myself for control, I was tired of being uncertain, and I was tired of being so tired and confused. The one piece of good news was that I wasn't drinking anymore. Incidentally, this was also the bad news (depending on what time of day you asked me). However, despite the turmoil, I was starting to feel pretty good. But what did this mean for my future? Was I truly done—forever? No more celebratory champagne? No more fine bottles of scotch, even on the rare special occasion?

I had no other choice as I saw it; I had already surrendered to the fact that I would never be able to drink "normally," so no need to revisit it again. I realized that if I could never drink responsibly, it only makes sense that I can never drink at all—an obvious point and I knew it was very dangerous to start thinking into the future. The only thing I had control over long-term was the present moment. Maybe I would decide to drink again one day; maybe I wouldn't, but I didn't have to drink now. It seems so easy, so obvious: "just quit," right? No, it's not nearly that simple or that easy.

Alcohol affects your brain. It affects the way you see and interpret the world, and it also affects how you handle the world you live in. I had learned to use alcohol to experience life. Good things happen; celebrate. Bad things happen; drink your cares away. Vacation; drink to relax. There wasn't anything that happened in my life that I didn't immediately associate with alcohol. I had what on the surface seemed like a nice innocent thought, one of those first sober days while playing catch with my son. "What if Davey plays for the New York Yankees one day?" Pretty nice thought for a dad to have, right? Well my jacked-up addict brain wouldn't allow me to just think of baseball; I thought, "How amazing would it feel to sit in the luxury box at Yankee Stadium and watch him play *and drink scotch*." I was insane, I thought, and shook it off. But it did prove a point—my entire way of thinking was going to need to change.

The most insidious part of battling for sanity and sobriety is that the only weapon you have to use against yourself is your brain, so this creates a paradox of monumental proportions. We damage our brains with alcohol and then we try to use the malfunctioning organ to convince itself that it doesn't want the magic liquid that will make it all better again! It's not a very fair fight, if you ask me, and the weight and confusion of the struggle is immense. I tried to ignore the prospect of living my whole life without alcohol because no matter how hard I tried, I couldn't digest the thought of never drinking again. It was too big, too powerful, so I danced my ass off to go around the issue. I wouldn't allow myself to spend time thinking about anything other than not drinking right in the moment. I couldn't think about next Christmas with no wine, or the next time I go camping without beer. I knew that there would come many times in my life that a compelling reason to drink would present itself, but I was going to have to trust myself to make a good judgment at the time. Until then as long as I wasn't on a bar stool, I was doing good work.

I started to deconstruct the image I had built of myself over the last 10 years or so and I saw vividly how much I was losing to the addiction. The addiction wasn't changing me as much as it was erasing me. I was withdrawing farther and farther into the shadows. I could see that most clearly when I was home with my kids and wife; I wasn't really there. When I was at a family function or party—or even by myself alone in a room—I wasn't there. Only the leftover shell of what the alcohol had created was there. And each time I filled my body to capacity with chemicals, I pushed more of me out of that shell and, in turn, awoke even more hollow the next day. I wasn't living at all; I was slowly dying. And as confused as I was at who I was at the moment, I was concrete on a couple things: I loved my kids more than anything on the planet. I was willing to do anything to protect them, and I knew deep inside that I was meant to be on this planet for a reason; we all are. I may have gotten sidetracked, but I felt that I had a mission to discover and complete. I was not ready to die; I was not ready to give up.

Although I was spending considerable effort to "live in the moment" and trust the future to work itself out, I also had to examine what type of person I wanted to be, moving forward. I refused to be the person I had been for the last several years. I was tired of being weak and tentative; I was tired of feeling that everyone else in the world knew some secret to happiness and I was the schmo who didn't get it. I had spent several years of my life being a leader and I was committed to getting that personal respect back. Everything was going to change. I promised myself that I would pull myself back up to sanity and control, and if I was ever fortunate to get back on top, I would never forget how low I was right now. I wanted to remember exactly how it felt to be at the bottom of the world's trashcan.

I never thought of myself as the "recovery guy" or the 12-stepper that would sip club soda while everyone parties their ass off. But I did start to think of myself as the guy who didn't need to drink alcohol to have fun. My first reaction was to just "become the old me," the one that was doing ok before alcohol wrecked his life. But as I considered that, it seemed way off. If I was in control before, how did I end up here? Maybe I was never truly in control of anything, maybe it was all an illusion—one that I had been chasing my whole life, and caused me to drink to escape from the reality that I was just as lost as everyone else. And so I asked myself, "Was I ever really successful?" I guess only if I could consider being fat, broke and drunk successful—because that's where my thinking lead me.

Be the Change

What type of life do I want for myself? It's a good question to ask. What would I look like? And what would I do with my time each day if I weren't 320 pounds and if I were healthy and sober and happy? I wanted to see a crystal-clear picture of this life, down to the way I would dress and what I would say. I could close my eyes and almost feel what it would be like waking up in the morning free of the sickness of the previous night. I could almost touch the peace of mind that must come with being free from alcohol and unencumbered by the worries of deteriorating health. How much better a father, a husband, could I be as this man? I reviewed all of the goals I had when I was younger. What had I wanted to do when I was a kid? Grow up to be an athlete or author, musician? I remember always being struck by the lure of impossible feats of endurance. I remember watching the Ironman Triathlon in Hawaii, and I remember how inspiring it was to think of Terry Fox running across Canada. I even revisited my childhood plan to bike ride across the US.

I had written down "run a marathon" on my life goals list many times as either a New Year's resolution or my "five-year plan." In recent years, I had even used the dream of running as a goal to try to get back to health and sobriety. Even though I was still battling the demons of my addictions daily, every day that I didn't drink, all these dreams and goals seemed more tangible, more vivid and more real in my mind's eye. Without alcohol in my life there was no reason I couldn't start making my dreams a reality; there was nothing to distract me. In fact, every moment spent not taking an action that would bring about my desired outcome felt like wasted time.

I was starting to feel the momentum of change building. I was starting to feel like I was directing my life and not just reacting to it. I gave up the illusion that I could control the world or other people. But I certainly didn't have to sit adrift at sea, so I picked up a paddle and started to row towards shore. In the midst of the most humbling (and perhaps humiliating) time of my life, I was finding myself. I was searching for the essence me—the me that existed in my first days on the planet, the me that was pure energy and light, the source that makes a human unique. The me that was unencumbered by life and hurt, the person that was never cynical or addicted to alcohol. This potential energy inside would allow me to become a new creature, forged in the fire of recovery, alive for the first time.

I wanted to be man at peace and in control of my life and physical well-being. I liked that. That was a better image than the tragic entrepreneur with a destructive alter ego. I knew I was flawed. I accepted that I was weak. But despite being powerless over alcohol, I did have complete control over how I responded to this "weakness."

I decided I was going to run a marathon—it was as if it chose me. I think

I said it out loud before I ever even decided to run a race of any length. I owned the reality of this instantly, and before I could talk myself out of it, I told people—lots of people. I always enjoyed the looks I received when I mentioned this particular goal, and I loved to watch as their eyes moved up and down my 6-foot, 320-pound frame. I could see them doing the math, calculating the permanent damage to my knees, and the slim odds of my finishing 26.2 miles of running. I think most people thought I was being a little over enthusiastic on this one, to say the least.

"It's not that easy to lose weight in your late 30's, trust me—I have tried," my friends would say. Or my all-time favorite sentiment was, "You know running is really bad for you—how about some hiking?"

I didn't even think about how my body would respond to the rigors of training for a marathon; I figured I would work all that out along the way. What I needed now was time—time to continue to find my spiritual self, time to detox and time to lose weight. I would trust that if I took care of these roadblocks, I would be getting closer and closer to my running goals. The first part of my training, though, was going to be the hard work of changing my thoughts.

I quickly discarded the old picture of me and replaced it with a new one. Well, that isn't exactly right; I decided to not only replace the picture, but actually become a new person instantly. I was no longer thinking of how it would feel to be living the life I wanted, I was behaving as if I was already there. I started to research marathon distance events and training, and I learned everything I could on the subject of running. I started to think of myself as a runner. I started to dress like and talk like a runner. Fuck everyone if they thought I looked ridiculous walking around in track pants and running shoes at 320 pounds. I didn't care what they said. I used to worry about what others thought and it got me drunk. Now I was doing something for me, to make me a better person, father and son. So every time I ate, or planned my day, or even sat on the couch, I imagined myself as an Olympic marathoner. I wasn't "relaxing," I was recovering from training. I didn't "eat," I fueled my body for tough workouts. All my thoughts and actions were filtered through my new lens.

Eventually I chose the 2006 Denver Marathon as the event for the launch site of my spiritual and physical rebirth. It was a little over a year away, and I thought it would be a fitting way to celebrate a year of sobriety (if I were fortunate enough to make it that far). I was only 2 weeks into my sobriety at this point, and I had only recently stopped shaking enough to sleep through the night. I had dreamed my whole life of doing something like this, and I couldn't think of a better time to undertake it. This was going to be hard, this was going to be humbling, and this was sure to be the ultimate test of whether I was talking out of my ass, or if I was in this for keeps. I think it's hard for people to understand the subtle difference between using running to escape addiction and running to celebrate sobriety. As odd as it sounds, I did not quit drinking by becoming a runner as much as I became a runner after I decided I was no longer an addict. In past years I tried to do things the other way around and always fell on my face, drunk.

I was serious about running, at least as much as a guy who is a hundred and fifty pounds overweight can be. I even went so far as to custom-order some white silicon bracelets that had "26.2" printed on them. This was inspired by the distance of the marathon, which is 26.2 miles. I solicited all my willing friends to wear these bracelets in support of my effort to capture a new life through running. Incidentally, I had very few takers and I still have a large number of these bracelets, unused and still in the plastic, if you happen to need any.

Running for 26 miles when you can't even run for 26 seconds can be intimidating, and due to the nature of my large frame, I hadn't as of yet been able to do much actual running for any amount of time. My running consisted of a 15- or 20-second jog on the treadmill, followed by 1 minute of walking to keep my hammering heart from exploding in my chest. I would repeat this walk/run effort for 20 minutes every day in the hotel when I traveled or at the gym when I was home. My workout plan was pretty simple at first: get 20 minutes of cardio every day. If I could get more, that was even better. Each day I promised myself that if I could just get to the gym, no matter what else was going on, I was moving forward.

This became my daily affirmation of change. If I could force myself, no matter how hard it was, to get on the treadmill, I was moving farther away from my past. As every mile ticked off on the treadmill, I was farther from the drunken 320-pound version of myself that had to go away in order for me to live. At first I didn't even worry about numbers on the scale or how many miles I was logging. It was simple; go sweat and see how I felt. I even told myself it was ok to scrap a workout if I felt sore or tired, but before I skipped the workout entirely, I had to go get on the treadmill first—then if I still felt tired, I could go home after 10 minutes. I should add that never once did I scrap the workout. After a few minutes of cardio, I always felt better—or at least no worse. And I never regretted getting my workout done.

But my feet hurt, my back hurt. And I was NOT a very good runner. In fact, I think I sucked at it. But I have rarely let not being good at something prevent me from doing well at it. As I blindly trusted that not drinking was making me stronger, I also trusted that getting on the treadmill or stair machine was part of the healing. I kept coming back. I kept putting my headphones on and my shoes on, and I just ran. Two minutes of non-stop running eventually became 20 minutes, and the sore muscles started to grow strong. I was starting to feel like a runner and it was about time, because I had been living as if I was a runner for some time now—way before my stubborn body was able to actually run.

I had a background in chemistry and biology, and I tried to put that to work for me while I tried to figure out a new approach to this whole dieting thing. I knew I was going to need to do two things with my nutrition and eating habits if I was to be successful: number one, I was going to have to make sure I didn't do anything that I had tried before. I didn't need to prove to myself that I knew how to lose 50 pounds and gain it back; I had that mastered. Secondly, I decided I was going to look to the root of my behaviors and attitudes toward food. Basically, I wanted to take a business-style approach (results-focused) and mix it with what I knew of the body and how people gain fat chemically.

What is physically happening when people gain weight? Certainly it is more complicated than simply eating too much. There had to be a reason that there were so many people out there that didn't have an issue with gaining weight. Is the problem really that I am just weak? Or that I eat more than all those people do? Certainly it is true that I seemed to overeat, but is that somehow affected by chemistry? Is there any truth to the idea that skinny people can just eat whatever they want while the rest of us have to deprive ourselves?

Even though on the face of it I used to believe these things, I knew upon a deeper glance that something was off. I started to look at the people in line next to me at McDonalds. Were there healthy skinny people here? I was surprised to notice that, in fact, the overwhelming majority of people eating at my favorite restaurants (with the possible exception of those under 19 years old) all seemed to be overweight. I compared this to the times in the past that I took note of healthy or skinny people eating what I called "rabbit food" or very light and healthy options. Obviously I had it all backwards. I wasn't thinking, "Wow that person is really lean because they eat really well." I was thinking, "Look at that skinny dude eating the salad! What gives? You can eat anything you want, why not go grab a burger or three?" It was becoming obvious that I needed to start being very mindful of the reality of food.

I was ever cognizant of the fact that many times I had lost weight in the past, only to gain it back. And I didn't want to lose 50 pounds again—only to find myself back in the Big and Tall section looking for the perfect pair of size 50 stretchy dress slacks. I wanted to insure that this time was different, completely different. The other times I lost weigh it seemed as if it were by some sort of trick. I would leverage a large amount of will power or motivation to force myself to change my behavior long enough for my body to respond, only to later slip right back into my old habits.

Talk about insanity! If I went back to doing the things that got me fat in the first place, how could I ever expect to stay thin? It seemed that I was losing weight in the worst way possible—by cutting calories or eliminating entire foods groups in order to force my body to respond dramatically. Then I was always confused as to why I could never keep the weight off. What I needed was an entirely different paradigm, a whole new way of approaching my situation. I knew that if I wanted a result I had never received previously (to lose weight and keep it off), I needed to do things that I had never done before. Hmmm, now we are getting somewhere. Now we are "digging where the taters are," as us Paddys say.

So all that sounds well and good, but how do I lose weight while I am establishing new thoughts and behaviors—and make sure that I can continue these habits after I achieve my goal weight? Not so easy to answer. In fact, I had to ask myself some very uncomfortable questions to get to the heart of this. Questions like, "Why do I self-destruct?" and "Why do I always fail ultimately at losing weight?" As I pondered these questions, my brain started pulling files and establishing all the sufficient data from my past memories to supply answers to those questions. Dude, you have always struggled with your weight because you enjoy food too much—you don't want to live life like a monk. My biology is fat, my metabolism is slow, I am Irish...

No sooner did I start to analyze the results when a thought hit me, "Hey, I don't always fail. In fact, I have been very successful at times in my life. So why did I only come up with answers to the failure side of the equation? That's easy; that's all I asked for!" I realized in an instant how powerful the construction of my internal questions really was. If I rephrased the question a little to, "What have I done in the past to get lasting results in other endeavors?" Holy crap! I got an entirely different set of answers from my brain. I got answers like: "You were 100% committed to the outcome, you didn't entertain any thoughts of failure, you acted immediately and you changed your way of thinking!" The more I really delved into this, the more I saw the biggest problem I had to overcome was not surprisingly—me. Not my diet or my eating habits—if I changed only those, I knew what would happen—I'd go back to the old me eventually. What I needed to change was who I thought I was.

I am not a fat person. In fact, I am not sure there is such thing as a "fat person." Neither God nor evolution designed me to have a 50-inch waist and a 29-inch inseam. So why is it that I keep assuming what I am today is what I am supposed to be? It was a very interesting question to ask. Somewhere in my rise to 320 pounds I had decided that I was "just a big guy." I struggled with my weight on and off my whole life, and I finally gave in to the inevitable outcome—I was always going to be fat someday. But if I truly believed that I was a victim of my pre-determined biology, that would mean I felt that everything was already mapped out and I had no control. This was not a concept with which I was familiar. It did not fit with my life. I knew from all my experiences that people can change almost everything about their lives. People can overcome injury, poverty, mental conditions and oppression to become anything they aspire to be. So if I am not a fat person, why am I fat? Maybe, just maybe, I was fat because I *accepted* that I was fat and I came to redefine myself as a fat person.

How we view ourselves and define ourselves is perhaps the most essential paradigm we have as human beings. It determines all of our actions and reactions. I had witnessed first-hand that once I changed my vision of who I was in my career, my actions and behaviors in my work life changed immediately, permanently. Conversely, other times when I just tried to modify what I was doing daily in my behavior (follow up more on calls, be more organized, etc.), those changes were fleeting and I ended up right back where I started. The bottom line is this—we act in ways that support our true image of who we are. We do it without effort or struggle; we simple "are that person."

Isn't this really the struggle that faces every alcoholic or drug addict who is faced with the prospect of a new life? We view ourselves as "the drunk" or the "bad guy," the "tortured-soul artist" or any other picture. The picture we have isn't necessarily accurate or true; it simply "is." And by default, this image of self creates supporting actions. If you change the actions through willpower (abstaining from substance abuse without changing internal ideas, for instance), you eventually reach the point where you think, "This isn't me. What I am doing here? I will never be able to live like this forever." Game over, you go back to your old ways.

So if I am not a fat person and I am no longer a party-go-lucky business owner, who am I? How exactly do I define myself in my head now? What would I say if someone asked, "Who are you?" Do I describe myself as a father? A hard worker? An American? The answer is very tough. I see myself as all these things, but those are just labels. I needed to get deeper to the question of who I was in the absence of all those external things. The answer came to me on the stair machine as I was working out. "I am a child of the universe," I thought. Call it God or nature or whatever you like, but I was put on this planet for a purpose. Now, I don't think any one person was meant to be a plumber, banker or mechanic, but I do believe we all have a place to occupy in life. As I see it, my job is to maximize my talents and experiences in a way that will help make the world better—to carry my own weight in impacting the universal trajectory of mankind. (Damn that was deep. And kind of corny from a guy who still tells fart jokes... but it was true).

I have always defined myself as a person willing to accept the challenge, no matter what it was. I knew I could persevere. I knew I could go on and on—because I had to, there was really no other option in life. But somewhere along the way, I became a victim. I choose to define myself as someone who was tragically knocked off course. I had become someone who had endured enough physical and spiritual hardship to generate circumstantial evidence that I was born unworthy, that I was, in fact, faking it all those years and afraid people would learn the truth about me—that I was not as good as everyone else, that I was almost sub-human.

I started to chronicle with great detail, my past attempts at weight loss and life change. I got it all down on paper and catalogued my exact mistakes so that they were never repeated—like one time, I was so determined to lose weight that I decided I was going to go an entire week without eating. I set up an elaborate plan and started on a Monday. No food whatsoever but I did allow myself diet soda and coffee... sounds pretty healthy right? What do you think my chances were of making an entire 7 days without eating? Well, if you said 100%, you would be right. I did go an entire week without the benefit of a single calorie ingested. Did I lose weight? Yes. Did I continue with this new lifestyle change? Most certainly I did not.

Another time, after summoning another dose of will power sufficient enough to send me back to the "new body" drawing table, I decided that I was only going to eat canned vegetables. That was it—only canned vegetables. Sure, it was more healthy that the "all diet-soda" plan, but I wasn't exactly setting myself up for success here either. I made it a few weeks, believe it or not, and I lost a lot of weight. In fact, I felt pretty good on this diet—high energy, new outlook on life. I remember going on a fishing boat with my dad and being keenly aware of how much smaller I felt just walking around the boat. I was really proud of myself. When we got back to our place later that night, I decided that I had earned a treat. I can't remember what I ate for my "treat" but it was the end of that diet plan forever. I guess you could say I kicked the can down the road and went back to good old American fare—hot dogs, burgers, and cheese... oh my!

All protein, no protein, no fat, high fat, no sugar—you name it. Atkins, South Beach, and Mayo Clinic. I tried them all. I am pretty certain this type of behavior will be familiar for many people who have struggled with their weight—maybe not the exact same diet choices for the exact same duration, but the same extreme thinking, perhaps. Maybe you didn't forgo eating for a whole week, or maybe you went even longer. Maybe your diet included only eating foods of one color, or from one section of the grocery store, but my guess is that you have been able to execute some of these crazy plans successfully for short periods of time. The big point here is that changing your body is not all about will power.

Let me say that one more time. Changing your body and losing weight long-term is not about will power. We all have the strength we need to do things if we make them important enough to us. This strength is written in our DNA; you simply cannot hide from it. The problem is you cannot rely on these "strong" moments of will to carry you for the rest of your life. If you want to change yourself long term, you have to change the way you think and change the way you perceive the world. You have to come up with a new set of eyes to view yourself with. You need a new way of communicating internally with yourself and you need to ask yourself different questions.

Instinctively, I could feel a change in the power behind what I was doing in my life now. There was a weight and depth to it. I felt like I had a damn good chance at getting through to the other side. I felt as if there was an ease to the process that was absent in my past attempts at losing weight or quitting drinking. It felt easy. Now all I could think of was how to keep it going.

It occurred to me many years later what happened. I saw from the distance so clearly why I was able to so quickly drop the weight of all my past failures and never look back—I was simply being me. Certainly not the old me that struggled so many times and failed at losing weight, but the "new me" I wanted to create. No struggle, no will power needed. I was being the new person I created in my mind. Once I changed the vision of who I really was, my behaviors changed automatically. Sounds straightforward, but how did that vision of me change?

I think as human beings we can justify almost anything if we try hard enough. We see proof of this in our everyday lives. We see people steal, cheat, drive aggressively, endanger other people or just be plain rude. Are these people really all just "bad"? I think not. Chances are many of these are regular people that love their kids and want to live good lives just like you and I do, but they feel justified in their actions based on the current circumstances or impulse. They stole that item from work because they got screwed out of that promotion, or they lied because telling the truth would have hurt someone, or they cheated because it was better for their long-term relationships, etc. Are these valid justifications? For most of us the answer is no. But many times as humans, we aren't really seeking the truth in these situations; we are only seeking the permission to do what we subconsciously know is probably wrong. We used our internal images to work against ourselves.

We are constantly bombarded with enough input from our senses to simultaneously destroy our self-images or prove their validity. If we are, for instance, in a circumstance where we are questioning our personal ethics and we come across a movie or TV show that shows the leading character engaging in a series of underhanded and shady deals to get ahead, as caretakers of our thoughts, we have a couple of choices. We can choose to view this as proof that everyone in the world is corrupt and our bad ethics are no better or worse than the next person's. Or we can choose to view the television character as an illustration of how ugly it is when someone exploits others for personal gain. Or I guess the third choice would be to change the channel and find another show that may be a better fit for your current mindset, life or inner monologue. But make no mistake—whether consciously or unconsciously, we are making always connections and saving the images we see on TV or in movies for future reference.

As my pages were filing with notes, it was becoming crystal clear that the mental part of life change was not only the "secret sauce" or missing ingredient—it might be the single biggest part of all change. I was 100% committed to changing my personal images and paradigms and, in fact, changing who I was internally became a life practice and a daily game—a big game with life and death consequences. This game involved proving and supporting the new concept of whom I was in every moment. I had to approach my days with almost insane determination to not give in to old habits and to find affirmation that I was on the right track. I was greedy for anything I could do to prove to myself that I had it all wrong before. I wasn't born to be fat—that was the lie. I am a runner now. I eat healthy now. I am that guy, the guy who orders food from the healthy menus to the approving stares of others. I am the guy drinking the club soda while others drink alcohol. In fact, every time that I ate or went to the grocery store or gym, I viewed it as an opportunity to prove to myself that I was an athlete... and that I ate and trained like one.

I heard it said once that we are just like computers. Our minds are capable of perceiving, processing and executing millions of bits of information at all moments. And like computers, we all have a large, but somewhat limited, memory capacity. And just as computers are governed by their operating programs, so are we also governed by our perceptions and beliefs. A Christian woman will behave in a different way than a Jewish woman when invited to a pig roast BBQ; conversely, a Hindu might give you a funny look when you say, "What the hell? We only live once." The people and timing of the circumstance can be exactly the same, but the response will be very different based only on how the person views the world and the meaning they attach to the events. The same is true for us in every small interaction we have in our daily lives. Just like computers, we are constantly saving information to our hard drives that we feel is useful, and we are also simultaneously deleting information that we don't feel is valuable enough to store.

As I went about my daily activities of working and going to the gym, I was taking in feedback continuously. Some of this information was affirming that I was on the right track: weight-loss numbers, shrinking waistline, increased energy, clothes fitting differently, etc. Other times the information seemed to suggest I wasn't progressing: I looked bigger in the mirror, no change on the scale, not enough change on scale, too much change on scale, self-doubt. I had a choice to make. I chose to click the "save" button on all the positive results and send the rest of that shit to the recycle bin. If my clothes felt different, if I felt different and I was losing weight of any kind—I was happy. I refused to get sucked into the mental game that I knew would ultimately unwind my effort. Keep moving forward: eat right, work out, go run, don't drink.

I was more concerned with defending the image I had of myself as a healthy active runner than I was of getting my weight down. I figured that would take care of itself if I was just patient. I used the same thought process to steer myself from bad food choices. Whenever I thought about a particular food, I would filter the decision about whether to eat it through my new perception of the world. Would the person I wanted to be eat this? I wasn't fighting myself anymore. I didn't feel I was making a sacrifice; I was just being the person I wanted to be.

It's funny how we undermine our image of self without ever even being aware of the sabotage. For example, if you constantly update your Facebook page with pictures of bacon, and testimonials on how "whipped cream doughnuts" are the perfect food, you are probably going to be in for a struggle when you walk by Krispy Kreme or hear the sound of the grease bubbling in the frying pan. If you tie your very identity to an unhealthy and destructive food (or substance) what do you think your chances are of abstaining long term? Let me answer for you: low, *very* f-ing low. If you view yourself (even in humor) as someone who is in conflict and deprivation when healthy food is the only choice, how can you expect to eat healthy food and enjoy it? What are the chances that you will give in when confronted with temptation? After all, you are simply just "being you." So have that doughnut—it's *you* and you love doughnuts, right? Hey, I really like your new doughnut socks, BTW.

If however, you associate these desserts as poison, as items that will wreak havoc on your waistline, your blood sugar and your state of mind, you will treat them differently. If you look at these foods as devices of destruction, your behavior towards them will naturally change. Don't allow yourself to be a victim to food. You are in control of what you put in your body. Spend your time reading about and talking about healthy foods and how important they are. Research and learn how to cook healthy foods, share your love of healthy foods and exercise with the world, and your chances of eating in line with your beliefs are very high. Hey, I know it's really hard at first and being a fat person talking about eating healthy seems awkward and perhaps a little insane—but do it anyway. Crazy is a powerful tool.

So what exactly did my diet look like? If there was an overriding theme behind my diet philosophy it was this: eat in a way that won't be destructive in the aftermath. In other words, I wasn't interested in starving myself if it meant my metabolism was going to slow to nothing after I lost all the weight. I also didn't want to adapt an effective "trick" (such as zero carbs) that I wouldn't be able to sustain after the goal was hit. For me the science behind the Glycemic Index and Glycemic Load captured my interest and focus. As a chemistry guy, the science behind how my blood sugar affected my storing of fat seemed fascinating and on-point. And it just plain made sense to me that other factors besides calories were in play when it came to obesity. For those hardcore geeks like me, a quick Google search will provide many sources for in-depth analysis and hard scientific data, but here in a nutshell is the concept of why the Glycemic Index is so important:

The state or balance of your blood chemistry is a key factor in how your endocrine system operates. This system decides how and when to secret hormones in the body and basically regulates the entire sum of your metabolic activities through your glands. This includes energy production, handling stress, sleep, moods, fatigue, and yes—the storing and metabolizing fat. When your blood sugar and blood chemistry are in balance, your body is working very effectively and efficiently. There was very little in our ancestors' diets (meaning from 100 years ago or earlier) that would wreak long-term havoc on our blood chemistry balance. In today's day and age, however, this isn't the case. Many of the foods we eat regularly fall outside our current bodies' ability to manage them. Your body is a strong and magnificent machine, to say the least, and it is more than capable of pushing that Big Mac or bowl of Frosted Mini Wheat through the system without a long-term issue, but when the bombardment continues day in, day out for years. The body gets way behind and clogged up.

If you are one of the millions of people that think eating too many calories is your biggest problem, well you are only partially right. There are many factors in gaining weight, and calories are one of them. Actually, reducing your calories is probably the least effective way of losing weight long term. Before you go crazy on me, though, listen to my thoughts on this. If calories are the end-all and be-all, consider this scenario: if two people are both eating 2,000 calories a day, and one is eating spinach and fish and the other is eating lard, will these two people look and feel the same? If you think not, you understand the one of the most obvious and basic dynamics of food—how the quality of what we eat is as important as the quantity.

When you eat, the food travels along your esophagus and into your stomach, where it is broken down into a more manageable form. The remnants are slowly sent to your intestines and turned and into usable materials. These materials (in the form of chemicals) are digested and released into the blood. What happens at this point is a factor of what you have eaten as much as it is of how much you have eaten. When you consume a natural whole food, such as a piece of fruit or a portion of meat, the food is slowly broken down and released into your blood stream as the calories become available. This process is very efficient and designed to provide your system with the necessary energy, nutrients and building blocks for all metabolic activities.

Your hormonal system is constantly overseeing this process and making adjustments as need be by secreting hormones into the blood to maintain the proper balance. Many of today's foods are almost entirely artificially engineered—or at best, are chemically modified versions of the real thing. The manufacture and transport of easily accessible foods is the goal and the norm now. When these highly refined foods hit our stomachs and the digestion process begins, they break apart almost instantly. The result is high amounts of sugar or "potential energy" being dumped into our blood stream.

This is very confusing to our bodies. Our internal alarms go off as our blood sugar level skyrockets. Our management team decides its needs to take action immediately and get our blood sugar under control. The mechanism the body uses for this is insulin.

When your pancreas secrets and releases insulin into your blood, it immediately accomplishes its mission; your blood sugar drops. Unfortunately, the process doesn't end here. It may have only been a 100-calorie Oreo Snack Pack that caused your blood sugar to rise, but your body doesn't really recognize this highly refined sugar. It thinks you might have just eaten an entire 50-gallon bucket of strawberries as your sugar rose so sharply, so it releases a *lot* of insulin. As the 100-calorie snack pack wears off quickly, your body is still producing the hormone necessary to drop your sugar to normal levels. The result is your blood glucose level drops far below where it was before you raided the cookie jar. Two very important things have happened at this point. The unfortunate side effect of the production of insulin has caused your body to store fat... and more importantly, it has stopped burning its own fat as a preferred fuel... but wait, it gets worse.

The results of your now-lowered blood sugar level will trigger your body's preferred mechanism for raising your blood sugar—eating. Yes, you get hungry. Even if you still have a full belly of food, you will experience hunger. Certainly you have noticed this phenomenon. Have you ever been able to eat pretzels or chips or candy for hours on end while watching TV? This is a direct result of this yo-yo rising of the blood sugar and dropping, producing a new appetite. It's almost never ending. Still not seeing it? Let me ask you this—do you think you could spend an hour or two on the couch eating a basket of apples?

Believe it or not, your body does not have a rigid caloric metabolic set point. In other words, there isn't a one-calorie "breaking point" for you where at 2,311 calories you are maintaining your weight, while at 2,312 you just stored 1 calorie as fat. Your body is the sum of millions of metabolic activities and it views food supply and calorie burning as "cleaning the house." Sometimes you have a lot of work to do (high calorie day) and other times you have very little work to do to just maintain body functions (low calorie day).

In the absence of spiking your blood sugar and insulin levels, your body is able to efficiently regulate your hunger and your fat levels. Trust me, your body does not wish to be fat. It wants to be lean and fast. I am sure there will be many people out there who will get their panties in a knot and accuse me of oversimplifying things or glossing over others... so be it. I have no agenda here other than to tell you what has worked for me and countless others and to give you a basic overview that will help you make better choices with food. This is not, however, a permission slip to eat as many calories as you wish. You must combine a healthy reduction of calories with smart food choices. Sorry, no magic tricks.

I know it's hard to make change. But as humans we are powerful beyond measure. Our bodies are capable of surviving incredible hardship and damage. As discussed, we can survive loss of limbs, car crashes, emotional devastation and even drug abuse. What we put into our bodies in the form of our daily food is no exception. We can survive on almost anything, including bugs, leaves and plants, if needed. And when we consider all the different diet and lifestyle choices of today, we can surmise that there is no one perfect diet that's perfect for all. There are both healthy and unhealthy people who are vegetarian, vegan, raw-foodies, high-protein Paleo enthusiasts and no-carbers. The body can function with all these diets, and the one common thread is that people who eat this way for long periods of time don't typically think of the way they eat as being "on a diet." They just eat a certain way—they crave or limit themselves to certain foods that might seem foreign or odd to others, but seem quite normal and enjoyable to them.

My point is simply that the body seems to crave what you feed it. Eat lots of veggies and eventually your body finds it normal to eat lots of veggies. Eat lots of Twinkies... well, you get the picture. If you were stranded on an island and all there was to eat was pineapple, you could survive. Or if all there was to eat was rabbits, you could survive—and even if all your body is getting is fast food burgers, it will do its utmost to keep functioning. So, the biggest problem we face is that it seems once your body has made the change to eating fast food and junk food, it actually adapts to the damage. And once you hit this new "accepted norm" (even though you are being malnourished, storing fat at alarming rates and suffering a whole host of negative side effects), you will begin to crave only the foods that you have poisoned yourself with. Call it the nutritional Stockholm Syndrome.

It takes some time and patience when you start a new lifestyle change—not just time for your mind to accept the new changes, but time for your body to adjust to the new supply of energy-rich foods. If you can stay in the game long enough for your body to make the switch, I can promise you that you will feel better and look better than you could ever have imagined.

But what about me? Why did I eat so recklessly to begin with? Why did I drink like I did? How did I get so far off track? These are tricky questions and I am not the type of person to give myself, or others for that matter, a "free pass." I believe in taking responsibility for my actions and control over where I am heading. So in keeping true to my beliefs, I can say to anyone who is morbidly obese or struggling with addiction—you are not a victim and neither was I. Perhaps I was a victim of my own ignorance, or a victim of poor timing, living in an age where we have 500 cookie choices, but I was the last stop on the pass-the-buck train. I had simply chosen to not think about my food habits. I strayed so far from the road, I couldn't even remember there was a road, much less see the path back.

⑪
"Fairing" Well

Many people these days say things to me like, "Sure, I could lose weight too if I became an ultra marathoner!" For those people and others, I want to share a little about what my training was like as I was losing weight. I can tell you that there were no 6-hour training runs during this period and, in fact, there was very little "distance running" of any kind until after I lost the weight. My first weeks and months of workouts were almost entirely on the stair machine with the occasional treadmill worked in. As I mentioned earlier I was barely able to put together about 15 seconds of running before my shins caught fire, and I felt like vomiting. Almost all of my training was done with 20 minutes of HIGH intensity cardio intervals on the treadmill, followed by longer sessions of lower intensity on the stair machine or stationary bike. Mostly this was because it was all that I was able to do. Going out and running was simply not an option.

The first time I got on the treadmill at the gym must have been a very funny picture for the 5% body-fat folks at the club. I was not laughing, however. In fact, I was quite pissed off, as I recall. For some strange reason, I was very conscious of buying increasingly larger clothes as I ballooned up. I guess I never wanted to be the 320-pound guy who seemed to think he was 250 when he bought his shirt. My selection of gym clothes was no different. When I got up on the treadmill wearing my size 50 basketball shorts (that I probably could have tucked into the top of my socks, they were so long) I took a quick side glance around to see if anyone was looking at me. Thank God I wore a 4XL shirt and the authentic Shaquille O'Neil uniform pants. "I don't want to look like an idiot," I thought.

I set the treadmill on 5 mph and took off in a dead sprint. I held the pace for about 8 seconds before I had to step off and regroup. Maybe I should start at 4 mph for about 15 seconds... this was going to be long process. Sticking to my plan of only indulging in positive thoughts that supported my new vision of me, I just put my head down and sweated. I worked hard, as hard as I possibly could. I may not have been able to run for more than a few seconds at a time but I was working hard. I did as many intervals as I possibly could within 20 minutes. Work out #1 was done. Eventually 15-second intervals became 30 seconds and then 60 seconds, to 2 minutes and then 5 minutes long. With some patience (stubbornness) over a couple of months, I got to the point that I could run the entire 20 minutes non-stop. It was slow, but fuck it—I was a runner.

As a side note, I have actually logged every single workout I have done from that first day until right now—every session, every treadmill run, every bike ride—it's all there and I suggest to anyone starting a program that they do the same. You won't have an accurate picture in your head of your progress without doing this, and it is very helpful to be able to look back and see how far you have come. I never would have remembered how slow I started if I didn't have it all staring back at me. Sometimes I am really not sure what kept me coming back day after day, but I was like a machine. My schedule wouldn't allow me to go to the gym at the same time every day, but I made sure somehow, some way, that I went every single day. The truth is, I was afraid to miss a day. I didn't truly trust myself yet. I was really afraid of talking myself out of all this silliness.

Being a runner was great. But for any of this change to really make a lasting impact, I had to get myself out of the financial gutter and find a job. I was sober. I was getting healthy, but my finances were an absolutely wreck. I was barely keeping my mortgage paid, and even though the bankruptcy had eliminated the business debt, I still had bills to pay. My wife was working part-time and I was kind of at a loss as to what I was going to do with my life. The one thing I was sure of was I wasn't going back into my old world for a while. I needed a change. I had really adopted the attitude in all this that it just didn't matter—I knew that as long as didn't get drunk, I could handle the rest.

In my last three months before my rock-bottom day, I had gone to work for a small hot tub retailer in Denver. I hated the job. It didn't pay anything to speak of, but it allowed me to coast on my previous sales experience and, more importantly, it was the type of job where I could drink. Newly sober and afraid of being tempted into drinking on the job again, I immediately quit without much thought as to what was going to replace it. I remembered once a friend from the hot tub business mentioned that he had made a lot of money travelling around to state fairs to sell hot tubs for out-of-state retailers. The first time he said it, I was quite sure I had heard wrong. "Who the hell would buy a hot tub at a STATE FAIR?" I said, literally laughing out loud. He explained to me that actually hot tubs had been selling at state fairs for years and it wasn't quite as bizarre as it sounded.

So now, months later after walking out (in spectacular fashion), I decided I might give that buddy of mine a call and ask about this "traveling spa gig." I could use a change of scenery, I thought as I dialed his number. After a quick exchange of ridiculously politically incorrect humor (as was our ritual), he said he would pass my name around and see if maybe he could find me a show or two. Since my performance in the hot tub world was "sub-par" to say the least, I really didn't hold out much hope that I would be receiving any calls. But being willing to do the things that no one else will do, is always a quick way to find work. I was driving down the road when my phone rang:

"Is this David Clark?"

"Yes it is," I said, wondering what unpaid bill this guy was calling to collect on.

"David, this is Larry Giles. I am the VP of Sales for [_____] Spa Company and I understand you are looking for work?"

I remember thinking that this guy must be really desperate to be calling me. I was right. It seemed he had a big dealer in the Sacramento area that had a large commercial booth at the California State Fair. The good news was the hot tubs were selling like pancakes. The bad news was he wasn't calling to ask me to come sell hot tubs in California. He was calling to see if I wanted to come sell high end BBQ grills.

"Uh... ok, sure," I managed to reply.

The deal was this: the dealer had been talked into putting these high-end custom outdoor kitchens on display at the fair and none of the sales people could sell one. I always like a challenge, and since I was little over 2 weeks sober without a single other thing to do and since my world was pretty much on bizarro autopilot anyway, I said yes.

"When do you want me out there?" I asked.

The response was a little unexpected, "How about tonight?"

What happened in Sacramento now seems like a small miracle. Not more than a few weeks into my new sobriety I was heading right into the enemy camp—the airport. There are no two places on the planet that I enjoyed drinking more than on a plane or in a hotel. Traveling was my most romantic and most deviant drinking buddy. Many times I checked myself into hotel rooms only to stay inside and drink for days. I loved to drink in hotel lobbies for hours and hours during conventions and business trips only to retreat to my preciously dark and quiet room to drink all night. Hell, if I were even just picking someone up from the airport, I would arrive 2-3 hours early so I could go sit at the bar and watch the flight updates inside the terminal. Looking back now, it was probably a little foolhardy to put myself in harm's way so soon, but then again...

I hit Sacramento and was picked up at the airport by three guys I had never met and who had apparently left the bar (literally) to come get me. It seemed they were set on skipping the part where they dropped me off at the hotel and wanted to go back to the bar where they had previously been imbibing. Worse still, was their challenge to me—delivered in a laughing way, yet it was an unintended bomb. They wanted to watch me drink and talk to girls to test my ability to sell, the theory being that if I could do that, then certainly I could sell these BBQ Islands. They laughed, thinking this was a great idea. Oh boy, what the hell had I gotten myself into here?

"Actually, I don't drink," I said. As the words rolled of my tongue they seemed to drop into my hands and the weight of it was heavy to hold.

We had made the trip back to the bar from the airport (which, thankfully, was the bar in the lobby of the hotel I was to be staying) and we were sitting at the bar discussing the details of the event I was walking into tomorrow. Larry (the VP of sales) was sitting at the bar with me now.

"Really? You don't drink at all?" he said.

"Nope," I said as I was still marveling at what my new life was to be. "I am a recovering alcoholic."

"No shit? That's cool," Larry said. "Good for you. Let's discuss tomorrow," he said without another thought. Just like that, with a simple—yet profoundly honest exchange—I changed the entire trajectory of my life. This IS me, thought. I am an alcoholic. And it's not a weakness. It's just a simple fact.

I hit the sales floor with a basic plan—just be honest and friendly with the customers, make some new friends and see if that results in some sales. I didn't know a damn thing about BBQs but I didn't need to. I did know people and I trusted my ability to connect with customers and find solutions to their problems. As the next 2 weeks unfolded, I sold almost a quarter of a million dollars in BBQs at the state fair. Every day I showed up awake, alert and—more importantly, not hung-over. I was having a blast. I made friends every day, I made money every day and I made an impression on some people in the spa industry. I was a dream come true for spa dealers. I was now a proven producer and, more importantly, unlike all the roughnecks and party boys on the traveling spa circuit, I was sober and reliable.

I can't help but think what would have happened if I had chosen to throw away my sobriety when I first touched down in California for that show. It would have been an easy sale. In the past I threw away longer bouts of sobriety with less thought. I would have drank my ass off every night in that hotel and slugged through the event and made a couple dollars, only to have my phone fall silent when it was over. Instead, I continued my commitment to work and to workout. I went to the hotel gym every morning before I went to the fair. I read my AA Big Book at night. I ate a healthy breakfast each morning and I sometimes even went to spin on a bike later in the evening after dinner.

Each time I went to the gym I felt like I was farther away from the mess of my life that no one here knew anything about. I was driven by a survival instinct, an understanding that I was not quite in the clear yet. I could feel the beast of my past and addiction chasing me and I couldn't slow down. I was running, not just away from my past, but as fast as I could to a new future. I also wrote in my journal and continued to explore the 12 steps of AA every day. I knew I had to change what was wrong inside me as I was changing my body. Everything had to be different this time. I believe now that I wouldn't have made it through another fall. I had to make it work that time, or I would have died. Of course I'll never know if that is, in fact, true—but at night when I think about it now, I know it is.

What a 180 my professional life took at that point. In what seemed like an instant (but was actually a slow grind) I was being offered work all over the country and I was making quite a bit of money. If you figure I was paid from 8-10% commission, you can do some quick math to see I was having no problem paying my bills again. For years past, I made my living for the most part by connecting to people and simply sharing my life experiences. I did this with my customers in our showrooms and with my employees in our sales meetings on a daily basis, and my new business endeavor in the spa world was no different. But now I was anxious to share everything from a new life perspective.

In the past I shared every detail of my inner thoughts only as it pertained to business. I shared everything from my own lowest motivational moments to my proudest achievements with the intention of helping others harness the power they have to improve their own professional performance. And I shared openly with customers the thought processes I used to set prices and design my product line and service polices. However, I always held back on my personal demons and struggles, for obvious reasons. But now I was about to up the ante, and continue this open nature on a never-before "personal" level. I decided that for me to stay sober and true to myself, I had to give it all away, all the hiding, all the secrecy and every detail that I instinctively wanted to withhold from my story. Now, when meeting new people, I gave of myself unashamedly and completely.

I told people that I was recently sober. I told people I was training to run a marathon, I told people how I lost my ass in business, and I told them what I learned from both my success and failures. I didn't feel the need to "preface" my story or build up my successes before I shared my failures—I just let it fly, and I smiled. What I found was a blessing, a gift for getting through to people and being able to connect immediately. By sharing so much hardship without any fear of humiliation, people would let their own guards down and shared with me. It was the most amazing thing I had ever seen. Some people were relating to my story instantly and it was overwhelming, touching, and very much unexpected. It is a good thing that I didn't know then that my trials were not over. In fact, we were only just starting.

Now We're Running

It had been close to 4 months since I woke up on the bathroom floor, drunk for the last time. My head was clear now but I was far from being "cured." It was November and the holidays were approaching fast. My entire life was different from any I had ever known before. Sure, it was amazing and exciting but I was also still very nervous about getting through this time of year without drinking. The good news was I was still sober and I was losing weight; in fact I had lost almost 60 pounds at this point. My running wasn't great yet but I could do 20 minutes of steady jogging without stopping and that made me feel pretty good about my progress. I still had the goal of running the Denver Marathon in the back of my mind, but it seemed so impossible that I tried not to carry the weight of it very often. For now, I was focused on improving my running and getting lighter. I felt that was ultimately the key to getting to the start line next October.

I was still spending a considerable amount of time reading all that I could about both running and sobriety. I was also savoring the small moments of life that being sober was giving me, the things that I could never wrap my hands around when I was using—simple things like sitting in the living room and reading or driving to the 7/11 for a diet Mountain Dew at midnight. I can tell you that there is a huge difference between a casual, cool evening drive to the convenience store for a soda and a last-minute midnight run to the liquor store. I remember the first time I left for one of these (what was to become regular) trips to the 7/11 around midnight. There was an overwhelming sense of freedom that I will never be able to relate. I felt as if I was recently paroled from a long imprisonment. The fact that I wasn't drunk at this time of night, alone, was liberating.

The feeling of freedom accompanied by the peace of mind that I was driving sober, simply driving my car down the road at night sober, with no fear of being pulled over and going to jail was irresistibly comfortable. I would always drive with the window down no matter how cold it was outside. I could feel the air on my face, feel the weight of the accelerator on my foot, the feel of the leather steering wheel in my hand and I would relax back into the seat with an almost childlike feeling of security—no jail, no booze, no threat of penalty—just a damn drive.

As I was driving one night, I remembered a night drive in the past. I had slammed into someone's car in the liquor store parking lot. Confused as to what happened, the other driver and I both were standing in the parking lot looking for the police to arrive. As it turned out we were both drunk. We decided to get the hell out of there. As I sat in the 7/11 parking lot with that night's horrible memory fading away, I noticed across the street from where I was parked there was a large running track wrapped around a soccer field. I thought it might be time to take my running off the treadmill and give this track a try on Saturday. And just as I was pondering this, on cue, a police car drove through the 7/11 parking lot. I looked right at the officer and smiled. He smiled back and kept driving.

After reading about how many different types of running shoes there are and being sufficiently scared about injury, I decided to go to the local running store and look at shoes. It was a little intimidating to go into the store (especially in Boulder, Colorado) and see all the amazing athletes meandering around the shop. I have often told people that even if you do an Ironman Triathlon, if you live in Boulder, no one will be impressed. In fact, they will probably ask you what your "bike split" was. But I walked into the store and looked at all the shoes on the walls and, instead of being intimidated, I was proud. I was proud of how far I had come, and I wasn't going to be embarrassed that I didn't fit in with the elite crowd.

I told the shoe guy that I had lost 60 pounds and I wanted to run a marathon. "What shoes do you recommend?" I asked. He was amazingly helpful, supportive and even encouraging. I couldn't believe it. Here was this guy who talks to elite marathoners and triathletes in Boulder, no less, taking a genuine interest in my story. He asked a lot of questions about me and how I was feeling, and I left thinking I made an actual friend. He gave me something much more valuable than a new pair of Asics; he gave me the sense of camaraderie within the running community. It was a simple exchange between customer and associate, but it was so much more to me. This would later prove to be a very important lesson of my recovery.

Up to this point, my running had been entirely on the treadmill and entirely based on time, 20 minutes to be exact. My workouts were hard and progressive, but it took all I had to make the 20 minutes each day. In fact, I could never decide what was harder—the burning in my lungs and legs or the excruciating boredom of trying to get through the time. Sometimes I would add some stationary cycling after my runs to get in what I called a "super cardio fat burn," but I had never been past the 20-minute running barrier. I was now entering new territory; the mileage zone.

It might not seem like much to the runners out there, but I can tell you this was a huge change. My pace those days was about a 12-13 minute mile, so committing to running a minimum of 2 miles EVERY time I ran was large. The extra 4-5 minutes was a 25% increase in an already tough workout. It's hard to remember that feeling now when a 3-hour run seems rather casual, but I am very thankful for the meticulous tracking I did of my workouts—and my state of mind—in these first days and months. Without that, I don't think I would correctly remember my progress.

I will never forget the tiny 2-inch by 3-inch horror film that the treadmill display became as 20 minutes ticked off and I was still running. I had one focus during these workouts. A very real and very intense thought kept me going:

This place where I am right now—the burning in my legs, the pressure in my head to stop running, and this general pain—it's exactly where I have to be to get better. The longer I could stay in this place, the stronger I would become—mentally, physically, emotionally. So I ran—two miles—every single day.

While at the running store, I noticed a poster for a Thanksgiving Day 5k run. The "Turkey Trot" was put on by the University of Colorado and promised "a low key two-loop jaunt around the research center." The prospect of running in an actual race, while still being 80 pounds overweight, seemed a little unnerving. I was very intrigued by the thought of doing a real race, but having never been in a running race of any kind, and given the typical size and make-up of a typical Boulder runner, I figured I would be two times heavier than everyone there. It turns out I was wrong. In fact, much to my surprise there were runners of all shapes and sizes there and I wasn't close to being the only person who was overweight. But I will never forget how difficult it was and how intimidated I felt when I walked into the running store to register for the race. To say I felt conspicuous would be championing the obvious. I didn't have (that I can recall) any real expectation of what doing a 5k race might feel like—in fact, if I felt anything, it was a lot of anxiety mixed with a tiny whiff of excitement. But what I did know, and what I was focused on, was what the race meant. I simply had to do this race if I was really going to run a marathon next year.

When I paid my $25 for the entry, the clerk took my money and told me what time the race started and where to show up. They also handed me a race-bib number and some safety pins. I looked down at the paper number in my hands and took in everything about it. The way it felt, the size and color of it and, most importantly, the Nike swoosh and word "RUN" on it. It was fantastic; it made me feel like an official runner. I was scared shitless that night as I lay in bed and thought of trying to run 3.1 miles in front of what seemed like the entire world watching.

Race morning (Thanksgiving Day) I woke up early and I was very excited. I had run 2 miles a few times now, but I still couldn't escape the extra 1.1 miles looming in the upcoming 5k. I could already taste the turkey that was cooking in the oven as I packed the kids and wife into the car and headed to Boulder. My plan was simple—DON'T WALK. I wanted to run the entire race no matter how long it took me. For most people, when they are new to running, they really only have two paces—running and not running and I was no exception. The thought occurred to me that I could probably walk the race faster than I could run it. Certainly it would be quicker if I ran hard for a couple of minutes and then walked for a few seconds to recover, but I just didn't care. The finish time was insignificant compared to finishing—feeling like I ran the race. Just before the race started my wife took a photo of me in my huge cotton sweatshirt and basketball shorts. I am not sure exactly what I was thinking at the moment of the photo, but you can tell by looking at it that I was out of my comfort zone.

I felt ridiculously energized and elated standing at the starting line. I lined up way in the back by the runners with strollers and dogs. The sound of Bruce Springsteen's *Born to Run* was blaring in the PA speakers and people were trotting in place to warm up. Many were doing that "runner's stretch" where you hold your foot behind your butt. I just stood there with my hands at my side wondering how exactly I got there.

With a quick countdown and a happy Thanksgiving wish from the race director, the gun went off! It took a few long moments before the back of the pack was able to start going, as we were held up by the lag of the front line, but eventually I started to slowly jog forward. Heather shouted something to me as I went past her and the kids, but I didn't even hear what it was. I concentrated on just keeping my head down and moving forward. It wasn't exactly an exhibit of graceful running form, but I was moving. By the time I finished the first of the two loops around the CU Research Center, I was being lapped by the leading runners. Eventually the mid-pack runners lapped me too. I remember seeing the 2-mile marker go by and thinking, "I got this."

The next thing I knew, I was running down the final stretch of road on onto the Potts Field running track where the finish line was waiting. When the volunteers steered me off the road and onto the oval running track, I felt for the first time the feel of the soft surface and saw up close the white lines that marked the runner's lanes. I got a little emotional as I made my way around the final 400 meters. The images I had seen on TV of Steve Prefontaine and other pro runners flashed into my mind. It probably seems strange for me to react to such a mundane running experience, but it was my very first time on an official running track, and it happened to take place on my very first race day. I made my loop around and hit the finish feeling fantastic. I believe my official time was 39:22. I was never more proud.

The next logical step was training to do a half marathon. My plan was to give myself plenty of time to train for this event and use it as a ramp up to my eventual goal of a full marathon in October. My weight loss was progressing nicely and I felt I was literally and figuratively putting some serious distance between me and my old life. When I started running, one of my most romantic concepts of what I wanted running to be was the ability to simply run without effort. I wanted to know what it felt like to be the person on the cover of *Runner's World* magazine, running through the snow and taking in a beautiful winter day… and those days were approaching rapidly.

I was now regularly running outside. In fact, I took my training to the running track at the Thornton Rec Center that I had observed from my late night 7/11 drives. I had structured my training to include my two-mile treadmill runs and a longer run outside once a week. That long run was 3 miles long then, and after my experience of completing the 5k, I was no longer worried about running the 3-mile mark. In fact, my 3-mile long run became the 4-mile long run and the 5-mile in the blink of an eye.

As I was looking online for a half marathon to make my target race, I was also becoming a student of online training plans for runners. I read everything there was to read about running—and there were a lot of resources to pour over. I finally settled on a modified plan that combined a "Cool Running Half Marathon Plan" and one of Hal Higden's classics. I religiously went to the gym, day in and day out, to get my treadmill training done. My 2-mile runs were now being blended into an organized training schedule that included 3- and 4-mile runs during the week, as well. The main focus, however, was on my once a week long run. For this epic training day, I drove my car to "the track" (as I called it) for my long run around the .8-mile concrete track surrounding the soccer fields at Thornton Rec. One day will always stick in my mind as a milestone of not only my progress towards my half marathon goal—but also as a very substantive moment of my journey.

The training plan called for an 8-mile run. I had been dreading it since I first saw the day charted out in my plan. There was something very foreboding about that number. Maybe it was the fact that it was exactly 10 laps around my regular running route, or maybe it was the fact that the math kept leading me to the realization that I was going to be running for close to 2 hours. Be that as it may, the day had arrived. As fate would have it, the weather was crappy—a rain-snow mix and a high of around 35 degrees, but I didn't let that stop me. I pulled on my cotton sweat pants (the kind that would have probably made Rocky Balboa grimace in embarrassment) put on a raincoat, my headphones, grabbed a sugar-free Monster Energy drink and headed out for my date with the concrete path.

I was miserable. I kept moving forward and employing every trick in the book to not think how many laps I had left to run. This was very difficult to do while constantly repeating the number of the lap I was currently on. I had no fancy running watch with a lap counter so I had to run saying "5, 5, 5, 5… 6, 6, 6, 6," etc. As the laps ticked off, my lower back started to give me some input—input of the screeching-hot, horrible burning-pain variety—ok maybe not that bad, but I was in serious discomfort for the last 3 miles or more.

The soccer fields whirled around me as I trudged on and on around the loop. As I got closer and closer to the final lap, I could almost feel the reality of my running goals moving closer to me. I tried not to think too much about it while I was running, but a huge grin was forming on my wet, frozen face. When I finished the final lap, I came to a stop and just looked around in every direction. It was a very surreal moment. I felt the distance I had run and I felt the distance my sobriety had taken me in the same breath. I was 6 months sober and I weighed about 230 pounds now (down well over 80 pounds) and standing there in my current state, it seemed the gods were using a new kind of paint to color the world—a much more vibrant, bright selection than I had previously noticed. I sat on the wet grass and just looked out at the mountains in the background and felt the calm and serene feeling of empty thoughts. No stress about my next drink. No feeling of anxiousness about my health, just an open channel to broadcast whatever signal was strong. I thought, "8 miles… that's a long way from 13.1 miles, but I can see the finish from here."

As I got up off the grass and walked back to the car, I took off my soaking-wet coat and hat and started to think about a nice hot coffee on the way home. Before I made it to the car, I discovered that there was one piece of the running puzzle I needed to address before my next run. I was horrified to notice the entire front of my shirt was streaked with blood. As I pondered all the possibilities of how this could have happened—unnoticed attack by serial killer being the least likely scenario—I realized my nipples had been rubbed raw against my shirt—a real, live runner's problem to be solved. How great is that. I'm now part of the club that thinks of Band-Aids in a whole new way.

I rented a nice condo in Steamboat Springs for my half marathon debut and made it a small family weekend getaway. It was June in the Rockies and the mountains were spectacular. I had long ago dispensed with the idea of weighing myself regularly, but I was somewhere near the 190-pound mark by this point and I was ready for my biggest challenge to date. My grandmother's somewhat recent passing was weighing heavy on my mind and I decided that I was going to run this race in her honor.

She was a beautiful woman, born in Belgium, who met my grandpa after the D-Day invasion in Normandy. On that day, she was a volunteer helping to take care of the wounded allied troops, but I knew her as the graceful woman who spoke French to me and made me marmalade and buttered toast cut into triangles. She called these treats "trumpets." We had lost contact with her and many members of the family due to a big falling out between her and my father. It had caused a huge rift, and I just recently had made contact with the extended family to find out of her untimely death. I was crushed.

That was about a year earlier. Now, here it was the morning of my first half marathon and I was thinking of her as I got ready for the race. I was experiencing a wide range of emotions as I pinned my bid number to my shorts, applied some Vaseline to my sensitive areas and wrote her initials in marker on my arm. It was early on race morning and I was standing in the bathroom looking at myself in the mirror. "Who is this guy?" I thought. I was wearing a sleeveless red Nike shirt and matching red shorts and I looked… well, thin. It shouldn't have been that big of a shock since I had seen myself every day for almost my entire life, but something about this context and this morning made it really hit me hard. "Never forget where you came from," I said. I snapped a couple gratuitous self-photos for posterity and headed out to the starting line.

The race was a point-to-point course and almost completely downhill. The logistics were pretty simple: they drive us 13.1 miles out to the starting line in buses and then we run back to the finish and to our families—easy enough, but it was freezing cold at the start and I was horribly underdressed. I was shaking violently from the cold and it was all I could do to keep from unleashing every known profanity in an unending and rather lengthy stream. And now that I think of it, there is no proof that I didn't do just that; after all, I am from New York. Somehow I managed to make it a few more minutes without being frozen solid and I found myself in the second running race of my life. It was a very good place to be. I had really picked up my training in terms of effort and intensity and I wanted to finished somewhere near the 2-hour mark, but I really didn't have a lot of meaning attached to any specific finishing time. I just wanted to finish and be 13.1 miles closer to my overall goal, the Denver Marathon.

The scenery was nothing short of amazing. We were running down a long winding mountain road with a rolling river alongside. I could hear the water cascading over the rocks and the chit-chatter of other runners talking about running. I stayed pretty much to myself, this being only my second time ever in an organized run, and my mind started to drift in and out of the present moment and the last 10 months. I was getting flashes of my first sober holiday, that first 8-mile run in the snow and rain, and all the mornings of waking up still drunk and sick from the night before. The mile markers ticked by as I took in all there was to see—my fellow runners, the aid station volunteers and the wildlife. I also caught sight of the 8-mile marker and nodded in respect—all good so far.

In fact, I was fine until about mile 11. The course flattened out and I no longer had the benefit of the downhill, and I had run past any of my training to this point. I knew I was going to be ok to finish if I could just hold on, but I was very uncomfortable and I really wanted to be done. I looked at my grandmother's initials on my arm and thought of her. This gave me some strength and I continued to run from road marker to road marker and mailbox to mailbox along the rural residential street heading into Steamboat Springs. I said out loud, "If you are there, Grandma, I miss you." A butterfly flew right into my face and tried to park itself on my nose. I don't know if it was a beautiful coincidence or gift from my "Gramere" but I didn't waste a second—I ran hard as I could to the finish. I finished in 2:09.

I was travelling a lot these days but I was still religiously getting in my healthy eating and training. I was enjoying my new life, and I was enjoying the way other people were seeing this "new me." I was no longer the fun party guy—I was "that crazy running guy." In the circles I travelled, my story was circulating around. Most of the national dealer network of the company I was contracted by heard about "the amazing shrinking man" who was coming to town to sell spas and do a sales training. I was sincerely touched when folks would approach me and ask how I had lost so much weight. I think, as people, we are very good at building walls to protect ourselves from reality, but even though we are closing ourselves off, we know what's on the other side of the barrier.

When we are unhealthy and overweight we are not happy; it's that simple. Those of us who have been morbidly obese know that we aren't "overweight." We are broken. It doesn't mean we cannot enjoy life at times, or laugh, or even be ok with how we look on the surface. But deep inside, we know there is a better version of us. I was amazed at how much people were willing to share with me about their most personal thoughts, fears, and even guilt, over not taking better care of themselves. When people are vulnerable with you, it really touches you in a way that changes you forever. And after hearing my story, some people would look me directly in the eyes and ask, "Do you think I could lose that much weight too?"

Sometimes the questions broke my heart, but they were always answered with encouragement and empathy. I have said before, I am certainly no special case and I stand by it. If I can do it, you can—and that's just the plain, hard truth.

As for me, I was at about 185 pounds and locked in. I felt great, I felt strong, and I was focused on maintaining my new lifestyle. Each time I planned a new work trip I immediately researched the area to find a long trail or route for my weekend long run. My travel ritual was firmly established. I would fly to the airport-of-the-day, get my rental car and head to my hotel. As soon as I found my hotel, I went to the nearest grocery store and purchased my food for the trip. Many of the places I worked were state fairs and home shows, so eating healthy was not only difficult; it might even get you beat up.

Most days I would wake up early and run before the workday's event started. Sometimes this meant running really early before sunrise, but I simply couldn't let myself off the hook—the stakes were too high. If I felt like staying in bed, it felt like I was deciding to go back to my old life. No way. Screw it—I'll run. It took a big commitment, but this was how I was able to continue to lose weight while I was travelling. And now I was getting in my longest training days while on the road. In fact, the majority of all of my long runs—14, 16, 18 and even my 20-mile long run, came while I was traveling. I like to bring this part up to people these days when the "I don't have time to work-out" argument comes up.

Somewhere along the way, and I can't remember how or where, I found two very valuable resources for support and training advice: the Cool Running network and Slowtwitch.com. These two groups were almost polar opposites in terms of personality and user etiquette. On an almost daily basis, I would post about my training—how I was feeling, and ask the more experienced runners if the aches and pains I was feeling were normal. I was not afraid to ask questions and share exactly what was going on in my brain. I shared race reports, thoughts on being sober, and even some of my "world-famous" politically incorrect humor.

I remember the way the guy at the running store made me feel when he so seamlessly welcomed me into the running world. I wanted more; I wanted to feel connected to others and what they were doing out there on the trails. I needed it. I craved the affirmation and the support I was able to give and get as a result of my online friends. In many ways, my blogging and posting became an internet non-12 step-based group therapy outlet for me. There were times when I would post 10 or 20 times a day. I was feeling something I had almost never felt in my 30 some-odd years on the planet—I felt like I was part of a community, like I belonged somewhere. I was actually one of the members of the group, not just an outsider trying to fit in.

Running 20 miles is kind of a rite of passage for a first-time marathoner in training. I was nervous about it, to say the least, but I was also anxious to prove to myself that I could make it through and stake a claim on the real possibility of being able to run a marathon. I read everything there was about the logistics of trying such a long distance endeavor. I had questions that needed answering: What should I carry? What route should I take? Will I get blisters? And what if I just can't make it? Will I have to actually call and get a ride home?

I was traveling in Utah when the date arrived to earn my "20-mile badge." I was working the state fair for one of the spa manufacturers I was in business with so I had to wake up early and hit the roads to allow for the 4 hours the run would take me. Hopefully, this would leave enough time to shower, get to the exhibitor's booth and work on my feet all day. I guess I was ultra training before I even knew what it was. With some solid advice from a local running store, I mapped out a great "out and back" route on the South Jordan River Parkway. It's an asphalt bike path that travels all along the Salt Lake metro area.

I parked my rental car in the lot as the sun was rising and I set off on my run. I was nervous and excited as the first few miles ticked by. I was working hard to distract myself from how long I was going to be out there. I knew it was going to be at least 3:45 to 4 hours for sure. Everything was great as I made the 10-mile turn around, and even though my energy was fading a little, I was still ok until about mile 17. All of a sudden I couldn't believe how dead I felt. My legs were concrete. My brain just wanted to stop. I needed to be done... and now. Somehow I soldiered through and felt very happy to see my rental car approaching around the turn as I reached the end of my last long run before the Denver Marathon.

Most of the times we are afraid of doing something, it is our fear and irrational imagination that are far worse than the reality of the looming event, and running 20 miles was no different. Don't get me wrong—it was hard, very hard. And it left me with some lingering doubts as to how I was going to summon the strength to run 6.2 miles farther on race day, but I was done with the hardest run of my life—and I felt great as I drove back to the hotel.

There is basically no way that I could ever really describe the level of electric nervous tension that buzzed in my head and body the day before I was to run my first marathon. It was October of 2006, I was 35 years old and, for me, every single part of this process was unfamiliar. I had never run this far, I had never been at a huge race expo before. I had never seen so many runners together in one place at one time. I felt like I was on another planet and everything that I knew about doing even the most basic of tasks had to be abandoned in favor of a new "marathon prep" version. Should I eat this cookie? I wonder if I should shower before I sleep. Should I brush my teeth differently? I got through the night on about 2 hours of sleep and 5 hours of flip, toss and twitch.

Standing at the start the next morning as the national anthem was sung, I was already fighting back the emotions. I couldn't believe how much my life had changed in just over a year. I had lost 140 pounds, and somehow, I had gone more than a year without getting drunk. I had my confidence back, I felt thankful to be alive, and I was ready to see what would happen over the next few hours as I tried to do what simply seemed 100% impossible only a few months ago.

I felt like a pinball launched into a machine as the thousands of runners bounced along on all sides of me and we all started our 26.2-mile journey through Denver. There was a huge sense of relief as I slowly wound my way through the city, completing the first 3-4 miles of the day.

"This is it—I'm finally here," I thought. "Now I just have to keep going..."

I read all the signs from spectators there to cheer on their loved ones and I could hear the conversations of people watching on the roadside. I remember feeling like I was genuinely alive for the first time in years. When you are locked into addiction, your life stops. It's almost like a song stuck on a skip—the disc keeps spinning, but you never get anywhere. My life had been so entirely focused on feeding my addiction and managing how it was affecting my family that I almost forgot how many other people there were in the world—people all just trying their best to be alive and live life. But here I was, in the midst of thousands of strangers—and I never felt more connected.

As I approached the 12-mile mark, I was starting to feel the miles building up as fatigue in my body. I tried not to let my mind focus on anything other than the moment I was in—no thinking too far ahead. At this point in the course, there was a sharp split in the road—half marathoners went right, full marathoners to the left. I watched as most of the people I had been running with took the right turn and headed in to the finish chute and into the arms of their families. Taking the left turn were only a scarce few. It seemed like I was going to get my alone time anyway.

Mile 13 became mile 17. I remember getting a little boost of energy between 18 and 20 miles. It lifted me to a renewed sense of mission. The music bumped into my ears from my headphones and I knew that particular moment would always be vivid in my mind. I can still recall, in perfect snapshots, the smallest of details of the park and path as we circled through the neighborhood and back out onto the streets of Denver. This was crunch time, the dreaded wall... mile 20. I don't remember actually hitting "the wall" but it sure felt like something hit me—something like a fire truck. All of a sudden my legs were Jell-O. The pain that was just annoying a few minutes ago was now intense and spreading. My feet, my knees, and my quads were all screaming for me to stop. I didn't. I had never been in any situation like this before. Never had I either unintentionally or on purpose put myself into such excruciating pain. The worst part was that I knew if I just stopped running it would be ok. This was a mental battle I was in, not a physical one, I quickly realized. Keep going. Keep going.

I remember repeating to myself, "If I don't quit in this second, I'll make it—second by second and minute by minute, I will make it." I could hear the finish line ahead; I knew I must be close but I kept my head down. I looked at my GPS and couldn't believe what I saw! 26.2 miles!!! I did it.

Only, wait. What the holy hell is going on? I wasn't at the finish line at all. In fact, I looked up to see it was still almost a mile ahead. #@$#&!!!! I was pissed! It's funny to me now, but to think I actually ran the 26.2 miles that is a marathon and yet I wasn't done, was infuriating. Now I know that it is quite common for races to vary a little in distance and that GPS isn't always accurate, but I wasn't feeling ok about it then as my feet were screaming and I was still going. Just then, a Dropkick Murphy song came on my iPod. It was an instrumental punk version of *Amazing Grace*.

I didn't wait any longer. It was an act that would be repeated by me over and over in the years to come—I put my eyes on the road ahead of me—and ran hard until I hit that finish line.

Don't Panic

"Now what?" my wife asked me as I stood at the finish line. I still had the foil blanket wrapped around me and I was wearing my Denver Marathon finisher's medal. I smiled at her; she knew me very well. The truth is I had already decided what I wanted to do while I was still training for the marathon. I was going to do something that was a childhood dream, something that scared the ever-loving shit out of me. I was going to do a triathlon. The fact that I couldn't swim, seemed like a minor detail.

I was just a kid when I first heard of the Ironman Triathlon. I didn't know what the exact distances of the events were, but I knew it was commonly held out to be the ultimate test of endurance. The 17-hour race pitted athletes against each other to swim, bike and run great distances in extreme conditions, all in one day. Years later when I saw my first broadcast of the live event on TV, I learned it was a 2.4-mile swim and a 112-mile bike race followed by an entire 26.2-mile marathon. All done consecutively.

In researching triathlons, I learned of a local Colorado event that featured this ultimate event in a slightly different format. It was called Ironman 70.3 and it covered half the distances of the better-known Hawaii Ironman, a 1.2-mile swim, a 56-mile bike ride, and a half marathon run of 13.1 miles. It had only been a month since my first marathon but, "Go big or go home," I thought. I signed up. What's the worst that could happen?

My first time swimming a lap in a pool came when I was 36 years old, and it happened at my local gym. I donned my new triathlon-specialized swimsuit, squeezed into my Speedo swim cap, tugged on my goggles and tried to do my best impression of a "pre-swim stretch" while standing in the water. Eventually I pushed off the wall and started what may have looked like actual swimming for perhaps 10 yards before it turned into an all-out panic-induced survival act. Somehow I made it the entire 25 yards to the opposite end of the pool just in time to catch my breath before I passed out and drowned.

No sooner than my heart rate started to settle down to triple digits and the fear of death started to ease, than I noticed a lady of perhaps 70 years of age and 250 pounds swimming towards me. I watched with growing concern. She approached gracefully, effortlessly gliding up the end of the lane next to me before she did an underwater summersault, planted her feet perfectly on the pool wall next to me and pushed off like a rocket. She surfaced about 20 yards later, swimming away from me without so much as a hitch in her stroke. I watched for about 10 whole minutes before I cursed under my breath in disgust. I have run a marathon for God's sake. How the hell is she doing that? What the hell is wrong with me?

I needed a coach… and maybe a nap.

I looked online and found a local a local masters swim group. I read *Total*

Immersion by Terry McLaughlin, and I became a student of swimming. Day after day I came to the pool and day after day I left unsettled and concerned as to how I was going to swim 1.2 miles without drowning. In the meantime, my cycling and running were coming around nicely; I was getting a feel for what it was like to run off the bike and I felt confident that I was going to be able to finish. Finish, that is, if my body didn't sink to the bottom of the Boulder Reservoir.

Each day I had to battle the mental demons and voices telling me I was running out of time. It was late April (race in August) and I was still unable to swim more than 100 yards continuously without stopping. Each day I would leave and find a way to convince myself to "trust the process," a concept and catch phrase that I would use repeatedly as a coach in the years to come. One day in May, I discovered a new toy. It was called a "pull buoy." I was swimming with the Boulder masters group and the coach came over to the deck and tossed me a piece of blue and white foam. It was shaped like a peanut and I had no idea what to do with it. "Put it between your legs and swim with your upper body," he said. Just roll from side to side. It will feel like you are wearing a wetsuit."

"What a minute," I said. Are you telling me that it feels different to swim in a wetsuit?

"Oh, man—you are in for a treat," he said. "It feels like you can't sink." *I had a ray of hope.*

I put the pull buoy between my legs and I swam. And I swam and swam—for 20 minutes nonstop! I couldn't believe it. I knew I still had a lot of work to do, but this was just the confidence boost I needed. Day after day I started to combine swimming long periods with the pull buoy and swimming free. I learned perhaps the most valuable lesson of all during those early days of swimming with the aid—I learned to slow down and swim easy. Before long, I was "warming up" in the pool with 500 yards of free-style swimming and doing longer and longer sets with and without the pull buoy. I was still scared to death of jumping into the open water on race day, but I was at least willing to give it a shot. Game on.

I spent every day leading up to race day experiencing at least one panic attack when I thought about swimming 1.2 miles in the open water at the Ironman 70.3. I started to fantasize about making it out of the water and turning around to "flip off" the reservoir if I made it out alive. It was as if the water itself was an enemy to be defeated. Never had death seemed so real. Funny that I could toss 5 Percocets into my mouth during a night of drinking, but a swim scared the crap out of me.

The sun rose and fell in Boulder and once again I was standing at a starting line—although this was unlike any starting line I had ever experienced before. I was standing with my bare feet in the sand for one, and I was wearing a suit made of rubber—and not to mention that when the gun went off this time, I was supposed to run right towards the water and swim away from safety... oh boy.

BANG!! The race started. "Aw shit!"

I let everyone go ahead of me after the gun went off. I slowly walked to the water and started to wade in. When the water got to my hips, I fell forward and started to swim. "Take it easy," I told myself. "Remember, breathe when your face is OUT of the water." I made it about 200 yards from shore before I started to feel like my wetsuit was choking me. All of a sudden it was getting very difficult to breathe. I started to do the breaststroke to slow things down. My thoughts sped up with my heart rate. I was panicking. I started to clutch and grab at the collar of the suit. I was doggy paddling now. I was starting to flail wildly and I was in a full-on panic attack. It seemed I was fucked before I was 10 minutes into my race...

I looked around for help. I could see a race official in a kayak out in the distance and we made eye contact. He could tell I was in trouble so he started to paddle towards me quickly. I wasn't going to wait for him. Instead, I turned around and started swimming... towards the shore. Yup, that's right. I was now swimming "salmon style" against the oncoming traffic and back the way I came. As I was already towards the back of the pack, it didn't take long before I passed the last of the swimmers and was swimming by myself toward the shore. Just then I heard a gunshot. I was confused—certainly no one was shooting at me, were they? It seems the starter was sending off the next wave of approximately 200 swimmers—and now they were heading right towards me. I stopped in my tracks, still in the water again. I was floating up and down in the current as I tried to calculate the impossible. How exactly was I going to die today? Run over by oncoming swimmers? Hit by angry kayak volunteer? Or maybe casual drowning...?

I looked past the fast-approaching swimmers and saw the shore behind them. I could see spectators and family members standing on the beach to cheer on the athletes. I noticed that some of the spectators had taken notice of my newly plotted trajectory and were staring at me in disbelief. Some people witness this confused facial expression of strangers more often than others. I seem to see it quite frequently. As I looked at those indescribable expressions of confusion, it hit me—I was going to have to actually swim UP to the shore and get out of the water and be greeted by these people. That meant FAILURE. It meant that I was going to have to live with my actions here forever. That really slowed down my mind for a second. I looked up at the sun. I thought about my sobriety, I thought about the 2-year sober coin I was carrying under my wetsuit that I had received just a few days earlier. I thought about my kids, who were supposed to be here later to see me finish the swim and get out of the water. All of a sudden, dying in the lake didn't seem like such a bad option. In fact, I was quite sure I was better off doing that than swimming to the shore in defeat. I was done giving up on myself.

I heard movement behind me. The kayak had made its way over to me. "Are you ok?" he asked with a dreadfully contorted expression.

"Actually, I'm fine. I don't drink." I said to the confused volunteer.

I turned around and swam towards the center of the lake. I surrendered to it and accepted it, just like I did that day two years ago on my bathroom floor. Fuck it, let's move ahead. As I swam forward, each time my face turned into the water I yelled. I yelled under the water while exhaling. I could hear the muffled sound of my voice through the water and I could feel the bubbles as they rolled around my face to the water's surface. "NO... MORE... QUIT... NO... MORE... QUIT..." I repeated.

I think nothing makes us feel more alive than conquering fear. And in facing my demons and swimming into the unknown, I had found a new energy. I was committed. Swim or die were the only options, and dying was a little too melodramatic for the rest of the day's events. My heart rate settled in now and I swam better, more confidently, and more aggressively than I ever had before. Each stroke had a purpose; I was pulling myself toward the shore with an imaginary ladder. I was completely primal and I swam my damn ass off and passed swimmer after swimmer as I continued to work harder and harder forward.

When I hit the shore 1.2 miles from the starting point, I felt I was on a different planet. And then all of a sudden I could see my entire world below me. I could actually see it—only it wasn't a blue and white spinning ball called Earth. It was a 6-year old girl named Emily Lynn Clark and she was holding a sign that said, "Go Daddy Go."

I had finished the swim, climbed out of the water and was jogging onto to the beach when I saw my wife and kids waiting. I stopped and hugged little Em while feeling so indescribably happy, I thought I might just combust on the spot. I kissed her quickly and ran into the transition area to start the bike portion of the race. I found my bike in the sea of rigs, got out of my wetsuit, changed my shoes, put on my helmet and headed out to ride 56 miles. By the grace of God, I was going to finish this thing. I could still feel my sobriety coin pressing against my leg from under my tri-shorts as I pedaled out.

I was riding high now. Quite literally, actually—I was riding my bike at 5,430 feet in altitude around the foothills of Boulder, and I loved it. Still emotional over what happened to me in the water, I was always aware and grateful about how much my life had changed in just 24 months. I couldn't stop my mind from wandering as I turned the big crank on my bike and let the miles fly by. The road made a noise under my tires that was soothing to my ears. I could smell the wild grass and trees around me, and the vibration of the handle bars coming from my hands all the way through my body was like a symphony of sensory overload. There was so much to take in that I realized

I hadn't noticed the tightening in my calf.

It seemed that I had made a bit of a rookie mistake. As the miles were spinning out underneath me, I was failing to hydrate and fuel my body. It was starting to get hot and my body was cramping in response. I reached down and grabbed my water bottle to try to get on top of my fluids, but before I could go much farther, the cramp was so tight I had to stop. I got off my bike and tried to stretch the tight muscle. Other cyclists rode by and asked if I was ok.

"Yeah, it's cool," I replied. I jumped back on the bike and rode for a few more miles before the calf forced me to stop again. "Shit. Screw it," I thought. Not willing to be discouraged, I thought, "If I have to do the rest of the race 3 to 4 miles at a time, so be it." And I continued to try to cycle through the pain, but as the cramps came, I had to stop several more times to stretch and nurse my lower leg. I was getting on and off my bike at an alarming rate and I was starting to get worried about being able to run—if I could even make it to the end of the bike course.

I managed to complete the first lap of the 2-lap course and I was looking forward to seeing some friendly faces at the turnaround. Unfortunately, though, I didn't see any. My family had somehow missed me and I felt lonely and a touch sad as I set out to complete the last lap alone. Eventually the calf conceded and I was able to start pedaling hard again, and I did my best to make up for lost time by hammering hard all the way back to the transition area. "Done with this damn bike," I thought as I hoped off and racked it.

I had completed the 56 miles of the bike portion of the event. It wasn't pretty; in fact, it was quite slow but I didn't care. I had been going for almost 4 hours now, but I didn't care about that either—I was in this to finish no matter what. I slipped on my running shoes, swapped my bike helmet for sunglasses and limped out of the transition area and onto the run course.

"Cool, now I just have to run a half marathon." That thought was not particularly comforting.

The run course was two loops around the Boulder Rez, which was kind of cool in the sense that I had a chance to glance over my shoulder several times and look at the large body of water that I was swimming in just a few hours earlier. The water made me feel simultaneously thankful, proud and squeamish. Now that the swim and bike were over, it felt good to have only one task at hand—knock out these miles and victory awaits. I saw the kids as I started lap one of the run and that was a huge boost. In retrospect, I was glad they weren't there to see me at the low point when I came in after my first bike loop. Now feeling determined, I couldn't help but contrast the memories I was creating for them today with the ones I was making for them a couple of years ago.

I was smiling inside and out as I banged out mile after mile. I was by no means "crushing it" but I managed to run the first 6 miles or so at a sub 9-minute pace before the wheels came off. As I came in for lap two (once again) I couldn't find my family in the sea of spectators and I was suffering badly now. The temperature was approaching 100 degrees and I was not faring well in the heat. I had basically no concept of what fueling was and it's surprising I didn't feel worse, considering how dehydrated I must have been. I had consumed perhaps 200-300 calories in the last 4 hours and now doing the hardest part of the race, I was feeling the effects. To make things worse, there was zero shade on the course and the sun was beating me down. But my spirits were still high, even as my body was breaking. I set off for the last loop of the run.

"6.6 miles and I am an official Ironman 70.3 finisher," I thought.

I was forced to a "slog" (slow jog) pace that only resembled running in the sense that my arms were bent and swinging from my sides. The actual speed my body was moving at was a little over an "elderly mall-walk" pace. I stopped at each mile of the loop and put ice on my head. I drank Gatorade and dumped water on my back and I just kept going. I could see the finish area on the other side of the lake now. I knew it was, at most, 2 miles away but it felt like it was on the other side of the planet.

With a final burst of energy, I committed to running the last part of the course all the way to the finish. As I summoned up all I had in the will and guts department, I started to run. I picked up the pace and found I was ok even if I did feel like ass. I passed another runner who was staggering on the trail. He looked over at me as I ran by and grunted in disgust that I could possibly be smiling, much less running this late in the race. That gentleman will never know how many laughs I have received from recreating his particular "grunt/moan greeting" for my friends.

Finish lines are always emotional for me and this one was no exception. I was starting to tear up as I ran into the final finishing chute and as I heard the announcer call my name—and I let it all go.

I could feel the weight of the medal around my neck. It was a strange contrast to the light feeling in my heart, as if a spiritual load had been lifted from my shoulders. I looked out at the water again. I remember the cramps on the bike. I relived for a second the heat and horrible nausea on the run and it occurred to me that this was the most epic thing I had ever done in my life. In that moment, I didn't think I would ever do anything harder than what I had done that day. I decided I was going to get a tattoo to commemorate the event. I wanted an Ironman "M-Dot."

I realized that to some, this was a big no-no, first of all because I only did the 70.3, not the actual 140.6 event and second, because I barely finished it at all, coming in at over 6 hours for a finish time. But honestly, I just didn't care. I didn't want to give people the impression I did the full Ironman so I had the tattoo artist put in a "1/2" symbol on the tattoo. In the years since, there have been many times that I felt a twinge of embarrassment by this tattoo, but later I learned to love what it represented to me. It brings me back to the place when the thought of finishing a 6-hour event seemed impossible. I never want to forget that what was impossible yesterday can be routine today.

My mom and dad greeted me at the finish line and my wife and kids were there too. It was one of the best days of my life and I felt as proud as I did humbled. My dad had been struggling for some time with his own demons, only his weren't of the substance abuse kind; they came from a place of feeling unable to escape past failures. I wanted to return the greatest favor he ever did for me. I wanted to remind him to believe in his own ability to change his life in an instant. So without a thought or moment of hesitation, I grabbed the 2-year sobriety coin I had carried all day and handed it to him, saying, "Thank you for teaching me how to fight. I want you to have this."

My dad has always been my greatest hero.

Won't Back Down

"Did you ever hear of Dean Karnazes?" my wife asked me a few nights after my first marathon finish.

"Can't say I have," I responded.

"Oh, he just ran 50 marathons in 50 days. I saw an article in *The Denver Post*," she said casually.

"No. He did not." I said confidently.

"Yes, he did—here's the story," she said, handing me the newspaper.

What the fuck...?

I was still walking down the stairs backwards and inhaling through my clenched teeth when I first started to read *Ultramarathon Man* by Dean Karnazes. I couldn't imagine that there was one bit of truth to any of this. I will admit openly, though, that—like thousands of others—I was first introduced to ultra running by The Man, Dean. And what an introduction!

All night running, vomiting in cars after races, hallucinating, and accomplishing the seemingly impossible. These people it seemed not only did marathons like they did 30-minute aerobics classes; they ran races LONGER than marathons! I was stunned stupid—fifty miles in one race? 100 miles? Longer? I was hooked before I finished the first page. I knew somewhere deep inside that this strange, painful, yet somehow beautiful place, was where I was meant to be. This "ultra" stuff was obviously for crazy people—and I had been hearing that I was crazy my whole life.

After gobbling up *Ultramarathon Man*, I started researching and reading anything I could find online about this strange sport. I was reading about things like running all night long without sleeping. I read about vomiting on the side of the trail without the benefit of stopping the actual running. Hallucinations, blisters that take entire sheets of skin off the feet, crossing raging rivers during races, hypothermia and, of course, eating entire pizzas while running. Something in my soul compass shifted. It was significant and I knew somewhere deep inside that the trajectory of my life had changed as I read those first couple of stories about this crazy sport.

It didn't take long after my big day on the Boulder Ironman course before I started to think about what was next for me. Should I try to do a full Ironman 140.6? I liked that idea. Or should I try to be faster at some shorter triathlons, or maybe try to run a PR marathon? All of it sounded great, but each time I thought about the future, I couldn't help but think about Dean Karnazes and the ultra marathon world. In his book Dean talked about a race called the Badwater 135. I was intrigued, to say the least, and I read everything I could find about this ridiculous event... Here is an excerpt about the Badwater race from a blog post I wrote years later:

"Some things just speak to us. We don't know why, and rarely can we explain to others in a meaningful way what we see when our souls are moved to act. The first time I heard of the Badwater 135 I was speechless. The race puts runners on a 135-mile run across Death Valley on the hottest day of the year. And if that's not enough, to get to the finish, runners must climb three mountain ranges, including Mt. Whitney. As I watched a documentary about the event called *Running on the Sun* I felt a combination of disbelief, confusion and anxiety. I think the disbelief came from the simple observation that people could actually do something like this without dying. The confusion perhaps came from wondering why I was so moved by witnessing it, and the anxiety was still harder to define. Maybe it was a precognition of sorts, a vision that I may find myself out there in that very desert one day with the ultimate question ringing in my ears, 'Can I make it to Mt. Whitney?'"

After watching the movie *Running on the Sun*, it was settled. I was going to try to do an ultra marathon. Maybe not Badwater, but I wanted to do an epic race, nonetheless. I read a quote online that said, "Any idiot can run a marathon, but it takes a special kind of idiot to run an ultra marathon." I liked that. I was, in fact, a special kind of idiot—I had been hearing that my whole life. It seemed the ultra marathon community was full of characters, extremists, compulsives, thrill junkies and pure sluggers.

I think perhaps no one person better exemplifies the rugged individual of our sport than Ken Chlouber. He is the founder of the Leadville 100 Mile Trail race and is never at a loss for words about what it takes to run 100 miles—and why he started his race...

> From 5280 Magazine: *"The Leadville hospital director had his finger in Ken Chlouber's face, which wasn't good for his finger. If you've seen Ken, with those cowpuncher boots on his size 13 stompers and that miner's mug as craggy as the rock he blasted for a living, you'd figure out pretty quickly that you don't put a hand near his face unless you're dead drunk or dead serious.*
>
> *Dr. Bob Woodward wasn't drunk. "You cannot let people run a hundred miles at this altitude," he railed. "You're going to kill them."*
>
> *"Good!" Ken shot back. "At least that'll make us famous."*

Ken had spent too many nights in the Leadville mines with dynamite in his jacket and a blasting cap in his helmet to take life lightly. "Boys," he used to tell his crew on the graveyard shift, "we're going under that big rock and blowing it up, and if one of us gets out alive, it's going to be Ken. So if you want to walk out with me, you'll do exactly what I say." Ordinarily, he doesn't joke about carnage, but these were not ordinary times. His neighbors were drinking hard, punching their wives, sinking into depression or fleeing town. A sort of mass psychosis was overwhelming the town, which is one of the early stages of civic death: First, people lose the means to stick it out; then come fights, arrests, and robberies; finally, folks lose the desire. It was 1982, and overnight Leadville had become the most jobless region in North America.

The Climax Molybdenum mine had suddenly shut down, taking with it the paycheck of nearly every able-bodied man in town. Without Climax kicking in its enormous share of the property tax—in other words, without a local economy—schools and city budgets soon would be bankrupt. An epidemic of foreclosures was only a matter of time. A vision of the future was right across the mountains in Winfield and Vicksburg, and in dozens of other Colorado ghost towns that dried up after a boom. Leadville was ticking down to Deadville.

"Hell and half of Georgia couldn't get me to leave," Ken liked to say. He loved watching the sunrise over Mt. Massive as he left the mine tunnels at dawn, honking at buddies on Harrison Street from his black pickup with its flame-painted hood. He loved bringing his burro right into the bar for a beer every year after the Boom Days races. Ken loved Leadville, so he came up with a plan to save it.

Unfortunately, it was a really bad one. Ken wanted to start a 100-mile footrace through the mountains—a horrendous physical challenge. Actually, at that time, as far as anyone knew, the only people who ran ultra marathons were the Boulder housecleaners who called themselves "Divine Madness" (which everyone joked was a sex cult) and those Sri Chinmoyists from New York who shuffled around the block all night. As far as publicity, the spectacle of a few silent, skinny obsessives chasing each other through the woods in the dead of night had all the ingredients of terrible TV, except in the case of a horrific catastrophe, which, according to Leadville's leading medical expert, was a near certainty. Ken wouldn't turn Leadville into Vail; he'd turn it into Jonestown.

Ken organized the first race in 1983, and sure enough, the freaks were first in line. Some were burro racers who usually ran tied to a donkey; some were mountaineers missing toes; some, as predicted, were housecleaning cultists from Boulder. Interesting folks, certainly, but not the glam crowd that builds a tourist trade. However, that was only the beginning. The race has grown in ways that not even Ken, in his wildest, weirdest hopes, could have imagined. Llamas appeared, and a billionaire, and mystic guru Indians, along with a mysterious wanderer called The White Horse. Strange things began happening in Leadville—strange and wonderful things.

On August 27, 1983, less than a year after Ken's brainstorm—and at the exact hour the miners would usually be in the middle of a graveyard shift, dark shapes began moving through the Leadville streets. The ones who'd arrived the day before couldn't believe how cold it was, or how much their heads were aching. They now understood why, at around Leadville's 10,152-foot altitude, planes pressurize cabins. By 4 am, one woman and 44 men had gathered at Leadville's only traffic light. How many would still be alive the next morning was still in doubt. Cindy Corbin, the Leadville hospital obstetrics manager who gave pre-race physicals, was sure some contestants were going to die. "Why wouldn't they?" she said. "They'd be alone all night in the mountains, with those snowstorms we get. And they were already so wired, their blood pressure readings were off the charts." After Dr. Woodward protested that the race bordered on criminal negligence, Ken asked hospital Chief of Staff Dr. John Perna to be race medic. Perna knew his hospital director, Woodward, had a point—severe altitude sickness and exposure were the most obvious killers—and Ken's sales pitch only made it sound worse.

"It'll be in August," Ken had said.

Ok, Perna thought, "We can now add heat exhaustion to hypothermia..."

"We'll go over Hope Pass heading out and coming in," Ken continued.

"...plus possible dehydration, frostbite, fractures, and hypoxia-induced delirium and disorientation."

"And we'll cut the last ones off at 30 hours."

Which was way longer than the Geneva Convention allowed German prisoners of war to work at a stretch at nearby Camp Hale.

Once again, something deep was touched in me as I read about this man and this race. The fact that this event was in my backyard and (unlike most 100-mile races) had no prerequisites or qualifiers for entry was too much to resist. Ken has always said if you were dumb enough to sign up, you could run the Leadville 100. Lord help me, what did I get myself into? I started to think about Leadville every single time I ran. It was still August of 2007. That meant I had almost exactly one year to train and prepare for the Leadville 100 if I decided to do it.

In the last two years I had managed to put together a string of races and events that allowed me to feel some sort of reasonable argument as to my ability to train for a 100-mile ultra (and by "reasonable" I mean it made absolutely no sense whatsoever). The truth was I had no business at all doing this, but I have never let intelligence or reason convince me of anything. The human heart was my GPS system. It didn't matter how many time people told me that Leadville is one of the hardest 100-milers in the country. It didn't matter that on paper, that it was probably the absolute worst possible choice for a first 100-miler. I felt like the race chose me. I decided to do it.

When I first got to Colorado in 1994, I drove to Aspen. I was so excited to see this mountain town that has inspired so much attention in books, songs and film. Being an East Coast kid and seeing so much of the industrial and commercial topography of New York, I couldn't wait to see the mountains and slopes surrounding this storybook western village. But my heart never made the entire trip from Denver. It jumped out of my chest when we drove through an old mining town on the way to Independence Pass, a town filled with boarded-up houses, vacant stores and a still-functioning opera house where Molly Brown herself used to sit and watch the arts. There was also an Old West bar with a horse trough still out front and a sign over it reading "Silver Dollar Saloon 1879." I had to stop inside and have a beer; I can't describe why, but I just had to be in there. It was as if I was returning to a place I had been a thousand times. My jaw dropped open when I found out there were still bullet holes in the wall from when Doc Holliday had shot up the place. I was hooked on Leadville 10 years before I heard of ultra running or the Leadville 100.

Well, back to the reality of today. The shining star in all this was that over the last 24 months, I had completely transformed not just my body, not just my eating habits, but also my mind. I had a whole new standard of what was acceptable and what wasn't. I had new expectations of what I could endure physically and mentally, and I was pretty sure that this was in many ways what I had been searching for my whole life. I was searching for the end of me—how much can I endure? How close to complete mental and physical collapse can I get without failing? It didn't matter what that end was; it only mattered that I kept searching for it. As far as my fitness and athletic resume, I was going to go to Leadville with what I had in the tank—it had to be enough.

At this point, my racing resume looked something like this:

November 2005: CU Turkey Trot 39:22
October 2006: Denver Marathon 4:45
November 2006: CU Turkey Trot 22:15
May 2007: Colorado Marathon 3:58
August 2007: Half Ironman

A simple but deeply rooted question loomed in my mind: "Am I worthy of something like Leadville?" Hell, it was starting to seem like anyone could run a marathon—or even do a triathlon. But you simply cannot fake a race like this. It was a true ball-buster.

As I kid (and still today), I was a huge fan of the Rocky movies. You almost had to be a fan to even be considered for membership into my family. Our daily lives were peppered with example after example of one-liners from the entire franchise of Rocky movies. But one scene from the original movie always struck a deep chord and has caused me to stop, listen, and rewind the tape time and time again. It's when Rocky comes home after a long run and he sits next to Adrian who is sleeping...

Rocky: "I can't do it."
Adrian: "What?"
Rocky: "I can't beat him."
Adrian: "Apollo?"
Rocky: "Yeah. I been out there walkin' around, thinkin'. I mean, who am I kiddin'? I ain't even in the guy's league."
Adrian: "What are we gonna do?"

Rocky: "I don't know."

Adrian: "You worked so hard."

Rocky: "Yeah, that don't matter. Cause I was nobody before."

Adrian: "Don't say that."

Rocky: "Ah come on, Adrian, it's true. I was nobody. But that don't matter either, you know? 'Cause I was thinkin' it really don't matter if I lose this fight. It really don't matter if this guy opens my head, either. Cause all I wanna do is go the distance. Nobody's ever gone the distance with Creed, and if I can go that distance, you see, and that bell rings and I'm still standin', I'm gonna know for the first time in my life, see, that I weren't just another bum from the neighborhood."

Many nights throughout my entire life I have pondered what Rocky was saying. In the past, I had wondered if I "lucked" into my chain of stores. I wondered if being an alcoholic was "the real me." I always felt like an imposter as a kid. And I also wondered if all this running was just some sort of fluke too. "Anyone can run a marathon," I thought again. I want to do something big. Something that will teach me something about who I am inside, who I REALLY am inside. But perhaps for the first time ever, in that moment, I wasn't just wondering if I was worthy—I just wanted to know the truth. I wasn't afraid to see it anymore. I had to go to Leadville and find out.

When I first met Larry Giles on my travels along the highway of personal change, I knew he was a special guy. And he was one of the first people to enter my life in the "sober era." The fact that he was an Ironman athlete was on the surface very lucky—and more accurately, an example of divine providence moving in my life. Larry was the person who gave me my first spa show 2 years earlier and was also the first person outside of an AA meeting that I ever told I was a recovering alcoholic. I remember him telling a bartender once when we were on the road that he couldn't stay out late drinking because he was "in training for an Ironman." I thought that was pretty cool.

Over the years I stayed in contact with Larry, and he was very supportive of me during my journey. He saw me go from 320 pounds on the day he met me at the California State Fair all the way to where I was now. I asked him training questions and I was always willing to listen to what he was doing to prepare for Ironman Triathlons; he had done many of them. One of the things that really stood out to me was his unconventional run training. In a world dominated by complex training plans, software, GPS and heart-rate training, he just ran. No plan—just run. And in fact, he "just ran" marathons! His marathon training plan was to run as many marathons as possible. That seemed so stupid that I simply had to adopt it.

I decided that running marathons was going to be the heart of my training for the Leadville 100. Since there was absolutely no written-in-stone understanding of how to train for something like a 100-mile run, I decided running marathons "as speed work" was as sound an idea as any. Unlike running conventional road races or triathlons where there is a litany of conventional wisdom, people that ran ultras sometimes had nothing in common with each other in terms of training. Some people claimed to run as little as 30 or 40 miles a week; others, 250 miles per week. Some did cross training; others only ran a couple of times a week. I decided to run a base mileage of about 40-50 and throw in as many marathons as I could while travelling around the country for work. I was also about to learn a valuable lesson: Even though I was starting to feel like superman, I was very human.

There was a local marathon in Boulder in September that was about a month after my Boulder Ironman 70.3 finish. I had to travel to work in Sacramento for a couple weeks, so I decided to get in a couple of long runs on the road and give the Boulder Marathon a shot when I returned to town. It seemed only appropriate that the marathon started at the same exact place as the Boulder Ironman 70.3—so in a sense, I was returning to the scene of the crime.

"Hello Runners! Welcome to the 2007 Boulder Marathon!"

I was very glad I wouldn't be swimming, and I was aware of that gratitude as I stared out into the Boulder Reservoir from the starting corral. It was strange to be getting ready to run a marathon that was just going to be a "training race," as many ultra runners would say. And the training race was pretty uneventful as far as marathons go. I stayed true to my plan and ran slow and steady. I chatted with other runners, I took in all the sights, and somehow I still managed to run what was a respectable time for me, considering the effort. I think my time was in the 4:15-4:20 range. I wasn't trying to RACE this marathon—I just wanted to get used to grinding out the miles to prepare for the rigors of going 100 miles in one event. It was a warm and sunny day and I remember feeling like I had won the life lottery as I hit the finish line. It was my third marathon finish and I took pride in the fact that it was something I was able to do without too much mental difficulty. In fact, I ran through the finish line without stopping. And I kept running—I ran right to where my truck was parked, drove straight to the office and worked all day in the showroom.

I started to scavenge the online marathon race calendars to find another marathon that would match up with my travel schedule for work. I noticed right away that there was a marathon nearby while I was in Utah for the state fair. It was only two weeks away—perfect. Well, it wasn't perfect; the race was approximately 90 miles away from Salt Lake, in Logan, but with a little creative planning I could make it work. Even in running circles, my friends were starting to call me the crazy one. I was getting chastised for running too much, and I was hearing a little talk about being obsessive. Oh well. I once heard that, "obsessive is a word used by the lazy to describe the motivated."

I went with that. But I still remember the look on my co-workers faces when I explained my plans for the work weekend:

"So, I am going to work the booth with you guys on Friday night until 11:00 pm, and then I am going to drive to Logan. I should get there about 12:30 or 1:00 am and I'll check into a hotel. I'll sleep until about 4:00 am and then head to the marathon to be at the starting line by 6:00. I'll then run the marathon, jump in my car, and drive back to the fair. I should be there by noon on Saturday and I'll work with you until the fair ends at 11 pm... cool?"

What I got was total silence, a blank stare—and then a burst of laughter. After the laughter slowly petered out, my buddy Peter looked at me and said, "You are serious, aren't you?"

"Yes," I smiled back.

So I did it. Just like I outlined for my buddy, I worked the fair, drove to Logan, slept for a couple hours, ran the Top of The Utah Marathon, drove back to SLC and worked on my feet all day and night. It seemed pretty normal to me, actually. It was the only option I had to get the run in, so I did it. As I walked into the commercial booth on Saturday afternoon wearing my finisher's shirt, people that worked with me stared in disbelief. "You really just ran a marathon?" I was asked more than once. In fact, other than a sheepish smile, it never really occurred to me that it was pretty out there.

Two days after my adventurous state fair 26.2-mile run, I signed up for the 2007 Denver Marathon. I had just done two marathons two weeks apart, but I was still anxious to get more training in. More miles, the better! After all, I was in Leadville training, right? The Denver Marathon was approximately three weeks away, so it gave me a little time to rest... oh wait. No, that's not how it happened at all. Instead of resting, I continued to run. I had stopped listening to my body and completely adapted the "no pain-no gain" mentality, which in case you are wondering, is potentially the worst mentality in the world for designing your training plan.

I was very excited building up to the Denver Marathon because this race was my very first marathon a year earlier. I couldn't believe that an entire year had gone by since I first laced them up and ran 26.2 miles. When I say I couldn't believe it, I mean I couldn't believe it had ONLY been a year. It seemed to me like I had been running my whole life. I was a runner now. It felt natural in many ways. I continued to grind out 40-50 mile weeks. I was hitting hard 8-mile tempo runs on the concrete bike paths around my house, and unknowingly at the time, proceeding to pound my body to hamburger.

The miles were taking their toll. I felt weak in my core. My adductors and hips hurt and my back was starting to really give me some shit too. When I was a big man, I was always good for one or two major "back's gone out" escapades. These would always result in me lying on the floor on a futon mat for a week or more until I could move again. But now it seemed like I had a weapon to combat back pain—running made my back feel better! At least while I was running, that is. AFTER the running, I was starting to feel worse and worse.

One day I was on an 8-mile tempo run, I was on a route that I had done perhaps one hundred times or more, and I noticed my back was getting ridiculously tight. Even after some painful miles, I still paid little attention to it and just tried to focus on "running light on my feet." As the miles clicked off, the pain started to increase. By the time I hit the 4-mile turn-around point, it seemed every time my feet struck the ground, I was getting shooting pain in my back—and now my hamstrings too. I veered off the concrete path and onto the small dirt trail next to the sidewalk, and this seemed to make it a little better. I instinctively knew that this was not good and the pain was more than just something annoying—this could be bad. Occasionally I would run out of dirt path to run on and was forced to return to the concrete. Each time I switched surfaces, my body immediately let me know it was unhappy by cranking up the pain until I could barely keep going. I should have stopped. I should have listened to the signals my body was sending me. But I finished the run anyway.

Eventually, I made it back to my truck having completed the entire 8 miles of running. I was a wreck. Everything in my body hurt. It seemed like my body was doing its best to send me a rest signal, but I shut off the receiving unit. All I could think about was running the Denver Marathon in a few days. As I hobbled over to my truck, I started to stretch my tight and hurting body. What happened next should have been a big warning sign and, in fact, should have sent me immediately to the doctor's office. I reached out with one hand and grabbed a hold of the side of my pickup truck bed. I then proceeded to lower my hips down in an effort to stretch out my upper body and lower back at the same time. Before I could get more than a few inches into the stretch, a jolt of electrical current went charging through my legs. It was literally an electrical shock. I twitched violently for about 3 or 4 very long seconds and then fell over on the ground.

"What the fuck was that?" I said out loud to no one.

Ok, gang, it's official. I was scared. But I was also stubborn. I picked myself up off the ground and went to work immediately on rationalizing, telling my brain why this was a fluke of some sort. That didn't mean anything, I thought. I just "tweaked" a nerve. It could happen to anyone, I reasoned. I stood up and placed my hand on my truck bed again. Once again, I started to lower myself into the stretch. Once again, I was greeted by an electrical current of extreme pain coursing through my legs and back. "Ok, that was stupid. Of course it would do it again—my body is all pissed off now. It still doesn't mean I am hurt."

I decided to rest for a couple days before the marathon. I knew I should have been trying to convince myself that running the Denver Marathon was a mistake. But I was going to have nothing to do with that loser talk. I was very quiet on the way home. I stared ahead and drove.

As I stood in the starting corral before the start of the 2007 Denver Marathon, I made a deal with myself. As soon as I finished this race, I was going to rest. Leadville wasn't until August of 2008 and that was still 10 months away. I had plenty of time to train. My back was still bothering me, but at least I hadn't had a recurrence of the shock treatments—and that seemed like a small victory. But I still needed some time, I reasoned. Before I could go any further down the road of mental bargaining, we were off and running. I hadn't run in a few days because of the back pain and I felt terrible now as we got going. Mile after mile came and I just never felt good. I felt like I had a thousand miles on my legs.

Somehow I made it to the halfway point and somehow managed to keep from turning toward the finish line with the half marathoners and calling it an early day. I started to feel good at about 15 miles into the race. My body was warm and my back was finally loose. I picked up the pace a little and started to have fun—I even started to run fast. By the time I hit the finish line, I scarcely remembered anything about bargaining for rest or promising to take it easy. "Wow, I have run 5 marathons," I thought as I admired my finisher's medal. This is no fluke at all.

As fate would have it, there was a lull in the marathon calendar between the end of October and the beginning of December. The only marathon I could find that fit into my travel schedule was about 6 weeks between races. It was the 2007 Tucson Marathon. I had a ten-day special event scheduled for work in the Tucson market and my plan was to duplicate my Top of the Utah plan. I was going to run the marathon early before work and make it to the event immediately after the race. I was still experiencing issues with my body, however. My back was still sore, but even more troublesome now, were my hamstrings—it seemed like they were as tight guitar strings. I could only manage to run 3 or 4 miles without excruciating pain, yet somehow I had managed to twist things around in my head until I convinced myself that somehow I was going to be fine for the race which was in 8, 7, 6, 5, 4, 3, oh shit—2 days now.

You can't always pinpoint the exact moment when you have lost yourself to stupidity, but in this case I remember specifically. The final jump came the night before the race when I said out loud to my friend Pete (the same one who stared at me in disbelief as I ran my Utah State Fair plan at him), "I am injured. It's really that simple." I said this as I tried to mimic a running gait back and forth in the parking lot we were standing in. "Let me do a quick test," I said and I took off running at a very slow and careful pace around the mall parking lot. I ran perhaps 2 minutes before I completed the circle back to him.

"I'm fucked," I sighed. "I can't run and there isn't a coach on the planet that would tell me it's ok to run this marathon tomorrow."

"What are you gonna do, man?" he asked with genuine sympathy.

"I don't know," I shook my head and we drove back to the hotel.

Later that night we went out for dinner. We talked about the current sales event we were out in Arizona to work. We talked about upcoming shows we had. We talked about New York sports, but he was obviously avoiding the subject that was hanging out there like a big meatball. He was really hoping, for my own sake, that I wasn't going to try to run the marathon.

"Here's the deal," I said as I ate my steak. "I already paid for my entry. I would probably try to run tomorrow even if I convinced myself not to do the marathon. So I may as well go out in the morning and run the first 4 or 5 miles of the race with everyone else—get my money's worth, you know."

Pete looked at me and agreed. It seemed logical enough and I don't think he really understood what the big deal was anyway—he trusted me to make a good decision. "Yeah," I said, going back to my food. "Just a little jog in the morning from the starting line. You never know, maybe I will feel great."

But it was all just posturing. I knew what I was really committing to. This race is a point-to-point run, meaning they drive you out in buses to the starting line, and everyone runs the 26.2 miles back to the finish. For me to quit early would mean stopping at an aid station and asking for a ride back. Although this was in the realm of possibility, it was highly unlikely that I would ever exercise this option. I woke up the next morning at 4:00 and got on the bus to head to the start. My hamstrings were killing me.

I was at mile 8 of the 2007 Tucson Marathon when a thought hit me, "I'm not feeling any WORSE than I was when I started, so maybe I will just keep going?" So, I kept going.

Sometime later my hamstrings were still pulling hard on the brakes as I hit the 13.1 mark. "Half Marathon down," I thought. "Still no worse." I kept going. Hell, maybe I was even going to finish this thing...

At 18 miles the worst possible thing happened—I felt good. I actually felt GOOD. My hamstrings loosened up, my back felt strong and I was cruising. So, instead of just continuing to slow-jog my way towards home, I ran. And I ran hard. I started to think that I could run the last 8 miles faster than I have ever finished a marathon. And I did. I hit the finish line with a huge smile on my face. BOOM! Number 6 in the books—look out Leadville. My back and hamstrings were already tightening like a vise by the time I had walked the 100 feet past the finish line to the parking lot.

I was standing in line for my luggage at the Denver airport when something very bizarre happened. I was just getting back to town after my Arizona trip and I was feeling some ill effects from the race. My glutes and hamstrings were sore, but I had also developed a kind of numbness in my legs. It didn't feel quite like any post-race symptom I had before, but then again, I had never run 4 marathons within a few weeks of each other, either. "Shit happens—I'm a runner," I thought. "Let's see what happens..."

But before I could finish the thought, I screamed out loud, "Goddamn it!!! What the fuck!"

Something had just run into me from behind. I turned around and scanned the floor and areas around me looking for the cart or heavy equipment that just ran over my left leg. I was instantly covered in sweat. I could feel it pouring down my back under my shirt, and even running down my legs. The pain coming from my calf was so excruciating that I couldn't stand. I felt like someone had jammed a screwdriver right into my lower leg. I dropped my backpack on the ground without a thought for who might pick it up and run off with my laptop, wallet and other items and hobbled over to the nearest bench and tried to sit.

I was in trouble. I knew it, but I was very confused. I needed to sit down on the bench and see what sharp object or piece of metal had pierced my calf muscle. It was on fire and I was gasping for breath. I finally lowered myself to the bench and instantly the pain was gone. Just like that. As soon as my ass hit the chair, the pain was gone. I looked at my lower leg. No objects sticking out of the calf. No blood. No trauma of any kind, actually. My heart sank in my chest. What the hell was going on? The pain was coming from inside. I knew I was in deep shit.

As I stood up to go get my discarded backpack, the pain started to build again. Now, both lower legs started to twitch and shake. An electrical current started to flow, and within a few minutes the pain was full-on raging. Somehow I managed to walk, sit, shuffle, and hobble all the way to the passenger pick-up. As I got into the car, I told my wife Heather I needed to see a doctor immediately.

"Are you sure?" I knew it was a stupid question, but I had to ask him.

"Yes, I'm sure" the doctor said. "You have a massively herniated disc impinging on your sciatic nerve at S1/L5. You also have a severely bulging disc pushing at L4/L5."

My father Loren Clark with his first work truck.

Dad, my brother Loren, and me (*in red shirt*) fishing in upstate New York.

This truck became home for my family for many years as we traveled the country. We added a small camper shell on the back for shelter.

Heather and me at our wedding, May of 1997. She literally took my breath away when I saw her walk down the aisle.

One of the best days of my life.

Always the entertainer—keeping my mom Joan and my dad laughing on my wedding day.

Drunk at 3 am—just another normal day in 2001.

Heather and our newborn twins David Clark, Jr. and Emily Lynn in July of 2001.

My brother Chase and me loading up on 90-proof and beer in the summer of 2004.

I think the beer can on my head is a nice touch... I was rarely sober. This day was no different.

Christmas morning after the shameful electrical tape night-mare.

Me with my two favorite Yankees fans, David, Jr. and Emily.

My brother Chase and my beautiful mother Joan in 2000.

Dinner at Mom's in 2008. Left to right: My brother Shaun, my father Loren, me, my brother Chase, his girlfriend Krystal, my mom Joan, and my wife Heathert.

November 2005 at my first race, the CU Turkey Trot 5k. I finished in just under 40 minutes and ran the whole way.

November 2006. One year after my first 5k, I returned to the CU Turkey Trot 5k—this time at 180 lbs and running 22:35.

June of 2006. My first half marathon, Steamboat Springs, Colorado.

Ouch. October of 2006 at my first marathon finish.

One of the first pictures of me as a sober man, early August of 2005 in San Diego.

California State Fair 2005—my first adventure into the road show circuit, selling high-end BBQ's.

The spa store where I worked in 2005 before I started my journey into the world of sobriety and running. I used to drink here for hours and hours each day.

One of the first pictures of me as a sober man, early August of 2005 in San Diego.

First sober Christmas, 2005.

The shrinking man in January of 2006. I was in Arizona for a home show, but I got my running in each day on the hotel treadmill.

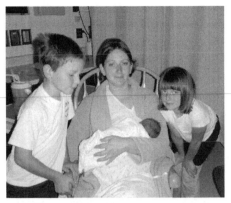

Heather with newborn Catie and the twins.

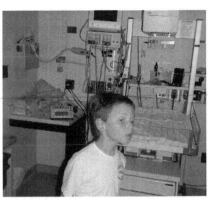

Davey up on his tippy toes to see Catie for the first time.

Little Catherine Mary hamming it up for the camera.

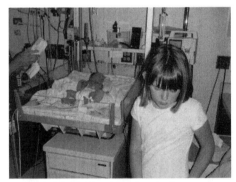

Emily with Catie sleeping in her protective crib.

Family photo at cabin before my first Leadville 100

A great shot taken during my panic-attack swim at the Boulder Ironman 70.3.

2007, my Ironman 70.3 surprise—seeing my daughter Emily after my struggle in the water was one of my best moments in the race.

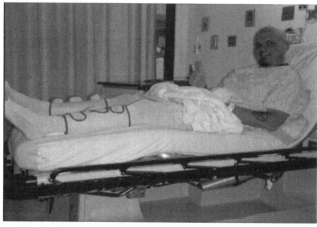

March of 2008, just minutes before undergoing spinal surgery for two herniated discs.

Bloated and stuck in a chair awaiting surgery, I show off my stash of pain killers. Inside, I was dying and confused as to what the future might bring.

Hours and hours on my trainer, rehabbing after surgery—fully committed to a comeback.

First trip up Bear Peak—got my ass kicked hard.

Top of Bear Peak after doing 12 hours of non- stop summits in training for the Leadville 100.

Nico and me on top of Torreys 14er—Leadville 100 training day, 2010.

4 am in Leadville, CO. The start of the Leadville 100 in 2010.

The 2010 Leadville 100—at 24 miles in and getting a bite to eat before heading out for 76 more.

A little over 13 miles into the 2010 Leadville 100.

After rallying at Winfield, Nick and I are passing a line of runners on Hope Pass.

Absolutely devastated at the 50-mile mark of the 2010 Leadville 100, I changed my shirt and got back on the course with little hope of finishing.

"Say goodbye to Hope Pass, David," Nick said to me at the summit.

Nick and me feeling strong as we climb Hope Pass at the 2010 Leadville 100.

Late in the night, approximately 70 miles into the 2010 Leadville 100.

My pacer Kelly getting me home, 5 miles to the finish of the 2010 Leadville 100.

Running in, flying our family's flag.

Not just another bum from the neighborhood.

Crew manager Jeff there to shake my hand.

The twins, Dad, Chase, and me at the finish of the 2010 Leadville 100.

The finish of the 2011 Leadville 100.

During my 300-mile Run Across Colorado for Sobriety in 2012.

100 miles into the Badwater 135.

The 2013 Badwater 135.

A New Kind of Recovery

If you have never had the pleasure of having an MRI, it must be because you were a good human being in your previous life. Being "coffined" into a 2-foot tube for 45 minutes, surrounded by whirling machinery and horrifically loud noises, all while being told, "Don't move or we have to start over," can only be retribution for once being a genocidal dictator.

So, I had a setback—a very painful, horrible setback, but it happens. The question was, "What will I chose to let this mean?" I have always believed that it is not what happens to us in life that matters; it's what we chose to let these things mean that can launch us to new heights or fold us up forever. Was I going to let this injury mean I was done as a runner? More importantly, what does it mean to my sobriety if I physically can't run again? Wow, that one was deep. It seemed like I had some serious soul searching to do while I was searching for medical solutions to the electric pain that was shooting through my legs.

Status check: I had a herniated disc that was impinging the sciatic nerve. I also had a bulging disc that may or may not be pushing on the nerve, as well. I had tingling and numbness in my foot and legs and I couldn't manage to stand for more than 10 or 15 minutes before the electrical storm would ground me, literally ground me. I couldn't run for now. But I wasn't going to let that shake me, not after I had come this far. I just had to figure out what I was going to do. I thought a good place to start was listening to the specialist.

After enduring the obligatory paperwork mountain in the orthopedic surgeon's office, I was finally sitting on the crinkly white paper in the examining room. I was there to discuss the results of the MRI. After what seemed like a week, my doctor Brian Castro, came in. He is a straightforward guy with the confidence that you would expect a surgeon to have. He looked me in the eyes and told me the truth, even if it was what I didn't want to hear. I liked him from the start.

"We need to get you into physical therapy for sure. From there we can talk about all the options." They were: PT, steroid injections or surgery. "You know that's an option, right?" Brian said.

"What is?" I asked.

"Surgery," he said.

"Yeah, I know."

But honestly, I had heard so many horror stories about back surgery that I was skeptical, to say the least. Brian somehow could see this skepticism in my body language and was trying to ferret it out. "I just want to give you all the scenarios for you to consider," he said. "I have done perhaps 10,000 of these particular surgeries, so if the time comes, I will take care of you. You should know, though, that there is always the possibility that the other disc will herniate too. Right now it's just bulging, but if it goes..."

"Yeah, I know," I conceded the point. I left the office feeling a little low on energy but still high in resolve. I had an appointment to see a therapist the following week.

"What the fuck is wrong with me?"

I said this out loud in complete exasperation. I was standing in the kitchen frozen in place. My legs were shaking violently and I was unable to move. I was completely paralyzed as my body twitched and jerked out of control. I stood there holding on to the refrigerator handle for dear life as I waited for the seizure to end. After about 45 seconds it abruptly stopped. I was left standing there in complete abject horror as the sweat from the pain and stress to my body lingered. I took deep breaths of air in to try to recover. I staggered back to the living room and sat down in my recliner. My symptoms were all over the map and didn't seem very concerned that I needed to file them in neat easy-to-understand files.

I met with the physical therapist, Diana, and she gave me a little hope. She said she wasn't 100% convinced that my disc herniation was causing all the hullabaloo. She thought maybe I had an inflammation of the piriformis (a large muscle that wraps around the glute) and that it was pushing on the sciatic nerve. She told me I had "a weak core," common to most endurance athletes who swim, bike and run themselves to death while ignoring the basic stability muscles of the spine.

To increase my spinal stability and take some pressure off the lower back, she had me doing exercises that honestly seemed like a complete waste of time. I would lie on my back and move my legs around a bit and balance on a ball, all the while thinking this was silly. Of course, the next morning would come and I was sore in places that I didn't even know had muscles. "Maybe there is something to all this," I thought. So I showed up for all my appointments and did my exercises at home each day. The one saving grace was that even though running was impossible, I did have the ok from the doctor and therapist to swim and cycle inside on the trainer.

I could ride my bike on the trainer for an hour—really hard. I would spin my legs fast and furiously to various metal songs thrashing in my ear buds. I could go to the pool and swim 2,000 or 3,000 meters until my arms felt like they would fall off. But I couldn't stand for more than 10-15 minutes. "How is that even possible?" I was asking Diana as she was working me over on the massage table.

She explained that as I stood up, it was as if a clock started. The vertebrae in my spine, once load-bearing from the gravity of standing, would start putting pressure on the disc. The disc would then expand under the pressure and push on the nerves in my spine. From there it was open season on the complex network of tissue and nerve endings in my back. Pain, tingling, numbness and, yes, even spasms that "took control of my legs." All normal responses. She told me to make sure I let the doctor know if I lost control of my bowels, as this was a symptom of something very serious. If this happened, I would need to go into surgery immediately.

"Great," I said. "You are telling me that if I crap in my pants, I'm in deep shit."

We both busted up laughing at the same time.

Despite my injury and subsequent rehab attempt, I still had a life to live. My kids and my family had always been the real inspiration for my recovery, not podiums and finisher's medals. And on some level, I was actually enjoying being unencumbered by work for the last several weeks. It was great being home and it was Christmas time, to boot! This was by far my best time of the year. To say I am a fan of Christmas is like saying that Marcos lady liked shoes. I LOVE Christmas. I even have an app on my phone that tells me each morning how many days until the magic night when Santa comes. I put on my red holiday-themed Yankees hat (yes, I actually have one of these), and my wife and I went out Christmas shopping for the evening. It seemed like a risky plan, given the time limit I currently had on standing or walking, but I left the house without a plan. I figured if I had to sit down on the floor inside Target every 10 minutes to make the pain stop, so be it.

It turns out this was exactly what I had to do. Shopping for gifts that year became one of the most painful things I have ever done. In the end, I had to grab a chair at the Starbucks inside and let my wife walk around the store to shop. But I didn't let it get to me; instead, I sipped on my Peppermint Mocha and listened to Dean Martin sing about the "marshmallow world we live in" over the store's speakers. "That's funny," I thought, "because I kinda feel like my spine is made of marshmallows."

After some time with no meaningful progress towards being pain free, I decided to talk to my doctor about doing a steroid injection into my spine. He had mentioned it as a possible treatment and I wanted to learn more. I was starting to think more about how nice it would be to just live my life without pain—and less about the prospects of continuing my running. I didn't like that direction of thinking one bit, but it was picking up momentum.

As we made our way into the parking lot of the hospital, I was still trying to be positive as I lifted my body, still in pain, out if the car. "I feel good about this," I said to my wife. "This will get me back on track in no time." The doctor said that he thought a steroid injection to the herniated disc was a great next step. He explained that the steroid will help clear up the inflammation and get the pressure off the nerve. He said there was a high success rate, and given the slow progress of our current plan, he made an immediate appointment for me to have the procedure done.

I was glad to being taking some sort of control over the situation. I made a commitment to myself to keep moving forward every day. "Find a way to stay in the game," I told myself. "Don't let cynicism creep in." I continued my daily research on all things back-injury related. I read about how the steroid inject is given, I found athletes that had the procedure done and went on to continue competing, I posted on all my internet forums and chat rooms, and I emailed people who were in my situation. Anytime I heard something negative, I went to work deleting the information from my mind.

"He didn't recover, because he didn't work as hard as I will in rehab," I would think when someone said they had the same injury and were still struggling years later.

"They were out of shape before they got injured; athletes set the bell curve on recovery," I submitted for no one in particular.

All these thoughts I needed. I needed them to *believe* and to keep hope alive. It might seem like a judgmental or harsh way of dismissing the struggle of others, but it was pure survival for me. I remembered how early in my recovery, I noted that we are all like computers in that we are always faced with saving or deleting files—we have to choose what is important enough to take up the limited space we have in our heads. Well, I was only interested in saving the information that supported a complete comeback; everything else was sent to the recycling bin.

One time, I was at my physical therapist's office and I was sitting on the examining table after my session. My therapist was printing off some exercises for me to do at home when another therapist walked over to me. "I heard about your injury and your story" she said. "I think if you want to have a decent quality of life, you should give up this idea of running ultra marathons. In fact, I would give up the idea of distance running all together. If you just did some 5k's and smaller triathlons you could stay healthy and not keep injuring yourself."

I stared at her in complete disbelief.

"I had to give up running to stay healthy too," she said, seeing my growing discomfort. "You will just be back here again if you keep going." That was the final straw. Just as she finished this last nugget of wisdom, my therapist Diana walked over to us with my homework for the day.

Without waiting for my new critic to walk away, I looked at Diana and said, "Keep her the fuck away from me." I was not sure, but I imagine I didn't enamor myself to the other therapist—but I didn't care. I consider that kind of negative garbage an act of violence. I don't care how many times someone tries to sell me the, "I'm only telling you this because I care," bullshit, I am not buying it. I show people I care by believing in them, not by trying to knock the wind out of them.

By then Diana, had gotten to know me a little and she smiled and said, "She's had that coming for a while—good for you!"

The day of the injection I was nervous. The thought of having to lie still on the table as they inserted a large needle into my back was a little unsettling. I mean, what happens if I move unexpectedly or roll over while a sharp piece of metal is in my spine? We are talking about being paralyzed here. Worse yet was the archaic manner in which they assure you that they are delivering the steroid to exactly the right part of your spine.

Here's the drill: The doctor will put the needle into your back while you are lying on your side. Then they do their best "guess-timate" to try to get the needle into the exact area in your spine where the herniated material has spilled. Then the doctor walks away and takes an x-ray picture to see exactly where the needle is in relation to the herniation. At this point, the doctor will come back to the patient and make needed "adjustments" to get on-target and once again take a picture to see what's going on under the hood. After several repeats of this ritual, eventually the needle will be at precisely the right location. With this done, the doctor will simply push the plunger down and release the steroid into the area—which, by the way, created possibly the strangest sensation I have ever experienced. All at once every nerve ending in my legs, feet, back and butt all seemed to grow alive and self-aware—in a moment. I felt like a million light switches were turned on all at once inside my body.

"My life is so bizarre," I thought as I lay on the table immediately after my injection.

"Give it 24 hours or so and let us know what happens," the doc said. "You should start to feel better immediately."

"When can I start to run?" *I can't believe I asked that question*, I thought.

"I see no reason that you can't at least give some light running a start in a week or so, but talk to your surgeon and see what he says. It all depends on how you feel and what symptoms you are still experiencing."

I remember joking around with the doctor as they processed my paperwork, I remember the white tile floor under my running shoes as I looked down on the way out of the hospital, and I remember looking at yet another prescription for painkillers that they gave me before I left. "Jesus," I thought. Back when I used to eat narcotics for breakfast, I had to beg and borrow for scripts from the doctor. These days, they seem to shove Percocet or Vicodin into my pockets like they're handing out breath mints. I had been very nervous about the pain medication, given my recovery and substance abuse history—and I had been doing a good job of staying away, but I couldn't help but feel the power of the drug, even if it was in the form of a paper license to use.

I had a post-injection follow-up with my surgeon and, I have to say, I was feeling great. I hadn't had any of the horrible stabbing pains or electrical shocks of the past. I could walk around for hours without any symptoms at all other than some numbness in my foot (which I was told was very normal).

I was beaming. I received the ok to return to some light running and normal activity and see what happened. Even though I now had the green "run light" I decided to play it conservative and wait a week or so before I laced up the shoes. In the meantime, I was going to hit the bike and pool again.

"I think I am going to sign up for a full Ironman," I thought as I left the office. "That might be a good break for my body. I can do Leadville in 2009."

I was hammering out 1- to 3-hour cycling sessions like I was on a mission. I felt alive again. I was not only able to train, I was getting stronger and stronger. I had put on a few pounds during the last 3 months and I was glad to have some intensity back to my workouts. Each day I rode, I swam, and I did all my core rehab exercises. I still saw my physical therapist 2-3 times a week and I was making huge gains in my core strength.

"Have you run yet?" Diana asked me as she was adjusting me on the table.

"No, I'm still afraid to," I confessed.

"Have you had any symptoms at all?"

"No, everything is going great," I said. "I just want to wait, but I'm going to start next week."

Diana agreed that I should start running again. *Aw right!*

I headed back to the house feeling really good about where things were going. I was still a little nervous about heading back out to the trails and roads with the memories of the severe pain still lingering, but I was a little excited too. In the meantime I was going to go ride on my bike trainer and then head to the pool in the morning. Life was good.

The next morning I was on my way out of the house, heading to the pool when I noticed my hamstrings were a little tight. "Oh well, I thought. I rode hard yesterday; maybe some time in the pool will be just what I need." I kissed my wife and yelled goodbye to the kids who were causing a little ruckus in the other room. As I left the living room, I grabbed my swim bag and, as I lifted the small pack to put it on my shoulder, I noticed my hamstrings were super tight. In fact, they were burning. "What the hell is this?" I turned to walk out the door and they were on fire. I couldn't stand up. The blood drained from my face as I leaned over to support myself and keep from falling.

"Are you ok?" asked my wife. She could tell something was seriously wrong.

"My hamstrings are killing!" I grunted.

Now the pain had spread to my glutes. I couldn't stand anymore. In fact, the pain was so intense that the need to sit or fall over (anything to get off my feet) was overwhelming my every thought. I was in deep trouble and I knew it. Something about the severity, depth and rapid onset of my symptoms told me this pain was from deep inside my body, not just from my muscles. I hopped once and fell onto the couch. I immediately rolled to my right side, bending all the way over the side arm of the couch in an instinctive self-defense measure. This seemed to ease the pain a little, but I noticed I was out of breath and covered in sweat.

My horror and pain quickly transformed into raw emotion—frustration, devastation and discouragement all fought for control, as my heart just felt limp. I cried.

"We are going to get you into surgery ASAP, Dave." The nurse at the doctor's office sounded very concerned and that made me at least feel that she understood on some level the amount of pain I was in. After a pause, she came back on the line. "We have you scheduled for March 17th."

"St. Paddy's Day," I thought. After a quick scan of the math, I protested. "That's over three weeks away!" The thought of spending three weeks in this condition was mind numbing. It had only been an hour since I was on my way to the gym for a swim and all hell broke loose. "I don't think I can make it that long. I can't stand up, for God's sake. How will I get to the bathroom?"

"We will call you in some painkillers and some heavy muscle relaxers to try to get you out of pain. If there are any openings in the surgery schedule, we will get you in right away."

I no longer cared about running. I no longer cared about Ironman or Leadville or even strolling through the neighborhood. I had devolved into a single purpose—stop the pain. It was constant and there seemed to be no way to shut it off. My resolve or concern about taking medication was gone. I wanted the drugs and I wanted them now.

The phone rang. It was the nurse from my doctor's office again. Awesome, I thought. They got me in for a sooner surgery time. Wrong. They made an appointment for me to have a pre-surgery MRI. "Are you telling me that I have to get into a car and ride all the way to the hospital, and then I have to get put into that MRI machine?" The hits just kept coming. That is simply physically impossible, I thought. They may as well have told me I had to triple summersault into a juice glass.

"We have to see what is going on inside your body before we open you up."

"Ok, I'll find a way," I said. My first thought was, "I wonder how much an ambulance would charge to take me to the hospital?" But when the day came, I made it to the car—one painful sideways step at a time, about 10 minutes after standing up from the couch, but I made it. I even managed to survive being lowered into the car. "Get me to the pharmacy... *now*," I said. We stopped and filled my prescriptions on the way to the hospital. I was very happy to see the single largest bottle of painkiller I have ever seen. I popped 2 or 3 into my mouth and tried to fall asleep as the car glided down the road, leaving its every bump and turn in the form of a new pain signal to light fire in my back and legs.

I survived the second trip to the MRI torture chamber and even managed to make it back to my new place of rest—right side of the couch, leaned over the arm. I guess it's amazing what we can get through when there is no choice but to do it. I had just gotten off the phone with the doctor's office; they called to discuss the MRI. It seems that the first herniated disc (S1/L5) was doing quite well. In fact, the steroid injection was a tremendous success; the herniation was almost entirely cleared. The second disc (L4/L5), however, was a different story. It seems that disc (at L4/L5) massively herniated and was completely impinging on the sciatic nerve. This one made the first impingement seem like a pinprick, the doctor said.

"So, it looks like this was going to happen one way or the other," I said to Brian, my surgeon.

"Actually, they are mostly unrelated," he replied, to my bewilderment.

"How could that be?"

"It's like a case of really bad luck. It doesn't appear that one caused the other to rupture at all. It's more like two separate injuries that occurred in the same area."

That was just great. Now I felt like my spine was made of glass and the remaining years of my life would be spent in hospitals and rehab centers as my discs exploded one by one, sending me into surgery after surgery, fat, addicted to pills and in chronic pain. I pushed the thought out as quickly as it came.

"I am going to come back from this," I said out loud.

"I have no doubt you will," he said immediately. "If anyone can do it, it's you. I think you can be better than you ever were."

"The Denver Marathon is in 7 months," I chimed back.

"Call me and I will come out and watch you finish," Brain said—and really meant it. The fact that my doctor never gave up hope in me was hugely instrumental in my recovery and my positive attitude. He later told me he thought I was a machine—a powerhouse of positive energy always moving forward, always grinding on any stone or rock that lay in the road ahead. It was one of the best compliments I have ever received.

"Did it go ok?" I asked.

"Fine," Brian said, laughing as they were wheeling me out of the operating room and I was just coming to consciousness.

"Why are you laughing?" I asked. I was very groggy and making no sense, apparently.

"Dude, you have asked me that question five times in a row." He was still smiling.

"Sorry," I mumbled.

"Everything went fine. We cleaned up the entire area, left you as much of the disc as possible, and I see no reason to be worried for now. I will meet you in the Recovery Room in a little bit."

And like that, he was gone.

The anesthesia was wearing off and for some reason, the side effect of this withdrawal was an irrationally bad mood. I knew I didn't have any reason to be upset, but I was pissed off nonetheless. I was once again lying in a hospital bed and I was nervous and scared to even move. I couldn't get the picture out of my head of all those doctors cutting me open and messing around in my back for over six hours. I knew they had to open my back, cut through all the muscles to expose my spine, and then clear away all the herniated material from my spine without causing permanent damage to the exposed nerves. Sometimes easy access to information isn't a positive thing.

My head was clearing and the desire—no scratch that—the *need* to get out of the hospital was growing. I had to use the bathroom too... now that was interesting. When I came into this hospital early that morning I couldn't walk, let alone stand or lift myself out of bed. How exactly was I going to wheel-chair over to the bathroom and relive myself? This just plain sucked. But I was laughing at least—that made me feel like everything was going to be ok again.

"All right. Gotta pee," I said to no one in particular.

The nurse said to be careful, but I should be able to walk now that the pressure was relived from my spine. I was skeptical and curious at the same time. It was only a few hours ago that I was immobile; how was it that I could be ok now? It is a strange place to be when you don't trust your body. We take for granted the simplest of things, like the ability to move around, grab the remote control or just sit up and stand. As I lifted my body up from the lying position, I was bracing for the pain. I had been paralyzed by not just pain, but the fear of pain, for four months now—and for the last couple of weeks I couldn't twist or talk without creating a light show of nerve explosions in my lower body. I sat up with no pain. Big challenge coming, though. Can I actually move my legs to get them off the side of the bed and put my feet on the floor? The answer was yes. I tentatively allowed my mom and the nurse to help me stand, all the while waiting for the impact of the pain train that never came. I stood. I walked.

"Holy shit," I thought. I was walking. I smiled. I felt like I was some miracle kid that just got healed in a holy tent rival. I threw my crutches onto the ground and PRAISE JESUS! I was walking! Well, despite the dramatic reaction, I was, in fact, very thankful to God for looking out for me. And I had to remind myself that as bad as things were, I wasn't in a horrible car crash, I wasn't born handicapped and my prospects for recovery were very high.

"Don't be so dramatic, Clark," I said inside my noggin.

I walked to the bathroom., took care of business and even made it back to my bed without assistance. Just like the doc said, I was going to be fine. But now I wanted the hell out of the hospital. After an argument with the nurse about hospital policy and a couple of phone calls, they agreed to release me against their recommendation.

"Mr. Clark, you were in surgery less than an hour ago. You should really spend the night…"

But Dr. Brian, my surgeon, and now my savior, told them to let me go if I was able to walk and if I was lucid. Love that guy. Before he left, he wanted to talk to me about what to expect in the days and weeks to come. "I want you to think of this whole injury as if you slammed your hand in a car door. The surgery was a success, but it was only to open the door and get your hand free. What happens from here is unknown. We don't how much damage there is to your hand."

"Ok," I said. That made perfect sense to me when I thought about it. "So the symptoms I had before, might still be there?" I asked.

"They might be," he explained. He told me that I could still have some pain if the nerves were damaged. There could be numbness and tingling that never goes way. But the bottom line is I should be able to return to activity quickly. In fact, he wanted me to start walking right away, swimming in as little as 3 weeks, and cycling in 6 weeks. He cautioned me that this was a best-case scenario, but I was chomping at the bit.

"How much walking can I do?" I asked

"As much as you want," he told me.

"Are you sure you want to say that to me? Are you sure I can't walk too much?"

"You have clearance…" he smiled.

When I got home from the hospital, I was exhausted and I was still feeling the effects of the anesthesia. It was weird to think that I was just in surgery a few hours earlier. No sooner had I lowered my body into my new "Zero Gravity Perfect Chair" (ordered specifically for my recovery), than I was asleep. After a few hours of fading in and out of slumberland, I finally woke to the smell of corned beef and potatoes cooking. We always have a traditional family dinner on St. Paddy's Day and I wasn't about to let something as trivial as having spinal surgery stop our tradition. I still had some hardcore pain relievers flowing through my body to help me move, but with our proud heritage intact, my family and I managed to keep our Irish tradition—we ate and shared our evening, and it felt good to be doing normal things so soon after the surgery. It felt like things had "rebooted" and this truly was a new start.

The next morning I woke up with a single thought: "Walk." The injury was over as far as I was concerned. It was in the past. No more worrying about the "ifs and buts." We had arrived at the end of the journey—we had THE SURGERY. The injury was corrected; now I just had to climb out of the aftermath. The last 4 months were a roller coaster of emotions. There were times when the symptoms had abated and I felt I was on the mend, only to have my world crash down on me.

"That's ok, back to the core exercises, be patient."

There were times when it seemed hopeless, so I did the only thing I could do—I got myself to move, I read something inspiring. Each step along the road, I stayed positive in the long haul. I never let the demons win. I kept my hope and I held steadfast to the idea that I was still going to live out the dream of life I'd made for myself. I was sober, I was no longer fat and I was going to be healthy again. I was going to return to the life I had clawed and fought for over the last two years. So what if I was at another crossroads. Fold up or die. I was going to move. And I was going to move *right now* in that moment.

I went for a walk. It was 24 hours since my surgery but the doc cleared me for take-off. I was going to keep it real easy today on the doctor's recommendation, but I was anxious to move after being trapped in a chair for so many weeks. There was a streetlight at the corner about 300 feet from my front door. Today's mission was simple: walk to the light, turn around and come home. A mere 600 feet of walking, I remember thinking, I ran a marathon a few months ago; this should be easy. About 35 minutes later I collapsed into my newly-purchased recovery chair in my living room. I was baffled. How could walking to the end of my street and back create this level of fatigue? To say I felt drained was woefully inaccurate. I was so exhausted, it seemed to be on a cellular level. I felt like I didn't have enough energy to maintain blood flow in my body, like all metabolic activity was going to just stop. I fell asleep and stayed there for 9 hours.

When I woke up I took my pain pills immediately. After my surgery I was given a painkiller schedule that included 6-8 Percocet a day for a couple days and then switched me to 6-10 Vicodin a day for a few more weeks. Eventually, I was to be weaned off the medication over a 4-6 week period. For some time now, I had been nervous about the incredibility high volume of painkillers I was taking. The truth is, once I surrendered to "not trying to be a hero," as Diana my physical therapist put it, and started taking the meds—I was already one foot into the rabbit hole. I had permission to use and there is nothing better than that to an addict. I was enjoying the pills way too much, and although I knew it in the back of my mind, I would never admit it out loud.

And I'm not sure if "enjoying them" is actually the exact right description, but I was always very aware of how many pills I had left in my supply and I knew exactly how much time was left until I was allowed to take the next dose. Eventually, the dose that was supposed to be every 4-6 hours "as needed" had become EXACTLY every 4 hours. And quickly every 4 hours became every 3.5 or 3 hours on occasion. I had said to several people up to that point in time that my substance abuse problems were limited primarily to alcohol. My reasoning was that I never abused drugs unless I was on alcohol. But I was starting to get the distinct feeling that my addictions were a little more dispersed. The first thought of throwing my pain medications in the toilet crossed my mind. I heard Diana's advice on pain management, "Don't be a hero..." I liked that because it meant I could keep that bottle of pills longer. I started to keep the bottle in my pocket at all times.

It was day two post-surgery and I was feeling very good. I had a serious goal for the day: I was 100% committed to walking 1 mile. That was a big jump from the 600 feet of yesterday but the doc said I couldn't walk too much and I was going to take him at his word. I put on my workout clothes just like I was back training for a marathon; in fact, I decided I was going to log all my post-surgery recovery walks just as I had all my training sessions since I started my journey in 2005. It was raining out but I didn't let that faze me one bit. I travelled along the sidewalk and past the end of my street without a blink. I took in all the sights that I never took note of when I was running by in previous months. I saw all the little alleyways and backyards and I saw each tree in all of its glory as I slowly plodded by. My back was sore and the muscles were tight, but I just kept going. I had my GPS watch on and before I knew it, I had made a big one mile loop through the neighborhood and I was back to my house. A huge smile crept up my face. I could walk, and walking was what I was going to do.

The next day was 2 miles, and 3 miles after that. By the end of the week I was doing long walks of 4 and 5 miles. I was treating it like a marathon training plan. Do short and mid-distance "runs" during the week; and then go long on the weekend. On day four I made a big decision. I knew I was at a tipping point in my life. The bottom line was I had no idea where this rehab stint was going to end. But I was going to do everything I could do to make sure I became 10 times the runner I was before my injury. But there were doubts... What if I couldn't? What if my body couldn't take the pounding anymore? And I needed to address the looming issue of my painkillers. I had to come face to face with a very old friend—my addiction. After countless nights of soul searching, I came to a very real conclusion. My sobriety was more important than anything else in my life. My kids, my wife would be lost if I were to fall again to substance abuse. I decided that fat and sober was better than running and addicted. So four days into my 6-week painkiller schedule, I went cold turkey. I had been taking pain medication for over 2 months on a daily basis. And I knew I was in for some tough times ahead.

The first couple of nights I was miserable as my body craved and searched for the simple relief that my medication had been delivering for the last few months. The insidious thing about opiates is that they are so easy for your body to use—they do their job. They make you feel good by attaching to the transmitters and pleasure receivers in your brain. After a while, your body stops producing its own chemicals to make you feel good because you are ingesting a synthetic and more readily available version. When you quit cold turkey, your body literally doesn't have anything to make you feel good. There is no pleasure or comfort available to you. You just have to wait and ride out the waves of pain and depression as your system tries desperately to refill the stores and meet the demand. After day one of cold turkey, I realized I was probably premature in my attempt to get rid of the narcotics. The incision on my back and spine were still really pissed off from the surgery and they didn't seem to care about my substance abuse issues... no turning back now—deal with the pain.

I journaled and chronicled each horrible thought and emotion as my pain-riddled body tried every trick in the book to convince me to take the narcotics I was still carrying in my pocket. I cried, I got angry, and I read more about addiction and the spiritual journey of self-discovery. Somehow, day by day, I was feeling better. My good moods returned in waves and by week two I was feeling great—I was clean again and I was walking 20 miles a week now. It felt great to sit in front of my computer and enter my walks into my training log. It felt like I was actually training again. In a blink, two weeks became four and I was swimming again. Six weeks crept up and I was on my bike riding indoors regularly. I was also using the stair machine in addition to walking. When the 8-week mark hit and I was cleared to return to running, I was nervous and unsure.

I inventoried myself again and I found a deeper peace with my addictions. Being at the brink of losing it all made me really re-evaluate my life, my recovery and what my life would look like if I were never able to run again. I realized I would be fine. No matter what happened in my life, as long as I didn't drink or use drugs I would be ok—I would figure it out. Making peace with this was the key to my gratitude and my serenity, but I was by no means ready to give up the idea of returning to running. I was going to be smart. I was going to continue to work my core, my running technique, and improve in the pool and on the bike—but it was only a matter of time as far as I was concerned. The Denver Marathon was looming in the distance about 5 months away.

I went back to work, travelling in the spa and hot tub industry. I made swimming my new passion. With visions of my Boulder Ironman swim retreat still in my head, I decided I was going to make my weakness my biggest strength. I did drills in the pool. I woke up at 5 am to swim at local gyms before work while on the road. I tried to hone my technique, and after many hard weeks of training, I was swimming 3,000-4,000 meters a day. I felt confident in the pool and my body felt strong.

After 10 weeks (I gave myself an extra 2 weeks from the doctor's timeline), I went to the gym to get on a treadmill and run. The treadmill looked like a giant slot machine to me as I walked up to it and placed my iPod and water bottle in the holders. Over the last several months with my injury, before my surgery, I never knew what I was going to get when I turned on the machine and pulled the handle. Sometimes I would hit the jackpot and run without issue, and other times it was three lemons and I was sent back to the doctor's office in confusion and pain. I wondered what I was going to get today as I stepped on and set the machine to 5 mph.

"Holy shit, I am running."

I was running, actually running. Step, step, step slow as a milk truck, but I was running. And I was fighting back tears, for Pete's sake. What a crybaby I am. I kept waiting for my back to seize up, kept expecting to get shooting pain in my hamstrings or perhaps some shock treatment from the glutes, but it never came. Instead, I ran a mile. It was a beautiful, horrible, and ridiculously difficult 12-minute mile that I will never forget. I must have registered every emotion there was to feel—triumph, sadness, inspiration, discouragement, redemption and hope—all in one sweat-drenched mile. I walked to the locker room and fought back tears as I showered. I honestly can't say if the emotion I was feeling was sadness over how far off I had fallen (I was doing all my 8 mile runs in the 7:30 pace range before my surgery) or how great it was to be running at all. Honestly it didn't matter; I was going to be a great runner (by my definition) one day—or collapse trying to be. Now that I had come to peace with the possibility that I could be ok even if I couldn't run again, I had no fear of failing. I had let go of the future and accepted any scenario—that left me free to control the moments of now.

The fitness was coming back more slowly than I would have preferred but I was making progress each week. I was running on the trails by my house again. Sure it was only three or four miles, but I felt like I had some momentum. My runs had a level of gratitude that I could have never imagined—thankful to be sober, thankful to be healthy and out of pain, thankful to have had a chance to become even stronger in my recovery, and thankful for family. And my family, it seemed, was changing again.

The Luckiest Man Alive

Earlier in January while I was in and out of the doctor's office like a whack-a-mole machine—knock this symptom down and another one comes up, etc., etc. There was one particular visit to the doctor that stood apart from the others in every way. The appointment wasn't with my physical therapist, it wasn't with my surgeon and it didn't even have anything to do with me at all. Well, not directly—not my body, anyway. This examination was for my wife. And It was also the time I found out for sure that I was going to be a dad again.

I was thrilled beyond belief, but I was playing it close to the vest, as well. When my wife had told me she was pregnant, it was a relief and it was also a little scary. We had lost her last pregnancy only a few months ago and we were both still a little raw with emotion. I think we were both trying to shield ourselves against the possibility that it could happen again. But as the doctor said everything was looking good for a healthy full-term pregnancy this time, I just knew somehow it was the truth. I knew this was going to be my chance to do it again—this time 100% sober and present. I was ever aware and filled with gratitude that I got out of the gutter before it had a lasting effect on the twins, but I was chomping at the bit to make this time around the parent merry-go-round my Shangri-La. I was a mess during the first years after Davey and Emmy were born, and this was going to be a whole new experience. I wanted to be present for all of it.

In the months after I found out I was to be a father again, I went about making sure we were set financially for this addition to the clan. I scheduled more travel dates and work events and did some retirement planning, but I was also intensely rehabbing from my surgery and mounting my comeback to running. I was relentless. I did core exercises every day (even the ones that seemed silly). I read about correct running form and the various schools of thought on form and mechanics. I changed my entire running gait—and I ran. I was logging 40-50 miles a week religiously before my injury and I wanted to get back there, plus some. But every run I couldn't help but let my mind wander to my little gift from god. Catherine Mary—what would she be like? Would she be a runner? Would she be funny? Aloof? I heard a song by Don Henley called *Annabelle* and it made my heart so full, I thought it would burst. I played it over and over in my iPod as I ran.

I was running about 4-6 miles a day at this point and I was ready to loosen the reins a bit, although still a little gun-shy. I hadn't gone for a long run (or anything that qualified as one in my head) since my surgery, which was 5 months almost to the date. But I did have one planned for the following week. I was travelling to Utah and I wanted to do a 10-miler before I left. The thought was if it went well, I was going to sign up for a half marathon that took place while I was in Salt Lake City. I was nervous with anticipation and (to be honest) dread fear as well. I wasn't sure if I would hold up to the pounding.

The night before I was scheduled to run my 10-miler I was in the living room working on my laptop once again when my wife walked into the room…

"She's here," she said with a smile.

We had a false alarm a few days earlier so I responded with, "Are you sure?"

"Well my water, broke… yes, I am pretty sure."

And just like that, we were on our way to the hospital again. It was August of 2008 and the entire world was aglow about Michael Phelps and his 7 gold medals; in fact, he was going for a record and 8th gold medal on this very day. Actually, he was in warm-ups for the swim and on every TV in the hospital as they wheeled my wife across the lobby, down the hall and into the private hospital room. I remember thinking how crazy it must be for my wife to be lying on the bed in painful contractions as the entire staff (her doctor included) literally jumped up and down screaming as Phelps swam his heart out and won the gold. She smiled at me and handled it with an amazing amount of grace. I rarely heard her complain about small stuff. I remember selfishly thinking that this Olympic buzz was an omen—Catie is going to be an amazing athlete, I decided. Maybe even an Olympian. By the time the Olympic celebration dance was over in the labor room, Heather was already about to give birth—the contractions were close together and lasting almost 2 minutes.

"This is going to be a quick one!" the doctor said as he apologized for his gold-medal distraction.

And as it turned out, just a couple of hours from the time we hit the door to the hospital entrance, Catherine Mary Clark came into the world and took over mine. She was incredible. I was so alive with emotions and color that I felt as if I was painting the scenery as I looked around. The doctors were going through the normal procedures and making sure that all was right with little Catherine while I just sat there and tried to burn it all into memory forever.

"How crazy is my life?" I thought.

I was on the brink of death and somehow made it out to find recovery. I was on the verge of never being able to walk again without pain, and here I was running again. I was already the father of two of the most amazing kids in the world, and yet once again, here I was in the same hospital where I first became a dad, the hospital where a few months ago I stood up an hour after my surgery and walked out. And now I was getting blessed once again with what I could only call "my angel of redemption and second chances."

"Hell, maybe, I am the luckiest man alive," I thought. "Maybe we all are."

Everyone was either sleeping (family) or being poked and prodded (baby), so instead of grabbing a bench in the cafeteria, I decided to go get my 10-miler in. The hospital was right on a popular running trail of mine and I brought my gym bag with me. I was feeling simply sublime so I couldn't imagine a better thing to do than try to get my long run in. I kissed my wife and headed out the door as she slept. I stopped at the convenience store and bought a 32 oz bottle of Powerade Zero (more fluid that I carry on a 5-6 hour run these days) and hit the trail. Like all of the moments in life where we are really tuned in to our place in space and time, I recorded every scant detail of the run. Time simultaneously stood still and flew by like a blink. I enjoyed every footfall, and it seems if I tried hard enough, I could recall every individual one right now some 5 years later. The 10 miles rolled by as if I were watching the movie of my life from afar, and the next thing I knew, I was back at the hospital room to see if I could get a chance to hold my little girl.

"What do mean there are some complications?" I said. I heard my voice come out of my mouth, but it was if I were miles away from my body.

The nurse said, "We need to run some tests; we are going to take your daughter to intensive care now and she will need to stay there for a day or so until we find out more."

The doctor came in shortly afterward and explained that there was something going on with her vitals and her blood work looked off. The cause for concern was that her immune system might be attacking her own body.

I wasn't about to let any unneeded drama or negative thoughts slip into my head so I put it all aside and focused on how amazing it was going to be to see little Catie come home, but my mind was running about a million miles per hour. I couldn't help it.

"She's a fighter, just like me," I said to my mother who was holding me ridiculously tight.

"Fighting hard is written in our DNA," I said as much to myself as to her.

I don't remember leaving the hospital at all for the next 36 hours or so. I paced up and down the hall, I prayed at the hospital chapel and I went to look at Catie lying in her protective crib, shielded from the outside world. I was on a roller coaster of emotion, to state the obvious. The minutes lasted for days, the hours were months, the 2 days were 2 years... Finally the news came back from the doctor. This was potentially the worst moment imaginable, the moment that causes parents to toss and turn in the sweat of their worst nightmares. The doctor started talking and I was so deep in my own head that I couldn't focus on his words. I was having a panic attack, and then I heard it...

"She is healthy."

I almost collapsed at the words. It was as if my legs could barely hold me steady and the weight of the entire planet was hoisted from my shoulders. I realized that I hadn't taken a full deep breath in days. As I inhaled deeply, my body shook and sputtered and my heart filled with gratitude and air at the same time. I wiped the tears from my cheeks and kissed my wife.

Finally, the twins were allowed to come in and see their new baby sister for the first time. It was the most amazing experience to witness the expressionless and almost nervous look on their faces as they got up "tippy-toed" to catch a glimpse of Catherine as they came into the room. I could see the excitement and curiosity through their eyes and it changed my perspective on the complete nature of the impact of this on our family. Our dynamic just changed forever—and it was by addition in every sense. We were now a "five-some" and everyone's roles had shifted. As we drove home I couldn't help but smile and feel as if I had received far more than my fair share of God's grace. The truth is, I was starting to feel like I had inherited a great responsibility—not just to my newest child but to give something back to the world to "balance" the gifts I have received. I wanted to change the world, for the better this time. And call me crazy, but I was starting to see all the horrible things that happened to me in my past as opportunities to share the gift of hope. Certainly if I was allowed to come so far from the gutter to this pinnacle of human happiness and fruition, there must be a debt to the universe.

It didn't take long for us to decide for sure to name our little girl Catherine Mary Clark, and if I hadn't known it before, I knew it was the perfect name the first time I saw her smile. She had a way about her that suggested she was in complete control of everyone around her. She was Catherine the Great. It was as if she already knew she was in charge and just hadn't quite developed the means to rule us yet. And as she has grown, she has proven my initial perception to be right.

She is always loving, always sharing, and always experiencing life at full speed... and yes, she is always in charge (if you ask her). She has a way of speaking to adults as if they were complete intellectual equals, but not in a disrespectful way. She has a confidence in who she is that belies her age. And I have never seen such a young child be so nurturing. Even as I have fallen asleep with her on the couch, I have noticed her stroking my cheek or my arm as I drifted off, comforting me, her father, and not the other way around. Who knows what the universe has in mind for my little angel, but I am sure her impact will be large on all those who are blessed to know her.

Seven months? It was hard to believe that just a few months ago I was being wheeled out of the operating room from spinal surgery. But it was true—I had the scar on my back and the pile of medical bills to prove it. It was a long road to get back to the starting line of the Denver Marathon but I was here—race morning at last. I had missed the feeling of standing at a starting line in anticipation of what lay ahead—and I'd thought, in fact, it might never happen again. But it was here and I was going to run 26.2 miles... again. I was dreadfully undertrained, but I was healthy. I knew I wasn't in shape to run a marathon but this wasn't a race so much as an affirmation of life—I was alive and I was moving on.

When I ran the Denver Marathon as my first-ever marathon in its inaugural year, I planned on making it a tradition for many years to come—maybe even a tradition that would include my children running beside me one day. The fact that the last 7 months were a litany of obstacles and reasons to give up meant something to me. I was lining up for my third straight attempt at this race even though I had every reason to quit and fall back into old habits. The reality is I could have cashed out. "Hey, I ran a couple of marathons and even did an Ironman 70.3... my body quit, I didn't." I could have polished my medals and put them on the shelf and headed to the pharmacy to get my never-ending prescriptions filled. It would have been easy—so, so easy to do. I could feel the lure of the pity and drug abuse calling. But there was a stronger voice alive in my head now. A voice that said, "FUCK the easy way. And fuck this injury. I can do anything I decide to!"

Just a month earlier I was back at my doctor's office for my 6-month post-surgery follow-up. I was pleased to report my rehab experiences with running, cross-training, and general health since our last follow-up at 90 days. After looking at my chart and asking me additional details on how much running I was doing, he put me through a flexibility and strength assessment. Then my doctor stopped abruptly and looked me directly in the eyes for what seemed like 2 minutes.

"You are a machine," he said. "Absolutely amazing recovery. I don't think we need to meet at all anymore unless you feel we need to."

"I'm good," I laughed.

"One more question," he said as I was standing up to leave. "When is the race? I want to be there."

I knew because of my lack of training I had to go out slow for the run. When the gun went off, I relaxed, let everyone else go out fast and started a nice slow jog. My longest run in training for the marathon (and longest run in almost a year) was a 16-miler that almost killed me. I had never felt so exhausted in my life. I couldn't worry about that now, though; I had to trust that somehow I was going to find a way to get that additional 10 miles done today. I didn't have any goal save for finishing and running the entire way. I wanted to be able to say "I ran" The Denver Marathon, not "I finished." I know it's a silly goal because, honestly, walking a little bit during the race would be better for my body and would probably result in a faster time. Oh well, the heart wants what it wants. I was nervous. I won't lie. I was nervous about not finishing. I was nervous about getting injured again. And I was nervous because my entire family was out to watch me finish this thing. I had inadvertently put a lot of pressure on myself, but that was part and parcel, honestly.

The first 6 or 7 miles went by quickly, as they usually do, but I was already starting to feel some tightness in my quads and that wasn't a very comforting sensation. By the time I made it 12 miles, my body was completely breaking down.

"Damn, I can't believe this," I thought.

I expected to have some pain in the legs as they didn't have the long miles on them. But I didn't expect to be limping before I was even halfway through. Thoughts entered my mind about quitting at the halfway point (13.1 miles) but I let go of the thoughts as quickly as they came. If I was going to fail, it would be trying to complete the race I signed up for. I guess it truly was "26.2 miles or bust," I thought as I saw the turn-off to the half marathon finish pass by.

My quads were burning now at mile 16 and people could see I was struggling. It was great to have so many spectators cheer me on as I plodded by in my slow painful pace. It didn't bother me a bit that I was so much faster just a few months ago. I was here for something more personal than a PR (personal record) finish—I was here for redemption, yet again. This time, from the powers of the universe that conspired to test my resolve and commitment to hold on to the new life I had forged. Yeah, I suppose I could have gone back to the barstool and told tales of all the amazing races I did before my back went out, but I wasn't interested in that. I was no fluke, no bum.

I chose to wear a yellow LiveStrong shirt for the race. When I ran this event in 2006 just a few months into my "transformation," I did so in honor of David Lynn. This time around was no different—with one possible exception. I took a black marker and wrote "3-17" on it, my surgery date. Many runners, not knowing the significance of the numbers, assumed it was a bible verse and cheered me on as they passed.

I later looked up the verse, "Matthew 3:17: This is my beloved son, in whom I am well pleased."

My legs were hamburger. The pain cave is a place inside of the body and brain that is hard to articulate, but one that expresses to me the essence of the human plight—we can always move forward. Each time my foot hit the ground, it sent an immediate signal to stop. The signal was delivered in the form of pain shooting through my quad, foot, and hamstring and directly into my brain. Before I had a chance to really process the information, my other foot would strike the ground and the process would repeat itself. Immediate pain, switching sides at all times, became my only reality. But the reality was tempered by one fact: as much as I wanted to quit, I COULD take one more step, and so I did. For miles and miles—I did just that.

I don't know how much time had passed but I knew I had been running for a long time. I looked up to see the sun in the sky, and instead, I saw the finish ahead. I saw the marker that said "Mile 25" and then I saw my family. There was my wife, there were the kids, and there were the tears. I stopped just long enough for a quick embrace and ran ahead. I wanted to speed up for the finish, but I just had nothing left. My legs were done. As I looked up to see the finish line just about a quarter of a mile ahead, I was treated to a nice little reminder of where I was. Life sure has a way of humbling us all, I thought as the 5-hour marathon pace group ran by me with balloons and cheers. 5 hours and 4 minutes was my final time. I was never a really fast runner, but I was almost an hour-and-a-half faster than this finish time in the past. But it just didn't matter at all. This day was the greatest day of my athletic life—it was the day I fell in love with running again.

Why did I think this was a good idea? Seriously, what the hell wire was loose in my head that caused me to link trying to run 100 miles with pleasure? I had been vomiting off and on for over 6 hours now. It was 2 am and I lost the ability to speak hours earlier. And it seemed that just a couple of hours in to this adventure, my once "sore and scratchy throat" advanced to "difficulty swallowing." And since then, had made it all the way to "my voice is gone." Let's add to the list of reasons to quit: "I AM SICK." It was the middle of the night and I was apparently in the middle of something called an "ultra marathon." Ultra *moron*-athon was more like it. I was no athlete. I had no hope of winning this thing, and even if I did win, there was no prize money anyway. I was doing this for the most insane reason of all—just to see if I could.

"I'm done," I said. My voice was just a harsh, gravelly sound that was more of a raspy vibration than anything else. I could barely make eye contact with my buddy Dan. "Dude, it's just not going to happen. I'm sick," I said. "It took me 2 hours to go the last 7 miles and I can barely move my feet."

As I was trying to explain to Dan why I was quitting, my pacer Nico was taking off his running gear and headlight. He knew the night was over; he knew I wasn't going to try to go any farther. I was toast. DNF (Did Not Finish) was my new name. I felt bad not just ego-wise, but because this 100-mile run attempt had been a fundraiser for LiveStrong and in honor of Dan's brother David Lynn. Of course, I have run in David's memory before, but this one was supposed to be big. I felt like a loser.

"It's ok," Dan said. "You are obviously really sick, brother. Thank you for even trying. You ran 63 miles! Dave would be honored."

Those heartfelt words only made it worse somehow, I thought, as I looked for a place to sit down. As I sat in a folding camp chair and stared at the fire that was blazing in the ring in front of me, my mind was turning over and over in a loop. I was done, I didn't want this, I thought. I am not tough enough, I thought. Maybe it's just because I'm sick, I countered. Fuck, I don't know. I looked into the dark night sky at the stars above me and I felt my heart sink into my chest. I actually felt my stomach turn—because I knew what I was going to do next. I knew I had to go back out and try again. I knew I couldn't quit yet. I stood up abruptly and said to my pacer Nico, "I am heading back out. You in?"

He looked at me like I was crazy (which makes sense) but without so much as a complaint, he started putting his gear back on and said, "Let's go."

This was the first time I had really gotten to know Nico, and he was selflessly volunteering to pace me for my first 100-mile attempt—which meant he had to run, walk, and hold my hand and move at a snail's pace all night long next to me with absolutely no logical reason to do so. You see, Nico wasn't just a good guy; he was and is an outstanding human being. He is a wonderful father, awesome husband and avid trail runner He also had the misfortune of responding to an email I sent out looking for people to run alongside me on my first ultra. A "pacer" is the brain of the ultra runner, if you will. Most 100-mile races will allow a pacer for a runner late in an ultra marathon. A runner, after spending 10-12 hours alone on the trail will eventually lose the ability to think clearly and stay on course. The pacer's job is simple. Keep the runner moving, make sure he is eating and drinking and let him take all the glory at the finish.

Although this was the first time Nico and I ran together, it was a small glimpse at what was to be (and still is) an amazing friendship. Nico has accompanied me to places I would have never imagined I could go, and all he has ever asked in return is nothing. He is the greatest friend a dude can have.

"I can't stop shaking," I said.

"I know. I am a little concerned that something is wrong," Nico said back to me matter-of-factly. We were barely moving and I couldn't manage to stagger a couple steps before dry heaving and shaking violently as my core temperature was dropping lower and lower.

"I am a giant pussy," I said. Nico couldn't help but laugh. And I suppose it was funny, but it was how I felt.

Somehow we kept moving (if you can call it that). When I left the campsite earlier, I knew I had to give it another try. I just had to go back out and see what would happen. I had heard all the ultra stories about how you could feel like you were dying only to feel like you were flying shortly afterwards. Well, so far all I felt was death. I knew when I left the cozy confines of the campfire that I was subjecting myself to what was sure would be a futile effort of stubbornness. Or worse, maybe I went back out because of a blind moment of bravado in front of my friend Dan. Either way, a new reality had arrived; I was quitting—for real this time. It took Nico and me three hours to go a little over 7 miles; that's about 2 miles per hour for the math lovers out there. At this pace I wasn't going to make the 30-hour cut-off, and I had little desire in trying to pick up the pace. As we made it back to the camp, I saw Dan again. Only now, I was refocused on a brand new outcome—I just wanted to go home.

It took me less than two minutes to tell everyone how sorry I was and to get the hell out of there. I was still wearing the race number on my shorts as I pulled the door to my truck shut and drove away from the Boulder Reservoir. It was October of 2009 and I had signed up for the Boulder 100 because I thought in light of my surgery, doing a local "easy" 100-mile race would be smarter than going right to Leadville for my first 100-miler. The Boulder 100 is a "looped course" with runners completing fourteen 7.17-mile loops to finish, and I had made it 71.17 (10 laps) miles before I quit.

As I drove home a thought crept into my head, and it wouldn't go away. "You quit this race before it ever got hard." I knew it was true but I pushed it down. "No," I said to no one but myself. "I was sick."

"You were not as sick as you made it seem..."

As I pulled into the driveway at my house, I didn't need to consider the matter any further. I was right. I quit. Sure I WAS sick, but I could have kept going. The more time I spent out there on the race course in the cold of the night with my feet sore, the more I was thinking about how much longer I had to go—and the more I thought about how nice it would be to just be at home. Well, now I was home and it didn't feel nice at all. In fact, I felt horrible. It was now Sunday morning as I walked into the living room (or about 24 hours after I started the Boulder 100), and my family was getting ready to head out to the race to see me finish. My wife was surprised to see me walk in.

"What happened?" she said.

"I quit."

Heather had never seen me quit like this before, and noticing my lack of a voice, she immediately assumed I must really be sick. I was sick all right—sick with failure. On my way to the bedroom I had to step over all the "Congratulations, Dad—You Did It!" signs lying on the living room floor. It seemed the kids had been up early and making the signs since yesterday as I ran laps in vain around the Boulder Reservoir. One sign said "You are 100 Miles Crazy." I couldn't look at the others. This is the most horrible feeling in the world, I thought, as I let go of consciousness and let sleep take me away. To this day, I have never felt pain more excruciating than what I felt as I lay there.

After nursing my wounds through the holidays and trying to make peace with my failure at the Boulder 100, I finally felt I was ready to move on. In the days following the race, I had told everyone that I was over the idea of running the Leadville 100 or any 100 until I got the hang of the whole "ultra thing" a little better. But after a much-needed break and time with the family, I was able to gain some perspective on my experience. I knew that DNF (Did Not Finish) was just a part of the game. For some reason, though, it's a part of the game we all assume doesn't apply to us. But it's a part of the game nonetheless. Being a stubborn person (perhaps my single genetic attribute for ultra), I decided I was not only going to let the pain of failure go—in fact, it wasn't failure at all unless I chose to file it as such. If I kept going forward, it was only a learning experience. I told my wife I was going to up the ante. Screw it—I was signing up for the Leadville 100. The race was 8 months away.

I knew that I was potentially setting myself up for another failure, but I always was aware that nothing big can happen without risk. If I failed at Leadville, it would be mentally and emotionally painful in a way that would make Boulder seem like a cakewalk. But fear is a reason to DO something, not a reason to walk away. I had already put about as much pressure on myself as humanly possible by making this race my "Rocky Balboa" litmus test, but now I was going from a flat "easy" beginner friendly 100-miler to one of the hardest 100-miler's in the country—a race that historically has almost a 60% failure rate. With just over 40% of the runners (including many people with several 100-mile finishes) not finishing the race each year, I knew I had to be accountable—and I knew I had to train harder than I ever had. So for leverage, I did what any sensible person would do—I told everyone I bumped into and everyone I knew that I was doing the Leadville 100 and how important it was. "Burn the bridge behind you—leave no retreat," as Manowar, one of my favorite metal bands of the 90's said.

Realizing that it was more than just a mentally weak moment that got me into trouble at the Boulder 100, I had to rethink everything about the way I trained—my body AND my mind gave out. I wanted to examine the way I ate, where I was running, how I was running and the way I mentally prepared for an ultra. Quite simply, I needed to be fitter in every way if I was going to finish the legendary Leadville 100. I emailed the various local trail-running groups, looking for a training partner with ultra experience, and I committed to going to some of the more epic runs that the infamous Boulder Trail Runners (BTR) held weekly. These were runs I had avoided in the past citing that these were elite runners and beyond what I was trying to do. I saw an interesting email from a friend about a BTR group going to run something called "Bear Peak." The group included several people training for Leadville, as well as some veteran Leadville finishers. Awesome, I thought. This seems extreme. Perfect—I was in.

Most of my long training runs up to this point consisted of long urban runs on streets and bike paths. I did occasionally take to what I called "trail running" but I was soon to find out I had no idea what that really was. Apparently, my idea of what a "hill" is and the ultra marathoner's idea of a "hill" were not even closely related. The moment that became most obvious was about to hit me. It was a cold January morning and several BTR runners and I met at my friend Shad's house in the Boulder foothills before heading up to Bear Peak. Shad had also paced me for a couple laps at my Boulder 100 disaster before Nico took over. He was a great guy and I was glad to pick his brain, as he was a very experienced runner and also preparing for Leadville this year.

I brought a friend with me named Jerry. He and I had recently met and had run a couple of times together previously, and we really hit it off. We were both willing to be dorks and generally had good conversation on the road. It turned out he was an experienced 100-mile runner and I was happy to have him as my new training partner. He was training for a different 100-mile run, the Western States 100, and we both had weekdays off, so it was a perfect for us to get in some long miles together over the summer. Jerry was also a "Bear Peak Virgin" and I wanted to have someone else on my side.

The plan was to run to the trailhead from Shad's house, hit the trail up to the summit of Bear Peak and run back. This would make the round trip about 11 miles or so. That didn't sound so tough, I thought. As we wound our way through the neighborhoods and towards the base of the flatirons, the peaks came into view. "You see the highest peak over there, the real sharp one?" Fred asked. "That's it—Bear Peak."

Fred was a very accomplished ultra runner and multiple finisher of the Leadville 100, as well as the Hardrock 100 (a race considered even more treacherous than Leadville). I liked Fred; he was quick to give advice (but only when asked) and is always in great spirits. It wasn't until I got home hours later that I was 100% certain I didn't soil myself the instant Fred pointed out Bear Peak. It was towering above us in the sky. And just as he described it, it was the highest visible peak in sight. As it turns out, it is in fact the second highest peak in the Boulder Range and sits at 8,461 feet. The trail gains about 3,400 feet to the summit, and most of that climbing comes in the last 1.5 miles. If I said I wasn't nervous, I might just ignite into flames on the spot.

We started the casual part of the climb (from the Bear Drive Trailhead) as a group. Everyone was taking it easy and mixing in some light jogging with some "power-hiking" (a very fast and brisk hike), a valuable tool for the ultra runner. The path starts out as a wide gravel path that winds for a bit as it carries you around the rolling hills and into the remote trails and rocky climbs of the tree-covered mountains. After about a mile on this fire road, we came to the start of the real climb—Fern Canyon. The Fern Canyon trail takes a sharp turn and goes straight up into a new world. It's hard to believe as you take those first few steep steps on the rugged single track that you are only a mile or so from civilization. It feels as if you are deep in the wilderness. To describe the trail as rocky would be beside the point. At times the rocks are so large that they are the entire trail itself and your only option is to raise your foot from one boulder and pull yourself up to the next. I could tell these guys were on a different planet when it came to power hiking. After about four minutes of climbing, everyone else was so far up the trail that I could scarcely still see them, including my buddy Jerry.

"Great, so it's just me, then?" I said out loud to no one, while smiling at my own joke.

After only ten minutes of slowly hiking straight uphill, I was already questioning if I was going to be able to make it to the top. My heart rate was through the roof. It was 20 degrees out and I was covered in sweat. This was crazy, I thought. I am not exactly out of shape here. I was running 50-60 miles a week and clocking about a 22 minute 5k—not world class, but definitely not a slouch either. How could these guys be going so fast?

I could hear the voices of Fred and Shad echoing down the canyon, carrying words of encouragement. They were telling me if I kept going I would get there. I wasn't so sure. One foot in front of the other, I kept saying to myself. There were parts of the trail that were so steep, I didn't think they were passable. Certainly I must be off the trail, I thought, only to see the trail come back into view above me. It felt like I was never going to get there. I was moving impossibly slow—10 steps, and then rest. 10 more, rest. Eventually I saw a beautiful sight. As the trail switched back and forth, I saw the summit. Everyone was standing there waiting for me.

"That was hard!" I said.

"This is just the saddle," Shad said. "Now the steep stuff starts..."

I dropped my head and looked down, because I knew he wasn't joking. My heart sank as I looked to my left and saw another 800 feet or so of vertical ascent waiting for me. Without a thought, I followed as they led the way up the final climb. Now it became a challenge to finish. I was committed at this point. My quads were on fire, I was soaked with sweat, my ears were ringing, but I would be damned if I wasn't going to summit. I had two looming demons clawing at the perimeter of my consciousness, and they were giving me that horrible hollow feeling that something was very wrong. But now wasn't the time to explore the source of this unsettled feeling, I thought. I had to let the battle go until after I was down off this mountain. I did pause long enough to identify the issues, however. One was the most obvious—after I made it to the "top" of this thing, I was only halfway done. That was troublesome for sure, but the other demon was much more menacing in its nature—it was in the form of a question: "How was I going to finish the Leadville 100 when I couldn't even stay within in sight of these other guys?"

My legs felt like they were made of Play-Doh as I hit the top of the climb about a half an hour later. We had to scamper hand over feet and crawl up for the last 100 feet, but I finally made it the summit. As I looked around, I felt a small measure of absolution. "It *should* be this hard to get to the top—this view is too good to get for free," I noted as took in the clean cold air and felt the chill drying my soaked clothes. I could see for miles in every direction. All the way to Pikes Pike to the south, Longs Peak to the north and, of course, Denver and Boulder below.

When you summit Bear Peak, you literally climb to the top of rocks that are jutting out of the landscape in the Boulder foothills. There are no flat areas and a bad step can send you falling for a long time. We all crouched down or leaned against a rock together and chatted about the climb. I was pleased to be done with the hardest part of the route and truly enjoyed the conversation, but my heart was still somber as my thoughts kept coming back to Leadville.

As for the return home from Bear Peak, instead of climbing down the steepest part of the canyon where we ascended, we opted for a long gradual downhill run around the back part of the mountain. This trail is known as the West Ridge trail and is about 4 miles long. I was surprised and encouraged by how quickly my legs recovered from the hard climbing, and I felt great that I could run the single-track trail that snaked through the mountains and canyons towards home. Once again, though, the group left me as if I were standing still. It seemed that the gap between these runners and me wasn't only in uphill fitness, but down-hilling, as well. I made a joke out of it and didn't let it get to me—I was on my own journey; they were on theirs. I would figure it out.

The boys didn't want to lose me in the Boulder wilderness, so whenever the trail provided more than one option for navigation, they would stop and wait for me to catch up. When I would catch sight of them waiting ahead for me up the trail, I would yell, "Here comes the Irish Fire truck! Whoop-Whoop!!"

This got many laughs and made me feel a little better about holding everyone back. Throughout my journey as a recovering alcoholic runner, no matter where my head might wander during a run or race, my gratitude to simply be alive and able to run was never too far away. And I found my joy again in those moments running the West Ridge. I laughed and "whooped" my way along the trail all the way back to Shad's house, and I decided that the day had its own value outside of Leadville or running or training of any kind. It was a great day, with friends new and old, and I had some great pictures and epic memories to share with the kids someday. I just started getting sucked into this thing called "Facebook" recently so I posted the pics from the day's run—and I drove home in silence.

Now was the perfect time to apply the David Clark "logic of insanity" to the information I gathered on my trip up Bear Peak. This process, I am sure, could be the subject of many scientific studies on the power of twisting events and facts to support any predetermined outcome of my choosing. Many people may think of this as a weakness; I always considered it a strength. It's simple. We all have the power to convince ourselves of anything we choose, regardless of the facts or evidence at hand. Why not use that to the advantage? So for me, I will turn the loose nuts in my head until I make the picture look the way I want it to. Even if it means I have to go back out into the world and do something crazy that will create a new memory that will support my theory... Yeah, I know how that sounds.

So now, I had a basic choice to make—use this Bear Peak run as proof that I am not currently capable of doing something like the Leadville 100 and make plans to run the race the following year (sounds reasonable enough) or figure out a way to make this a positive in my journey toward doing Leadville 100 this year. It was my choice. But I always say, "The heart wants what it wants."

"Fuck it. I don't discourage that easy," I told myself.

Getting my ass kicked on Bear Peak was going to be the mark of my rise. It was the moment when I saw the TRUTH of where I was and the reality of where I needed to be to make my Leadville dream come true. In fact, I want uphill running and power-hiking to become the strongest part of my running. I decided to make Bear Peak my new home—and I did just that.

The next day I went back to Bear Peak. I struggled, I pushed and I summited the peak again—this time while it was snowing. It was potentially the greatest turning point in my running career. Standing on the top of the summit, I was never more resolved and never more sure about what I had to do. I knew that if I could manage my emotions, leverage my desire to get that finisher's buckle into active motivation (and of course, continue to come back to this place), I was going to be standing at the starting line of the Leadville 100 in August.

Week after week, day after day, I returned to Bear Peak. Sometimes I went as many as 3 or 4 days in a week. My buddy Jerry and I also mixed in many other epic training routes such as a 13-mile run to the top of Mt. Evans at over 14,000 feet and a couple of runs through Rocky Mountain National Park. I was betting everything on this hand, and as a result, I did not miss any of my long training days. Sometimes because of work commitments, I had to run late. Several times I ran from 10 pm at night until the small hours of the morning, but I always put the work in.

After these night sessions, I would get home at 3 am, sleep and go back to work. The main reason for the extreme measures was that I was committed to make sure my family didn't suffer for my newfound level of training. It was tough, but it was doable. I ran for 4-5 hours starting at 4 am on weekends so that I was ready for family fun by the time by the time kids finished breakfast. I simply *found a way* to get in the training. Once I decided it was non-negotiable, there was always a way to get in long runs if I was creative enough. In fact, several times I ran for 20-30 miles to the start of a hockey tournament so I could get in my long run without missing Davey applying his skills on the ice. I made all the Girl Scout functions and choir recitals, too, as ultimately these were the main reason I was running—for a better life.

The training was paying off. It seemed like every day I was getting stronger and faster. I ran with other runners from all over the metro area and it seemed as the weeks and months were flying by, I was now leading the charge up the hills. I was the one setting the pace—the others were trying to keep up with me. It didn't take too long before I started to hear things like, "Watch out for Dave on those hills... he is a beast of a climber," or "How do you make it look so easy?" And I have to say, I was proud. It took a hell of a lot of resolve to get there. Now I looked for hills, I wanted the hills—and most importantly—I was attacking the hills with confidence. In May before the Leadville 100, I invited a group of friends to join me for what I called "An epic training day" of 12-hour Bear Peak repeats. I have always taken "you're crazy" as a compliment. And I'll tell you, it takes a lot of work to be called crazy when you live in a world of other crazy people.

So what did I do? For 12 hours, with the company of a few friends who joined me for a loop or two, I went up and down Bear Peak—the same peak that almost killed me a couple of months earlier. It was a complete transformation, but it wasn't magic. This day was paid for with hundreds of hours spent climbing endlessly, lost toenails, blisters, cramps and sore muscles. This currency purchased for me the tools to tackle the job at hand. On one of my summits that day, I was climbing up the canyon and I noticed that I had lost the group. I turned around and saw new friends smiling and moving together in a line climbing up the trail towards me. I pulled out my phone and snapped a photo. It was a gift to be here, and I wanted to remember it forever. As I was on top of Bear Peak for the final summit of the 12-hour run, the sun was going down and the view was stunning. Jerry was the only one with me at that point and we just kind of sat in silence, each of us replaying the day and the many steps we had taken individually and together in training for our own races. For me it was Leadville and for Jerry it was Western States. We never talked about what we were thinking, but I suspect we were thinking the same thing... "I'm ready."

The Leadville 100 is called "The Race across the Sky." The obvious reason for this name is the sheer altitude of the city where the event takes place. At 10,200 feet, Leadville is the highest incorporated city in the U.S. The race starts on 6th and Harrison Streets in downtown Leadville and journeys out 50 miles into the deep and treacherous Colorado Rockies. From the halfway point at the ghost town of Winfield, runners turn around and retrace their footsteps another 50 miles back to Leadville where the life-changing finish line waits. Runners have to cover the distance in less than 30 hours or they are not considered official finishers. Standing in between the starting line and the 50-mile turnaround point are many climbs and challenges, not the least of which is the epic journey over Hope Pass.

This is the place where dreams are crushed and people fall apart. The Hope climb comes at the 40-mile point of the race and is just a scant 3.5 miles to the top, but runners must go from a starting point of just over 9,000 feet to the summit at over 12,000 feet. The quick rise in altitude causes runners to experience a wide range of symptoms, including vomiting, light-headedness, hypothermia, passing out, and HAPE (High Altitude Pulmonary Edema), and due to the lack of oxygen, many runners are unable to digest calories efficiently and experience a slow painful, nutritionally deficient climb. Once on the top of Hope Pass, runners drop down a bone crushingly steep decent on single-track trails and rock fields and eventually out to Winfield (50 miles into the race). One of the reasons (other than the obvious) that this race is so notoriously difficult to finish, is the point at which this section occurs during the run. Most runners in any 100-mile race experience the lowest point (yes, you guessed it) during the 40-60 miles in the middle, exactly where the "double Hope Crossing" takes place.

Of the 400-600 hundred runners to line up and start the race, only a little over 40% will finish. And the vast majority of the 60% of runners that will not finish will drop out at the Winfield aid station. After having already run 50 miles, surviving Hope Pass and its many snares, the thought of going back over Hope Pass and running 50 more miles is just too much for most people.

Running 100 miles is not a solo effort. It requires the obvious race staff, volunteers all over the course, aid station workers, and course marshals to direct traffic. But also each runner has his or her own crew dedicated to taking care of them as the athlete battles the elements and distance. I had my own team in place and I had a bunch of total rock stars, if I do say so. My crew manager was a friend of mine named Jeff O'Reilly. He is veteran of the ultra marathon world, a local running figure, and he knew the Leadville course very well, having attempted the race a couple times himself. His job was to drive the crew car from aid station to aid station during the race in case I needed any "special gear" such as shoe changes or medical supplies. He was also there to coordinate the pacers and make sure I was moving through the course on schedule. In addition to Jeff, I had three pacers, including my best buddy Nico. I called him shortly after my Bear Peak epiphany and said, "How would you like to come see me redeem my Boulder 100 debacle at the Leadville 100?" He said yes before I finished the question.

My friend Nick was going to pace me 10 miles from the halfway point at Winfield over Hope Pass and to Twin Lakes (roughly miles 50 through 60 of the race). He had a tough section to cover with me, but he had finished the race himself the previous year so I knew I was in good hands. Nick and I had much in common with tough childhoods and both of us overcoming alcohol/drug addiction.

The plan was to have Nico pick me up at Twin Lakes after Nick delivered me safely over Hope Pass. Nico would pace me 27 miles from mile 60 to mile 87 (or from the Twin Lakes aid station to May Queen). Although not quite as gnarly as Hope Pass, this section of the course was no walk in the park. The last 13 miles from May Queen back to Leadville is rolling and slightly uphill. My friend Kelly got the best part of the journey—she got to carry me home to the finish of the race if I could make it to her. Sounds like the easy part, huh? Not so fast—that meant she had to basically stay up all night long, not knowing until the last minute if she drove 150 miles all the way to Leadville for nothing.

Kelly and I met when I reached out to a local charity that was doing amazing work by helping homeless people in Denver get back on their feet—literally. The program helped people on the street with substance abuse problems by training them for running events. This was a huge concept for me as running help change my life, as well. Kelly actually introduced me to my pacer, Nick. He had started the charity and I quickly became involved as a coach and mentor to the men and women in the program.

I also had Mom, Dad and my brother Chase on the crew. They were committed to being out on the course, following me around all day and night for support. I was pleased to have my dad and brother there as these two men are my dearest friends in the world and I knew I would turn myself inside out before I quit in front of them. Chase came up with me to a cabin I rented a few days before the race. I wanted to spend a couple days relaxing and getting my head right and he needed the time way from town as well. The cabin I rented was very secluded and sat right on the Colorado River. Chase and I had a ton of laughs and spent the days before the race relaxing, reading and putting together all the gear and supplies I was going to need for race day.

Chase was my number one drinking buddy back in the day. When I say number one, what I really mean is, other than being my closest friend and the person I drank with the most back in the day, he was also the only other human I had met face-to-face that lived the exact same way I did—full speed, no fear. Chase and I have seen the very worst of each other. We have seen each other irrational and angry as a result of intoxication, we have seen each other vomit, fall over, pass out and cry for no reason other than being so drunk we lost control of our emotions. Yet despite all that, we see the very best in each other today. Chase would be the call I would make if I needed to hide a body. (*New York humor, sorry.*)

Heather and the kids were all making the trek up to Leadville on race day. There was no need for anyone other than Chase and me (and my crew manager Jeff) to go to the 4 am start, as there would only be a minimal amount of action for the first several hours of the race. I knew I would see Heather, the kids and my mom at Twin lakes (mile 40) and again as I came back through Twin Lakes at mile 60. Although I would really like to see the family out on the course more, I knew this was the best plan. For people who aren't too familiar with the rigors of ultra running (such as moms and wives), having them around in the darkest moments isn't always wise. You need crew people who love you enough to lie to you, kick you square in the ass and send you on your way. Or in the case of one notable example of Leadville 100 crewing excellence, one runner decided to drop from the race and his crew locked themselves in the car and wouldn't let him inside (the runner went on to finish, by the way).

There Is Always Hope

The alarm went off at 2:30 am but it didn't wake me—I was already awake. The fact was, I'd barely slept a wink since I lay down. Drop bags. Shoes. Raincoats. Flashlights. Sunglasses. My mind had already raced a thousand miles and I hadn't taken a step yet. I climbed out of bed, ate a Cliff bar and started putting on my running clothes. I was relieved to know that finally all the worrying, planning and stressing were over. Now, I was going to get my chance to roll. It didn't seem like morning—it seemed more like the middle of the night as we jumped into the truck and headed for Leadville. The cabin was in nearby Buena Vista so we had about a 25-minute drive to get to town. It was an electric feeling on the drive. Maybe I was feeling melodramatic, but it seemed more like a heavyweight fight than a race we were going to. I was at peace. I did everything I could think of to prepare for this day. I had no regrets at all, now I was going to trust the process and see what happened. I knew above all that I was going to learn something about myself I didn't know... and there is no greater gift.

I had seen many YouTube videos of the starting line of the Leadville 100, but now it was me standing there in the corral as others filmed. It was odd to think that I might be in someone else's homemade video on YouTube now. There were flashes going off from every direction as the hundreds of runners looked around like deer in headlights at the cameras of friends and strangers. I couldn't help but think that less than half of these people would make it back here tomorrow for the finish. Would I be one of those? What will I endure over the next 30 hours? Whatever it was to be, I was ready.

"Dude, you are one crazy fucker," I heard Chase say from my left. I turned around to see him filming me. I smiled back and thought about it.

"I guess so," was all I could muster. Memories flooded my mind all at once. I thought about walking to the end of my street and back before collapsing in my chair, just a day after my surgery. I thought of a thousand mornings of vomiting and shaking. I saw little Catie lying in her protective hospital crib, already fighting just a couple hours after making it in to the world. And I thought about all those still out there struggling with addiction. How many people are staring into the mirror right now, asking themselves "Why? Why can't I stop?" I felt the weight of a thousand souls settle on my shoulders for just an instant, like the universe was letting me know what was out there. And then as soon as it was there, it was gone. The weight lifted and I felt like I was exactly where I was supposed to be—right here, right now—doing this very thing.

I looked back at Chase and said, "Crazy is gonna be different tomorrow."

As the race director Ken lifted the shotgun and fired into the sky to start the race, the entire crowd of runners let out a howl of excitement. It seemed like we were all connected forever now. We were the 2010 Leadville 100, all on the same course but each on our own journey. We were all given a blank canvas as the gun went off. Now we were going to paint the day with our footsteps and sheer determination.

I could feel the pressure building up inside of me. "I don't need to be strong forever," I thought... just for this one day." I ran off into the dark with my headlight on.

I was no stranger to feeling pressure. Some of the earliest memories I have are of being a child trapped in a place I didn't want to be. Being forced to handle the overwhelming need to be anywhere else in the world, but being powerless to do anything about it. I remember sitting at a picnic table at a roadside rest stop on I-95 on the East Coast. My family was trapped on the road again. We were homeless, to put it bluntly. We had nowhere to go. No food and no gas in the truck, meaning even if we did have somewhere to go, we couldn't get there. The truck I am speaking of was a 1970 green C-10 Chevy pickup with a camper shell on the back. The truck had a name; we called it "Babe." And we also had been calling it home for some time now. The truck is where my brother, mom, dad and I all lived for the moment.

As I sat at that picnic table, I put my hands over my face and I squeezed my head as hard as I could. My entire body was shaking with the effort as I pushed harder and harder on my temples. I thought if maybe I could squeeze hard enough, somehow this nightmare would end. I would open my eyes and, instead of sitting at an interstate toilet stop, I would be in the living room of a house—our house, any house. Instead of hearing trucks go by and car doors opening and closing, I would hear dishes rattling in the sink and Mom cooking something to eat in the kitchen. No such luck. I was here, and I was going to have to find a way to deal with it. I was having a panic attack. I know that now, because I have had them off and on my whole life, but I didn't know it then. I just felt overwhelmed and like I was going to crush under the weight of it all. I couldn't have been more than 8 years old, but I would wager that the universe would have set my soul's age at 50.

Although just a vulnerable child, I was not feeling the pressure for myself. I was feeling the hurt of my mother. I saw how hard it was for her to know we were hungry. I saw how torn up she was inside when she had to get on the phone and make collect call after collect call to strangers and local churches, looking for food or gas money to help. I saw the complete frustration as she was hung up on again and again until she finally found a soul willing to drive out to a rest stop to help complete strangers.

"Someone from the church will be here with some food and gas money," my mom said.

I could tell she was thankful for the help we were about to receive, but I knew it took something out of her to go through such an emotional beating to get there. My dad nodded his head and thanked her; then he walked off with his head hung low. Despite not having eaten for a day or two, he wasn't going to eat any of the food they were bringing us. That made me sad too. My dad gave up a thriving business to do God's work—a missionary of sorts, I suppose. But through some extraordinary circumstances over the last couple of years, we had ended up here. We had been chasing work all over the East Coast while living from church to church and prayer to prayer. He was conflicted, to say the least.

Later that night I was lying in the truck camper with my head next to the window. The camper had those little pane windows that opened in unison when you turn the crank round and round. I had a belly full of food, which was good. My mom and Dad were up front in the cab of the truck and my brother Loren and I were in the back. I already felt stronger having made it through my mini-breakdown earlier. In fact, I was hopeful; things are going to be ok.

When I touch these places in my past of my childhood and my family's struggles, running 100 miles all of a sudden doesn't seem like such a tough thing to do. I have to say that my life, although hard, was not tragic. As a family, we never fought each other and we never felt like victims—we were more like survivors. And although in our quest to find God, a better life, and a peaceful future, we would endure ridiculous hardship, we loved each other completely and we cared for each other and watched out for each other too. We were all we had. It undoubtedly made me stronger.

Now, I was doing it. I was running the Leadville 100. The thoughts of my DNF at the Boulder 100 entered my mind, and I let them out as soon as they arrived. No time for negative today. Instead, I focused my efforts on the task at hand. I took in a deep breath of the cold mountain air. The sun hadn't risen yet and we all had our headlights on as we moved into the Colorado Rockies. I stayed in the main group. The leaders went out fast and quick into the woods as the rest of us were content to run nice and easy as we went through our mental checklists and recommitted to our "stick to the plan." The greatest thing about ultra running is that, with the exception of a handful of elite runners, the entire field is not in competition with each other, but is in fact on a great journey of mutual experience. I might not have the same time-goal as the person next to me, but I am cheering for him to finish (as he is for me) and we feel a kinship that ties us to each other's finish.

The first part of the course took us out of Leadville on the roads of the city, but quickly launched us onto dirt paths and trails. Before I knew it, we were running on the soft single track that winds around the amazing Turquoise Lake. The sun was rising and I felt ready good as I took inventory of my current physical state. Legs felt strong, breathing was even and steady, my form was good and I felt light on my feet. I came into the May Queen aid station (13 miles into the race) and ditched my knit hat, headlight and gloves. I grabbed a couple of gels, refilled my water bottles and headed back out onto the race course. As I was leaving, I heard someone call my name from behind, "Hey, Dave, we're pulling for you man!"

I looked around and saw a small group of people smiling at me. I didn't recognize anyone there, so I smiled back and thought they must be looking at one of the other runners. I ran out of the aid station tent and back onto the road. We ran on the road for about a half mile before we jumped back on the trail and started the first climb of the day, a winding steep effort to the top of Hagerman Pass road and to the top of Powerline. As I left the aid station, my buddy Scott jumped out in front of me and snapped a few photos. I felt a huge grin spread across my face as I realized I was in many ways living my dream. "Time to suffer," I said and smiled as I ran by.

The trail went on and on and we climbed higher and higher into the thin mountain air. I knew from studying the course that we topped out of this climb at just over 11,200 feet and it was a blistering downhill from there. The words of my crew manager Jeff were rattling around in my brain. "Don't go out too fast. The downhill sections will kill your quads late in race. Be smart..."

As I hit the top of the pass I could see why they named this section "Powerline." The course ahead was a straight drop down from the summit along a steep washed-out road directly under the power lines built to carry electricity into Leadville. To say the section is steep and treacherous is simply not adequate. There are sections where the washed out parts of the trail would be waist deep if you had the misfortune of dropping into one—not to mention your day would surely be over as you would break your ankle or entire leg if you face-planted on this fast descent. The sounds of the transformers humming and cracking with electricity over your head add to the ambiance of danger already hanging in the air. I jumped, hopped and bombed down the trail with a huge smile on my face as I tried not to imagine what climbing up this section was going to be like, should I be lucky enough to make it back here with 80 miles of running already done.

"Fuck that—I'll jump off that bridge when I get there," I thought.

After several miles of the Powerline descent, I was finally down. I ran along a flat section of trail for a while and eventually was turned out of the woods and back onto a section of road. There were thick pine trees and a beautiful clear blue sky to behold. As I climbed the last quick little 20-foot rise out of the trail, I noticed many people up ahead lining the street. I felt like a rock star as I ran along the road with at least a hundred strangers all cheering, clanking cowbells, waving signs and yelling encouragement. I heard someone yell my name again. "We are all here for you, Dave! Thank you for running for my son!!"

I turned around and saw a woman looking directly at me, and even though it's a little disorienting trying to place people in this environment, I was sure that I had never met her. Yet, she was looking at me with familiarity in her eyes. Since I couldn't place where I might know her, I shouted back a response.

"Thank you!" I smiled back. I barely made it another 40 feet up the road before another person leaned out onto the road and said, "Give it hell, Dave. I have been sober 6 months now."

And then another. "Thank you, David. You are an inspiration. You can do this, man!"

The blood drained out of my face as it hit me. The reason I didn't recognize these people is obviously because I didn't know them. They were strangers who had come out to support my run. Through my friends at The Partnership@DrugFree and some Facebook posts, I had mentioned that I was dedicating my run to all those struggling with addiction. What I didn't know was out there in the cyber world, people were sharing my story with their friends. My heart expanded in my chest as the reality of that sank in. These people had been touched by something in my journey. Something about my struggle with food, drugs, demons and booze had made it all the way into their hearts and caused them to drive for hours to Leadville, Colorado just to come encourage me. It made me feel very small, and at the same time, I felt tremendous gratitude. It felt like the universe was watching and it knew that I had taken a huge withdrawal from the karma bank—and I owed for my sobriety. I should be dead—that's just the truth, but I wasn't. I was here and I was very much alive. And somehow it meant something to people I had never even met. I looked up and said "thank you." I picked up the pace and ran like my life depended on it.

I was about 9 years old when the family moved to Florida with all of our possessions in the back of a truck that also served as our home. The decision to move to Florida was two-fold: my Dad was chasing down some potential contracts for his renovation business and we also believed that God was directing us to head south. We were penniless, and we needed a new start to try to get back into a stable situation—and there was an opportunity for us to do just that in the Sunshine State. But the other reason was equally as magnetic. We had years ago turned over our lives to the will of God and after hours and hours of prayer; my mom and dad felt the Lord was moving the family in that direction. And by all accounts, that would prove to be persuasively true.

My father's will to find God (something the family called "the Quest") had brought us to Florida—Tampa Bay, more specifically, and if you want to get downright exact—to the parking lot of a large inner city church. We arrived at this church unannounced and completely by fate. No one there had ever heard of us or even knew we had been sleeping nearby. What happened was nothing short of a miracle. The next 18 months saw my family start a food bank through this church, and my father's work (with the help of my mom) created the largest and most successful ministry the state of Florida had ever seen.

A once unused and broken-down building on the church parking lot became a flourishing food bank with a huge outreach. The rooms once filled with dusty chairs and discarded items from the main church building, were now filled with families and people in need. People were lining up around the block to meet my father and experience his strange way of doing things. He was there to solve problems, not to hand people food and make them pray or show up for church service. He lead by example and left the preaching to others. As word spread, my father became known around town as "The Preacher," and there is nothing he wouldn't do to help someone that was down. I have seen him give away his last dollar, walk miles and miles to hand deliver food, and walk right into drug houses and gang dens to rescue trapped women. He walked the walk and talked the talk. As we walked through the low income neighborhoods in town, people we had never met came out of their houses to shake my dad's hand and thank him for the work he was doing.

My mind couldn't help but fall into these old memories as people I never met greeted me now around every turn of the Leadville 100 course. People who would likely never see me again were here to tell me they heard my story and that it touched them. You see, I think many people are cynical—not because they don't believe in the good of people, but because it has become increasingly rare for people to share the true essence of themselves. When we catch a glimpse of genuine human struggle—the determination, fearlessness and honesty required to make even a small positive change in the world, we all want to touch it. As if in the mere presence of this show of character, we all seem to drop our own barriers and choose to shamelessly believe in the good of ourselves and others. I tried to graciously accept the gift I was receiving from so many people and promised to never forget the responsibility that comes with such a blessing.

"Slow down, dude. You are pushing it."

My crew manager Jeff had been telling me that all day, every time I saw him. Most people that don't finish Leadville, drop out because they went out too fast and blew up late in the race. Jeff was trying to keep me in control to protect me.

"I feel good," I told him. I was riding a high that words are simply too cheap to buy a proper description of. Every aid station brought with it, not just what I needed to nourish my body, such as sports drinks and salty foods, but nourishment for my spirit in the form of words and signs of personal encouragement.

I was approximately 40 miles into the race and heading into the Twin Lakes aid station now, with the killer of dreams, Hope Pass, looming in the near future. The next 20 miles was the make-or-break part of the course. I reminded myself that many of the runners that started the race that day will drop just 10 miles from where I was standing. I told myself that no matter what, I wasn't going to be part of those that drop. The Twin Lakes aid station is perhaps the busiest spot on the course primarily because families can camp out all day and see their loved ones at both the 40- and 60-mile points without driving. There were hundreds of people scattered about as I walked through the crowds and made my way into the large metal garage that housed the volunteers and supplies. Jeff was waiting for me as I dropped down a short but steep trail and right into the Twin Lakes circus. And now he was doing his job, taking inventory of me and making sure I was on task.

"Don't run the back of the pass too hard," Jeff cautioned, snapping me back to the moment.

"My legs feel good, man—seriously, I'm cool," I said.

"Really? You aren't just saying that?" Jeff looked at me fiercely.

"Yeah... I mean, my quads are a tiny bit tight, but no big deal... really. I feel good," I promised.

"Fuck it," Jeff said. "You really are doing great. I am taking the reins off. Go hard if you feel good."

I smiled because I liked the sound of that. Let it rip baby. Just then, I saw the most beautiful thing I had ever seen in my life. My wife Heather was making her way through the crowd towards me with little Catie on her shoulders and Davey and Emily alongside. The twins ran up to me and started excitedly asking me how I was doing. I hugged them both tight. I told them I was doing great and that in my mind this was the start of the actual race.

"It was all just fun and games until now," I smiled.

This was the first time I had seen Heather and the kids since leaving Denver several days ago. My wife was a little worried but she could see I was ok (at least for now), so that set her at ease. "I feel good. But now I have to get up Hope Pass and back here and somehow still feel good enough to run 40 more miles at that point," I said to her with a nervous laugh.

I was also glad to see my brother Chase and my mom and dad, as well, who were now making their way over to me. It was starting to seem more like a picnic as I stood there eating potato chips and drinking Coke. I was holding a paper cup full of chips and I silently noticed the twins sneaking chips, hoping I wouldn't notice. I made a mental note to remember how cute they were as they went about it.

"Time to go to work," I said. I shrugged hard and rolled my head around from side to side as if trying to clear the cobwebs and knock any demons loose that might be hiding there. I kissed the kids goodbye and told everyone I was going to do my best. As I ran through a long line of cabins and spectators on the way out of the village that makes up the Twin Lakes aid station, once again I heard cheers of encouragement from friends as well as strangers—all doing their best to make me feel like a rock star. I felt more determined than ever as I made my way out of the village, across the road, and towards the marsh and Hope Pass.

"There is another one," I said with excitement... "and it's a Coke can."

I ran over to the discarded empty can and picked it up from its mud-crusted resting place alongside the road. The trash bag full of cans rattled a clunky song on my young 13-year old back as I ran. As I let the sack slide off my shoulder, the bag hit the ground with a loud clack as the butt end came to rest on the ground by my feet. I picked up and placed the Coke can in the bag with the others and went on about my search.

It had been a few years since my days as "The Preacher's" son at the Community Ministry in Tampa, Florida. The food bank and ministry program was shamefully discarded by the church board as a small but powerful group of church members were complaining of all the "undesirables" drawn into the parking lot to wait for food baskets. The end result was a parking lot expansion that leveled the ministry building and left my family, and hundreds of others, all without a prayer or a basket to put shit in... so to speak.

My brother Loren and I were collecting cans along the roadside for money. I can't remember where we were exactly. It was just another rest stop or campground in a long chain of places we slept in and lived as we made our way out of Florida and back up the East Coast toward New York and home. It was late 1983 and we had spent over 3 years in Florida, and we even added a couple new family members along the way, my brothers Shaun and Chase. We now we were a family of six, all travelling in the "Holy Pickup Truck," as I called it now. Chase Clark was 3 years old and Shaun Clark not even a year old came in April of 1983. We may have been struggling, but a cloud of love and spirit still hovered over our heads and camper as we continued to try to find a better life. Here we were now, though, totally busted... again.

We were collecting cans in hopes that we could get them to the recycling center before they closed later that night, thereby managing to scrape together enough aluminum to feed the six of us, put some gas in the truck and make some phone calls to see if my dad could get some renovation jobs scheduled and get us off the road. We had to collect a "shit bird ton" (my own unit of measure) to get that kind of money, so we decided to hit the most target-rich environment I could think of... dumpsters. I still say you haven't really grasped humility until you are standing in a trash container throwing out cans to your brother who is making a game of catching them with an open trash bags as tourists and commuters walk by in horror. Hell, we didn't care; we were excited to get back to camp with what was turning out to be the aluminum can mother lode. Looked like we were going to hit our goal after all.

Of all the cans and bottles we collected, for some reason, we put the highest value on the Coke variety as a brand. Perhaps it was because drinking a Coke was such a luxury those days and was a treat to be savored and celebrated. Sometimes my brother and I would vividly imagine what the ice cold taste of the sugary beverage would be as it rolled out of the frosty can and hit our tongues.

"I want a Coke, please."

They were my words, and it was my voice I heard, but it seemed it was coming from afar. I had only made it ¾ of the way up the top of Hope Pass and I was already spent. I was dizzy, and all the exuberance that I'd felt when I left the Twin Lakes aid station a couple of hours ago was gone. I was suffering, I was cold, I was discouraged, and my body was robbed of calories. I needed some sugar. I saw the discarded Coke cans lying around the ground and trash bags at the "Hopeless Aid Station." I thought again of the times I'd collected cans as a child—and then let the memory go as quickly as it came.

This aid station is an amazing place in that it sits at 12,000 feet altitude, just 400 feet below the summit of the pass. This is a no-car access area and all the food, water and medical supplies must be hiked some 12,000 feet in altitude up to the place. The volunteer crew uses llamas to do the heavy lifting, and it requires a huge commitment of time and resources to be there all day to help some freaks stupid enough to run this race. I knew this and made sure I thanked the volunteers for being there. No sooner had I had spoken my words of gratitude, though, than someone said something horrible to me:

"We are all out of Coke," the aid station worker said. I just stared back without saying anything. It was like getting kicked in the nuts by a pro soccer player.

"Would you like some sugar cubes?" she asked, with an apologetic smile.

"Sure, thank you," I managed.

I sat on a rock for a couple minutes and tried to make sense of what was happening. "I am not done," I said out loud. I am in a low, but I am still having a great race. Time to get up and take control back! We don't do this because it's easy, I mused. I popped 3 or 4 cubes of sugar in my mouth and got the hell out of the aid station before I could talk myself out of it. The trail is a winding switchback of single track that snakes up and up for a little while before dropping down steeply on the other side. It looked so close to the top, but the more I climbed, the farther away it seemed I was. I trudged on.

I made it to the summit of the pass. This brought with it a new sense of hope and excitement. I knew that I had a steep but fast couple of miles down and then 2.5 miles to the Winfield aid station—halfway done. I took just a quick second to look behind me and see the mountain range stretched out in the distance. I could see the trail below and I could see the town of Leadville way off in the distance. A quick adjustment of my shoes and pack and I was off running again.

The trail starts as a gradual descent and gets steeper after a short distance. I was hopping from rock to rock and feeling ok. I can't say I was feeling great, but at least I was moving fast again. I felt the rocks of the trails under my shoes and I was aware of the cold thin mountain air I was breathing. The terrain changes dramatically as we drop down to lower elevations, and I marveled at the how the barren expanses above the timber line quickly become rocky quarries of large boulders. Then trees started to appear in random places and before I knew it, I was surrounded by pine trees and vast national forest.

In theory, runners should start to feel better as they drop down to the lower altitude where the much-needed oxygen is available. This was not happening for me. In fact, I was feeling worse by the minute. I was no longer able to move forward in any reasonable pace, and my running posture was rapidly becoming a limp forward, then a march, a stagger, and finally into something the *Night of the Living Dead* zombies would have been proud of. I made it to the bottom of the Hope Pass trail and found my way on to the Winfield Road where the wide dirt road left me a slight uphill grade for 2.5 miles before dead ending at the 50-mile point of the race. I knew my first pacer would be waiting for me, but I knew it didn't matter. I wouldn't be moving on.

I was fighting to keep moving forward at any pace. I was staggering from side to side in 4- to 5-foot arcs along the road, and I just wanted to lie down and go to sleep. In fact, I found myself searching the roadside for places that looked suitably comfortable. I felt like I had been awake for a week. My legs felt empty and I was unable to even hold on to a thought long enough to form a coherent response. I was being greeted by runners coming directly at me from the road ahead. A couple of my friends from my first trip up Bear Peak passed me on the road and said their condolences (they assumed by the look on my face that my race was over).They had already made it out to Winfield, checked in at the half mark, picked up their pacers, and were heading back to Leadville toward the finish. They still had 50 miles to go, but they were doing it. I was happy for them, but I didn't care. It was the worst feeling of my life at the time. That is the only way I can't describe how I felt. Physically, I was a wreck. I had no energy, I was sick and my heart was sinking all the way down to the soles of my feet. I have never felt so bad in my life—and that was saying a lot for me. All the cells in my body felt as if they had broken apart and died. And I could barely breathe.

"I let everyone down," I said out loud.

I was still staggering down the Winfield road but now I could see all the people, tents and cars that make up this town in the middle of nowhere. The aid station looks more like the state fair as there are literally hundreds and hundreds of people milling around, cheering for friends and family and engaging in some sort of ultra running support. My pacer Nick came running up to me as I crossed the timing matt and was officially registered at the-50 mile point of the race. It had taken me well over an hour to go the last 2.5 miles.

"Dude, you ok?" Nick asked.

"I am done," I said.

"What can we get you?" he asked as he walked me into the tent and sat me in a chair. I looked around and I saw carnage. Outside, the runners that were doing well were strapping on fresh packs and heading back out, but here in the medical tent it was heavy and solemn. People were lying around on the ground, nursing wounds, and someone was actually crying. But most runners (like me) just stared into the space in front of them. I saw my dad and brother Chase walking up to me out of the corner of my eye. I thought I was hallucinating.

"Hey, son," my dad said in a very concerned tone. My brother Chase looked at me and said, "What going on, bro—you ok?" I couldn't even make eye contact with them. I was choking back tears.

"I don't know if I can do it," was all I could manage to say. I couldn't bring myself to say I was done out loud to them. As I sat there, Nick showed back up with a slice of watermelon with salt on it. "Eat this," he said. "What else do you need?"

I looked around the tent again at the other runners and my dad and brother. I thought of all the statistics about how everyone drops at Winfield and I thought, "Son of a bitch. Here I am, dropping at Winfield like every other bum..." It might not be flattering to the other runners, but it was what I thought at the time—and right now, it was about how I felt about me, not how I felt about them.

"Maybe I am just a fucking bum from the neighborhood after all—just a big pussy."

I sat. I didn't say anything for a long time. People were standing over me and talking, but none of it was getting through. For several minutes I just sat and let the fight start to build inside of me. I was hearing it from my demons— all of them. "You don't have this in you. You're a fucking drunk. You should have stayed with marathons. You can't escape who you are—just go home."

I was starting to get pissed off. Then another voice started to battle for control. "Just get going. The past does not equal the future. Don't lie down and die—stand and fight. I am better than this." That last one was the thought I was looking for.

But even though I had some fight lighting up inside me, I was still in a world of shit physically. I decided that I wasn't dropping here, not at Winfield. I wasn't being dramatic, and I was almost positive there was no way I could make it over Hope Pass again, but I was going to pass out on the mountain trying to get back over, so help me God. I choose to go down swinging. If they had to put me on a stretcher and carry me off the course, I was ok with that. But I was not going to quit here.

"Get up and move... NOW!" Came into my head as if shot from a canon.

I said, "Let's get going."

Nick grabbed my pack that I had been running with all day, threw it over his shoulder, and we headed out. I hugged my dad and Chase and I limped back out onto the trail. As we walked, I was starting to feel something else besides anger—I was starting to feel hope. I was starting to let it all go—the drama, the panic. The thoughts of what finishing meant or didn't mean. The past, the future—I let it all escape through every pore of my skin and through every breath that I exhaled. I was here. I was here and I felt like fucking shit. Now what? We fight, that's what. No more giving up on myself—that was my promise.

What was happening was literally my birth as an ultra runner—and I didn't even know it at the time. Nothing I did until now mattered. This was what it was all about. The moment when the runner is no longer wondering what will happen to him or her in a race, but starts to create it second by second, thought by thought, one ugly painful step at a time. I found a way out of my head and into my heart. The pain didn't matter. I had been dealing with pain my whole life. What mattered was what I did now that it hurt.

Nick was awesome. We were barely moving forward, but he was all positivity and he kept telling me I was doing great. The single greatest attribute in a pacer is the ability to look you right in the eyes and lie with conviction. Nick was a great pacer. I told him my earlier plan to just try to climb up Hope Pass and maybe get pulled off the course when I passed out. I am not sure if he believed me or if he even cared. His job was to take me as many miles as he could—forward.

As we walked down the road with the base of Hope Pass getting closer and closer, my mind was getting clearer. I was 100% committed to staying in the moment. Yes, I felt horrible; yes, I could hardly stand without losing consciousness. I was dizzy, out of breath and confused, but what if I didn't leave myself an option? What if I had to get over the pass to live? What if my life was on the line? Could I find a way? These thoughts were ringing in my ears as we approached the base of the climb. Without a second thought, I turned to Nick and said, "Let's try to get up this thing as fast as we can. It feels like I can't go any farther—so what if I tried to go faster?"

Nick didn't wait for a second thought; he jumped ahead of me and started leading the charge up the 3,000-foot climb to the summit. I was back to where I was just a couple of hours ago as the wheels fell off and my race day seemingly came to an abrupt demise. We picked up the pace, hiking hard up the steep trail, and my heart rate immediately skyrocketed in my chest. I took a deep breath and, instead of panicking and slowing down, I forced my body to accept what was happening. I am not stopping. "Figure it out," I said to the Gremlins inside my head that were running my body. I climbed. I felt like I was going to get my wish and pass out—but I didn't. I kept going. I tried to accept the mountain and stop fighting it. I could feel the first few drops of sweat trickling down my back. I hiked faster. I tried to find the sweet-spot perfect pace as my body adjusted and figured it out. I was in.

By the time we hit the 20-minute mark of the climb, I felt like I was a new man. The sugar and calories were mixing in my blood at the same time that the resources of determination were aligning. My body believed me that I wasn't going to quit—it was acting accordingly. I now entertained no thoughts of passing out on the trail, no thoughts of not finishing this race. I had one thought only now, "Get over this fucking pass as fast as you can."

Nick and I climbed higher and higher up the mountain. The trail is much steeper on the back side and my quads were screaming. The air was also getting thinner as we made our way up towards the summit but it didn't matter. Nothing mattered except moving as fast as I could. Head down, feet moving, stretching my strides out long and powering up the trail. We were approaching some runners up ahead on the single-track trail. "Coming through," Nick said with a grin. The slowing runners yielded and allowed us to pass. I couldn't believe it. I was dead a few minutes ago and now we were catching people.

"Faster," I thought.

"I feel good," I said to Nick. It was very business-like in its delivery. I wasn't bragging; I was telling him I was ok so he would know. He responded by picking up the pace. So did I. We were absolutely crushing it now. We were passing runners almost in a steady stream. One after another, Nick was calling out the runners as we approached from behind. "Runner back!" he would shout.

I was seeing the anguished faces of struggling runners as they turned around and dipped off the trail to let me pass. "How you feeling?" Nick shouted without turning back to look at me. He just held the pace steady up and up.

"I feel good," I shouted back. I continued to follow his heels up the trail. I was maintaining the pace about 3 feet behind him now as we continued to climb. It was almost a jog now, we were moving so well.

"HOOOPE PAAASSSS!!!" I shouted from the top of my lungs. Nick turned around and smiled at me.

"Fucking A, man!"

I couldn't believe it. We were practically running straight up the ridiculously steep mountain now.

"Runner back!" Nick again alerted the oncoming runners.

My heart jumped a beat in my throat. The group we were passing included two of my friends that had passed me earlier in the day when I was struggling. They were also there with me that first day on Bear Peak when I struggled so much. "David?" Shad said to me as I approached.

"Hey dude, how's it going?" I replied. I actually felt guilty for feeling so good while he was struggling. My heart dropped yet again.

"Good for you, man! Give it hell. I thought your race was over when I saw you at Winfield."

"Me too," I said. "Thanks brother."

We kept climbing. Time and time again we passed runners as we continued our miraculous comeback climb to the Hope Summit. With about a half mile of the climb left, Nick called back to me, "How you feeling, man?"

"Fucking awesome," I said.

"Ok, good. But I'm struggling," he chimed back.

I couldn't believe my ears. "Ok, I got the front," I said as I passed him and started leading the charge for the remainder of the climb.

I felt better in that moment than any drink or drug could have ever made me feel. There was no chemical high on earth that could hold a candle to one second of the feeling I had as I looked up the trail and saw nothing but blue sky. No pacer in front of me, no other runners—just clear trail. I put my head down and powered uphill with everything I had. I felt the weight of impeding failure and pressure release from my body the same way I had released in a slump of broken will on my bathroom floor 5 years earlier. Only now, I was in charge, and I was alive from the inside out.

"Say goodbye to Hope Pass," Nick said, as he snapped a picture of me at the summit.

From the Hope summit the trail drops down 3,000 feet over about 3.5 miles back into the Twin Lakes aid station. I knew my family was waiting for me there and I was anxious to see them. They had no idea what was happening out here, and the last they saw me, I was drawing my last breaths at Winfield. "Let's fucking roll down this thing fast," I said to Nick. He took the lead back and fired down the mountain like a banshee as I dropped in behind him with a huge grin on my face.

I was pumping the brakes and nothing was happening. The car continued to roll on, and even picked up speed as we dropped downhill along the interstate. That crazy reality-detached boy inside me smiled and released the fear of any consequences... "This should be interesting," I grinned as I surrendered to the fact that I was basically driving a 2,000-pound soapbox derby car. But the look on my father's face brought me back to reality again; he was worried and rightfully so.

I was 17 years old and i was feeling alive. Today I was with my dad and we were in Pennsylvania racing out to a job site to collect a deposit for a renovation project. The brakes on my car that were just recently labeled as "shaky" went to "complete failure" without (pardon the pun) stopping. The deposit money we were risking our lives for was going to be enough to feed the family, fix the car, and get us out of the campground we were living in. We knew we were up against the wall, and we knew it was cause for drastic action. We could only hope my faltering Chevy Impala that had somehow become the only running family car, could get us there safely and in time. We had to make it 40 miles to the job site in about 20 minutes, and then we had to collect a check and get to the bank before it closed. If we missed the bank, we didn't have enough gas money to get back to the campground and my mom and brothers would be alone with no food—and as it was Friday afternoon, we would be stuck until Monday morning when the bank re-opened. So we kept going. Not having brakes was just a detail that we didn't have the luxury of considering.

I was using the emergency brake in mid-flight when I needed to slow the car quickly or to stop, but I was also trying to coast as much as possible and anticipate the traffic farther ahead so I could glide to a stop when necessary and save straining the parking brake. I also figured out that if I drove with my right hand on the wheel, and my left hand pulling the emergency brake release handle from under the dash, I could use the emergency brake pedal almost like a normal brake, so it wouldn't lock down or click into a fixed brake position. That was what I had to work with, so I pulled, pushed, coasted—and even let the car veer off to the side of the road to use the grass to slow the car as we made our way through rural Pennsylvania and into our destination town. Somehow we made it without any accidents or damage to ourselves, others or property. I did have a couple of close calls that required creative improvisation through back alleys and parking lots to avoid stopped cars, but we did eventually roll into the parking lot and into an actual parking space with the smell of the burning emergency brake hanging in the air.

We had arrived with about 30 seconds to spare at the job site before they left for the day. In an incredible dance of delicate salesmanship, we closed the deal and got out of there within a few moments with check in hand. Now we had 5 minutes to make it a few more miles to the bank before it closed. I must confess that even though this came with a supremely high level of stress, I was alive with adrenaline. "Let's roll," I grinned as we jumped back into the car.

As we pulled up to the bank drive-up teller, someone had just put out an orange cone to signify that the line for cars was closed. I drove around the cone anyway and up to the teller. They said they were sorry, but we missed the time. The bank was closed and they didn't care how many miles we drove or what parts of the car were or were not working. We were screwed.

"Let me see the check," I said. "I have an idea. We need to buy groceries for the family anyway, right?"

"Yes," my dad said skeptically.

"Let's go to the grocery store and I will see if I can get the manager to cash the check."

"How are you going to do that?" he asked.

"I don't know," I replied.

Luckily, the manager was very helpful and decided to cash the check for us. It allowed us to buy groceries at his store for the family, put gas in the car and take care of all of our needs. Even at 17 years of age, I guess I realized the power of putting people on the spot and giving them the chance to do the right thing. I suppose I could have talked to him in private, but I knew it would have been easy for him to say no in private, yet very hard for him to turn me down in the busiest line of cashiers, with a cart full of groceries already rung up as I explained to him my circumstances. And of course, with many customers in line listening closely as he decided if he should make an exception to store policy in light of the nature of my circumstance.

He decided it would be ok to cash a check from a local business. The customers in line were happy with the choice. So was I—and I learned a valuable lesson that day. If the stakes are high enough, you will find a way.

I was hopping over rocks and roots and bombing downhill faster than I had at any point in any run or any race—ever. Only now, I was in the middle of a 100-miler. After climbing up Hope Pass and resurrecting myself from the depths of hell, I was back in the game. Simply put, I had found a way. We were clipping downhill at a sub-7 minute pace and passing runners at a rate of speed that was, honestly put—a little dangerous. At this point of the race, although we had made up a lot for ground on the field of runners, we were still towards the back of the pack and everyone on the trails seemed to be eeking through as best they could—and maybe looking for a comeback of their own.

A couple of runners even shouted at us as we flew by in a streak of laughter and joy. "Sandbagging much!" someone shouted. Nick actually laughed out loud and then took a hard fall. I had to slam on the brakes to keep from literally running over him. But before I could ask him if he was ok, he was up and running again—blood flying. We continued running hard, with no fear. At this point it was all fun. More than a few runners recognized me from seeing me hours earlier in my zombie-like state; they expressed words of encouragement.

"What a comeback!" I heard.

"Give it hell, Dave," someone said from behind me.

The miles were ticking off as we ran down the wooded trail and switchbacks. We ran along a rushing river and through open mountain meadows, and the scenery was amazing to behold. I had never felt so alive. We were running back towards Leadville, re-covering every painful step I had taken in the hours before. Only now I was going fast and I was feeling great. Before I knew it, we were down off the mountain and we were running in the flat marsh about a mile out from the Twin Lakes aid station.

Nick was already telling me about what the last 40 miles of the race were going to look like as we crossed the water and made our way in to pick up my next pacer, Nico. "Coming out of Twin Lakes, you have a big climb that seems to last forever—nothing like we just did, but steep. From there you have some flat and downhill that you can groove through," Nick reminded me. But I was barely hearing him. Now that Hope Pass was behind me, there was really only one part of the course I was thinking of—Powerline. If I could manage to get over that hill, I would have an easy jog of 13 miles to the finish. I was starting to think of it with a sick, detached curiosity.

I released the thought. "I'll be ready to turn myself inside out when the time comes," I decided. I had to run 20 more miles before I had to worry about Powerline anyway. As I ran into the Twin Lake aid station, I had no idea that my crew was in a state of panic. When I left the Winfield checkpoint before going back over Hope, I was in bad shape. My dad and brother left Winfield shortly after I did and drove back here to Twin Lakes to wait with the rest of the crew. They shared how bad I was feeling when I arrived into Winfield and how bad I felt when I left. They explained that my race might be over. My wife, crew managers, pacers, and dad and brother had all been in complete limbo, not knowing anything that had happened since I staggered back out onto the trail and left Winfield behind. They had been trying to stay positive; Jeff informed my family that I might still be able to finish the race within the 30-hour final cut-off time if I could make it back over Hope. Jeff estimated that it was going to take 4 hours for me to make it back over Hope Pass, in which case I was going to be cutting it close. They didn't know I was about to run into camp 2 hours before they were expecting me.

I could feel the anticipation building as we made our way through the crowds at the upcoming checkpoint. As we ran into the aid station, many spectators were cheering me and the other runners on, and once again I heard my name being called in the periphery. I looked around and tried to make eye contact but my gaze was lost in the sea of eyes looking out at all the runners coming in. There is no other 100-miler like Leadville in terms of crowds and runners. It was non-stop spectators and runners all over the place, hundreds of people on all sides. As we made our way through the course, I caught a glimpse of my brother Chase. As our eyes met, we somehow communicated everything that had happened. He saw the struggle, hardship and redemption of every step I had made over the mountain in the last couple hours, and I felt every anxiety he endured and every tear he had shed waiting for me. In a moment I will never forget, he ducked under the line separating the runners and spectators and ran up to me. We embraced in a frenzied celebration that somehow belied the fact that we had seen each other only a couple of hours earlier. It seemed like a reunion of years in the making.

"THAT'S HOW WE DO THAT MOTHERFUCKER!!!" I yelled at the top of my lungs, losing myself in the moment. People looked over and smiled along with us. We laughed and high-fived each other. My wife and kids came over to me and we also embraced. Then in a moment fueled by adrenaline and the desire to not lose a teaching moment, I bent down and pulled the twins close.

"Don't ever sell yourself short," I said to little Davey and Emily as they looked up into my eyes. My face was covered in salt and sweat and grime as they looked at me. "Do you understand?" I asked. "I want you to know that it's possible to be at the very brink of yourself, to feel like you can't take another step, that you are done for good—but if you believe and move forward with faith, you have strength waiting for you inside... don't quit before the miracle happens. Make sense?" They nodded their heads and smiled at me. I kissed them both and stood up. I kissed my wife and ran into the tent to grab some calories in the form of soup and Coke. My crew gathered around me and got to work on checking me in and changing out my gear for my next pacer.

I thanked Nick as everyone was fussing over me. "I'll never forget what just happened, brother," I said.

"Me either," he said, shaking his head and laughing a bit.

The sun was down as we left the Twin Lakes. Nico and I had our headlamps on and our water bottles full. I had no idea what to expect in the next several hours, but there was no doubt that this was a race now. I was dialed in and I was as determined as I possibly could be. We began the steep climb that Nick had told me about. It was just as he said—a straight-up gain. But I was a completely different runner now. Fueled by adrenaline, sugar, potatoes and a crazy rush of momentum, I was now in "mission mode." In the back of my mind, I was a little afraid of dropping back into the ugly dark pain cave I'd experienced earlier. Although I felt great, the pain of where I had been was still fresh in my mind. I made sure I did exactly as Nico told me. I ate when he said eat; I drank when he said drink. And I put my head down and started climbing hard again. Just like on the back of Hope Pass, my body was still able to carry me fast.

As we ran, I shared with Nico the details of the comeback and the climb over Hope. We chatted about the race, ultra in general and we relived the debacle at the Boulder 100 when Nico was with me as I DNF'd my first true ultra attempt. In fact, we talked about everything—everything except finishing this race. I wouldn't hear that. Maybe it was just left over superstition from my baseball days, but I didn't even want to hear the word "finisher."

We eventually made the top of the climb and I was still feeling great. I was becoming more and more confident with each step. We were still passing runners with steady progress as we made our way along the Colorado trail and through the beautiful forest. The sun had gone down some time ago, and the dancing orb of light coming from my headlamp was hypnotizing me as it bobbed along the trail lighting the way in front of me. It was very surreal to be out in the middle of the Rockies in the middle of the night, but it was familiar in a way I couldn't quite wrap my mind around. I thought of the many nights of staring out the window from the back of my father's camper as we drove through the night when I was a child. Strangely, those are not memories of anxiety, but of peace—as I knew I was ok. I knew I was going to be all right. That was exactly how I felt as we ran down the switchbacks, around the trees, over the small creek crossings and towards the next checkpoint. I was going to be all right.

I couldn't believe that I was 70 miles into The Leadville 100. Nico and I made our way in to the Half Pipe aid station and our plan was to keep it brief. This checkpoint is in the middle of nowhere and has no access for family or outside crew; only the runners and pacers were here. I was still feeling good, but my body was starting to show the signs of wear for running for almost 20 hours. My feet hurt, my quads were starting to feel dead, and my calves and hamstrings were suitable for banjo-strings. I lowered myself into a chair as Nico grabbed some food for me. That was a mistake.

As I lowered my body, every muscle tensed and strained, but as my ass hit the chair, I felt the most wonderful blanket of warm comfort fall over my entire lower body. It was as if 1,000 angels started to sing at once. A huge smile swept over my face and I closed my eyes... Fuck! I jerked my eyes open and stood up in one swift move. My quads buckled as I stood and I almost fell right back into the chair. My alarms were going off. Note to self—if you want to finish this race, don't sit down. As I stood there I looked around the tent. Many runners were lying down in cots nursing injuries or just staring into space. It was like the Winfield tent only worse. Here it was the middle of the night and a couple of runners were pulling from the race, having already travelled 70 miles towards glory. But I supposed if you are in the shit deep and your body is shutting down, 30 miles may as well be 300. I decided I wasn't going to do any more math. It was time to get back out on the trail. As if on cue, Nico came up to me and handed me a PB&J sandwich. We left the checkpoint and headed back out into the cold mountain night. 10 more miles to go to Powerline.

From Half Pipe we had a long section of flat road running ahead of us. This part of the race can really break you down physically and mentally. The road is hard and unforgiving on the body after so much time on the soft trail, and the road stretches out forever in front of you. After a couple of miles, you can actually see the lights of the May Queen checkpoint ahead in the distance, yet the distance seems fixed. As if you jumped on a treadmill, no matter how fast you run, it seems you are not getting any closer. The only thing you can do is put your head down and run—and we did. As we ran along the road, mixing in fast walking intervals to allow the aching body to regroup, the temperature was dropping rapidly. The wind was picking up and the nearby creek water was causing a deep biting cold to set in. We ran harder to keep warm. The headlights of the oncoming cars reminded me of something from my childhood. I couldn't quite place it but it was comforting and disconcerting at the same time. I shook it off as we ran into the May Queen aid station. We arrived. We were at the second-to-the-last checkpoint and we were at the base of the final climb. I was here. I was standing at mile 80 looking right up the mountain—Powerline.

I could almost hear the bell sound in my head as if my moment had come, time to step in the ring for the final round. "One more climb," I said to Nico.

I felt trapped. I was trapped, actually. I was just barely a teenager with few options and no way of getting out of my current predicament. But the truth is, I wouldn't leave if I could. There was no way I would abandon my family no matter how bad things were. We were at a truck stop—again. The truck stop was set back from the interstate and I could see a long line of trucks coming and going in both directions. Once again I wondered what it would be like to be in any of those cars—to be anywhere other than where I was now.

My parents were so stressed, I could hear the panic in their voices as they tried to figure a way out of this predicament. As an adult now, I can imagine the true depth of pain they must have been enduring—the pain of the moment, of being trapped and wanting to protect their children. But also the pain of feeling somehow "wronged." They were not in this situation because they were irresponsible, although some might argue otherwise, or because they were lazy or even incapable of being responsible members of society. My father had run large companies, designed complex electronic devices for the military, and had made a considerable amount of money in the past. That is what made all this so convoluted.

Many nights my dad just needed to sleep. To rest and shut down his mind from the never-ending onslaught that must have bombarded him as he drove us down the road on the way to the next destination. On some of these nights, my mom and I would sit inside an all-night Denny's restaurant or other diner and talk and sip coffee, buying my father a few hours of shut-eye in the camper. This was one of those nights, my mom and dad were discussing what the plan was for later on, but soon my mom and I would sit and chat. I was actually happy because I was hungry and we had enough money to buy me a kid's meal breakfast. These nights with my mom are some of the fondest memories I have of my childhood. The way she loved me came across in every word she spoke to me from the other side of the booth. We spent hours laughing and playing word games while my dad slept. She made me feel loved, important, and safe and sound all at the same time. How the hell did she do that while our whole world was in chaos?

I looked out the window from our booth and I watched the headlights of the vehicles coming in. I analyzed them with my 13-year old going on 30-year old brain. I remember thinking that every one of those sets of lights represented a life outside of me or the people around them. It was overwhelming to think of all those people, all within a few feet of each other, that would never know the details of the other's journey, but all connected somehow in this moment. I don't know why this memory stuck in my mind so clearly, but it is burned in and has remained intact for almost 30 years.

I shook off the childhood thoughts of my beautiful mother and the diner.

I was back with Nico at the Leadville 100. I smiled and I thought for a second that if I finished this thing, I needed to remember to give her an extra tight hug at the finish line. I was now standing on top of the Powerline trail. I made it up the long and brutal climb of 4 miles and now looking backwards, I could see a long line of headlamps stretched out as far as I could see. Once again, I took note of how each light represented not just a runner, but a dream, a support network of friends and family all equally committed to getting their runner home. We were all out here in our own race for our own reasons, but none of us were alone. We were all a permanent part of this race forever.

I had navigated the climb like a champ—there is no other way to say it. I was as light and fast and strong as I had been all day since my "Lazarus" moment at mile 52. My legs were rubber, my feet were torn up, but that was just pain, I was alive and moving well despite it. Another lesson from my childhood came to mind. Pain can be managed—it only meant I was still alive. Nico and I took in the moment together and savored the night air as if it were 30-year old scotch.

"Fun time!" I said. We turned our backs to the moving artwork of headlights snaking up the hill towards us and we began to run.

"It's all downhill from here," I thought as we ran down Hagerman Pass Road. I was doing my best job to keep my wandering mind from thinking about the finish line. Nico and I were still chatting it up as we ran towards the May Queen campground where I was going to pick up my final pacer, Kelly. We were on a long windy stretch of rocky dirt fire road and it was pretty steep in places. The downhill running was really testing my quads and tolerance for pain. Each step sent pain radiating into my bones, but I was thankful to be running. Eventually we took a sharp turn off the road and back onto the single-track trail that would carry us down from the mountain and to the base of Turquoise Lake.

"Well, looks like you are going to fin..."

"STOP!" I said abruptly, but my voice was friendly and light. "Don't say it, man," I grinned.

Nico, being a very matter-of-fact guy, said, "Well, I think it's safe to say that from here you are going to be able to finish the Leadville..."

"Don't do it!" I was almost panicked and laughing at the same time. I didn't want the words spoken. I didn't want any real finishing thoughts to enter my mind until I hit that red carpet on 6th street in Leadville. I was aware that as soon as we made it down to the final check in, it was all rolling to flat terrain, so barring a catastrophe I should be able to get home. The catastrophe, however, was exactly what I was worried about. I was thinking, "What if I rolled my ankle? What if my shaky weak legs just gave out?" The longest I had run in training for this race was 50 miles—and I only did that once. So every step I was taking was uncharted territory. 13 miles was still a long way to go. The good news was we had time. Due to the speed that we were moving through the night, we gained hours on the cut-off times and we had plenty of time to make it home within the 30 hours.

The sun was coming up as we came into the May Queen campground for the final aid station. It was still dark, but you could see the sky getting brighter in anticipation of the sun. My body was pretty beaten up at this point, and just to stand up hurt—but my mind was young and vibrant and healthy. There were many laughs exchanged as Nico and I entered the tent and met up with Kelly. I was also experiencing some serious chaffing issues between the "Twin Cheeks" behind me, and for the last mile or so I was constantly reminding myself to make sure I lubed up before we left for the final stretch. Nico, captured the moment for posterity as I grabbed the lube and busted up laughing putting the cream on my ass. You can see a wide range of emotions in the photo as I am laughing, standing there with my arm behind me, with crazy red bloodshot eyes. I don't know if I ever laughed as hard as in those few moments before Kelly and I left for the final trek back to Leadville.

"Where are Chase, and my dad?" I asked?

"You beat them here," crew manager Jeff said with a grin.

I smiled at the thought. "If I am able to make it, I will see them at the finish," I said, still managing my superstitious demons. I hugged Nico and thanked him, and then Kelly and I made our way out as the sun was rising on the lake.

"13 miles to go," Kelly said as she smiled at me brightly. She was a sweet sight to behold. And I was very glad to have her with me now. As we left May Queen, the sun was coming up. It was still dark enough to need our headlights, which was unfortunate because mine went out about 15 minutes after we left. In our haste to get moving, we forgot to change the batteries— oh well. Luckily, we only had to navigate for a few miles in the dark until the sun would take over. I had to keep reminding myself to keep my eyes on the trail. There were still plenty of technical parts of the course to trip you up and end your race with an abrupt face-plant or ankle-snap.

The trail winds around Turquoise Lake and the view is simply serene. In fact, the view was tempting me to watch it instead of the trial in front of me. Then just like that I was falling—a kicked rock, followed by a mad stumble-dance and subsequent last-minute save, and I was back on task with my eyes firmly following Kelly's shoes toward the finish. "That was close..." I said.

Kelly and I laughed and jogged and made our way forward in a light-hearted but purposeful pace. She did an amazing job, keeping me moving and keeping my mind off the pain that was being transmitted to my brain from seemingly every place on my body. At this stage of the game, my shoulders hurt, my ankles were swollen, my hamstrings were piano wire, my quads were rubber and my mind was jumping around like ticker-tape machine. I could feel the emotions welling up inside as we got closer to the finish, but each time I pushed them back.

"Almost," I whispered. I started to think of my mom and our nights in the diner when I was a kid and my eyes teared up. "Not yet," I warned myself—still got some work to do. We picked up the pace at times; others, we walked and jogged. It was all pain management now. Get to the finish. Keep moving.

The trail eventually gave way to a dirt path that winds along the lakeside and provides campsites for tourist and race spectators. We passed a wedding taking place on a boat ramp by the water. I later became friends on a complete whim with the couple getting married. The dirt path expelled us onto the road without much warning and the hard surface was making my ankles feel like they were made of glass. We were out of the woods now, literally. We were on the road outside of Leadville and we could see cars and people along the roadside looking for their runners. I saw Jeff standing at the roadside up ahead. He was taking pictures.

"Less than 5 miles now," he called out.

"I can do that," I thought and picked up the pace. Kelly responded by running harder next to me and encouraging me to follow. "Great work," she said. "You're looking awesome," she lied.

Despite my pace slowing considerably in the waning hours, we were still moving well compared to many other runners. I saw runners barely able to stand or put one foot in front of the other and my heart went out to them. I didn't know if they would make it or not, but I couldn't resist giving the best encouragement I could as we passed each runner and pacer. If I had to bet, I would say every one of them made it home. Each time we approached a runner/ pacer team, we spent some time chatting or exchanging embraces before we moved on. Sometimes we didn't even need to speak—just a knowing look and smile said it all. I felt personally connected to each of these souls and I suspect they felt the same. We were now all a part of something special—something that no one could EVER take away. We went deep into the dark forest of our own fears and pain, and we made it to the sunrise. It was a new day—literally, and we were close to home.

The course took us off the asphalt road, and onto a dirt road known as "The Boulevard." I knew from when we ran this section at the start of the race, that we were about 3 miles to the finish. The terrain becomes a mild uphill gradient to the finish and my legs were happy to see it. It sounds counterintuitive, but my running muscles were much more tired at this stage than my climbing muscles (thank you, Bear Peak) and the switch felt good. Kelly and I started moving as fast as we could towards home. We ran, we walked and hustled down The Boulevard and made our way onto the street by the Leadville High School. From here I could hear the crowds cheering at the finish line—we had less than a mile left. For the first time, I let go. My body started to shake. The rattle started in my feet and moved up my legs to my heart. My shoulders were heaving and the tears spilled out onto my cheeks.

"Even if my legs gave out, I could crawl to the finish from here," I thought. I released the superstition—I was going to finish the Leadville 100.

I laughed in the midst of the tears and started running. We made the final right turn onto 6th street and from the top of the hill, I could see the red carpet of the finish line way ahead in the distance. I was in shock. I hadn't allowed myself to think of this moment during the race, and the reality of seeing it now was heavy. I felt like I was floating. My feet were no longer touching the ground. The crowd was lining both sides of the street and seemed to be moving and clapping in slow motion.

The red carpet was getting closer. I was searching the side of the road for familiar faces.

"Son!"

I heard my father's voice. I looked over and saw him and my brother Chase standing just outside the finish area on the roadside. I ran over to them. My father was holding an old faded American flag. I recognized it immediately— we had come to call this family treasure our "Battle Flag."

More tears. We had carried that flag all across the country on our quest for truth. The flag first hung outside in our beautiful home in Sugarland before the quest started. Since, it had hung in tents, rest stops, trailers, churches and in the back of my dad's truck we called home during all those tough years. The flag was present as we sped down the road with no brakes in Pennsylvania. It was there as we collected cans so that we could eat as a family. It hung in the inner city ministry where my father touched so many people in Florida, and it actually spent some time at the corporate office of my company before it closed. And apparently it had been here in Leadville all day and night as I ran through the Rocky Mountains in search for the answer to a simple question...

I was not just another bum from the neighborhood. I was just a young man with an imperfect past. I was like all of us, searching to find something to fill the gaps and holes inside. I couldn't fill the gaps with alcohol or food. I couldn't make sense of any of the things that had happened in my life—and the truth was, I didn't need to. I just needed to step out and breathe—I just needed to let me happen.

Right there I saw myself in that moment—not as I actually must have appeared, covered in sweat and dirt and blood and muck—and not as I see me, or as my friends see me, but as my father saw me. I saw the pride, redemption and validation that a man can get watching his son succeed. And as he looked into my eyes and contemplated what this moment meant, I saw all the memories he might have of me as a drunk, a failure and a fool fade away forever. Then I saw my own son, and I realized that maybe today in finishing this race, I had given him the most valuable gift a father can give his son—better than an Ivy League education, a trust fund or even a house—the gift my dad gave me: the ability to believe in something even when everyone else in the world thinks it's hopeless, the desire to fight for what I wanted, and most importantly—the ability to endure for as long as it takes.

My father handed me the flag. "Let's finish this," I said. The red carpet was magic under my feet.

Keep Moving Forward

In many ways I never touched the finish line in 2010 at The Leadville 100. It was more of a *starting* line for me than I possibly could have imagined. I spent the remaining weeks and months of 2010 trying to put it all in perspective. I couldn't help but think of how lucky I was—how many people had taken me in, worked so selflessly for me, held my hand, and nursed me back to health as I trudged along and fumbled my way into recovery. The problem with me wasn't booze or food or workout schedules. I wasn't an alcoholic or a 320-pound addict by accident. It was my thinking that got me into trouble— the desire to control, the need to measure, the absence of being able to quiet myself and simply let life flow. These things broke me down into a person that needed to use something outside myself to find moments peace. I was trying to shut my brain off from the outside. I simply didn't know that, all those years, healing silence was available to me from the inside out.

My new life started in a strong and yet purely selfish moment. The moment I realized I could never be anything for my kids or for anyone until I healed my own fractured soul—I needed to take care of me. It is a strange thing, addiction. It is the most selfish thing a person can do, to put your own immediate gratification over everything else in the world. Yet for me, the paradox was that I was an addict in many ways because I never lived for myself at all. I never figured out how to just be me. And yet strangely, the solution to becoming a more loving and less selfish husband and father was to put my sobriety on the top of the list ahead of everything and everyone else. If I committed to doing that, I could give myself away entirely. I think the Creator has a sense of humor, after all.

I was true to my word; I never dismissed my accomplishment at the 2010 Leadville 100, as I did all my previous races. But I didn't let it get out of focus, either. I never felt like I was something special because I persevered out there. But I did learn a lot about myself that I didn't know, and that had tremendous value. I looked deep into the darkest corners of my soul when I was on Hope Pass—the places that in the past I was afraid to see, afraid because there might be hidden secrets that could expose my lack of character. Instead, I found strength, I found guts, and I found the me that was never discouraged by any of the things that happened in my life. All the drugs, alcohol, all the times I quit, and all hurt that I lived through never touched the true essence of me—they only colored the outer shell. Inside, I was a pure spirit of potential. I was free to do whatever I wanted. This is the truth of all human beings—we are all the same and all undamaged by life.

The next year brought with it a new level of expectation. Not just what I expected from myself in terms of running, but also my level of commitment to reach out to others. I started to talk more openly about my addiction and struggle. I listed my cell phone number on my Facebook page and asked people to call me 24/7 if they were struggling. I wrote race reports and spoke about my experience in Leadville and what it meant to me. In the process, I was finding that many people in my inner circle were struggling or had struggled in the past with addiction. I was shocked. People I had known for years never mentioned to me that they had been following my posts on Facebook and felt moved to share their own story of addiction with me. It was amazing—and very humbling to hear. I was also receiving much encouragement to keep doing what I was doing. "Please keep sharing so openly what you have been through," I was told in the locker at my gym or at starting lines of races.

As I shared and listened to others, I was learning more about myself, as well. I had to look deep into my own heart for answers to questions I had never asked myself. I had to search to see if I could accurately articulate my truth to other people. I was forced to search my own soul to see if I could relate in a meaningful and honest way to the other people fighting for a new life. I found that I could find a depth of understanding of my own soul that I thought was unobtainable. I sought the path of spiritual enlightenment. I read every book I could find, I wrote in my journal, and I worked on my own issues as I ran countless miles in the mountains. I spent hours on the phone, I visited alcoholics in the hospital and I sat next to heroin addicts detoxing. I blogged and posted and tried to get the message of hope out there as much as I could. And I was hearing from people all over the world now who were looking for some inspiration or a kind word of encouragement. Facebook can be an amazing tool, and I was discovering quickly how fast the word can spread if I put myself out there.

Working with alcoholics can be the most rewarding and depressing thing in the world on a moment-to-moment basis. The most difficult part to accept is the reality that I cannot help anyone. It sounds harsh, but it's true. I cannot bestow any wisdom or inspiration sufficient to bring a lost soul to the rock-bottom moment of clarity. That has to come from within the addict. What I can do is stand in the light. I can show that a new life is possible, and I can share my experiences with those trying to find a way out. I can relate only what I have been through in hopes that it strikes a familiar chord in those still out there. Although a draining process, the calling is there nonetheless. It is as they say, "the alcoholic alone is uniquely qualified to help other alcoholics." It is an odd contrast—the alcoholic himself must be the architect of his recovery in many ways, yet he cannot do it alone. It takes a village to raise a child; well, it takes a bunch of fucked-up former addicts to relate to a confused chemical abuser. I stand today on the shoulders of the many people who cared for me along the way.

I raised the bar on my running and commitment to excelling in the ultramarathon world, as well as in my spiritual plight. I routinely ran up Bear

Peak 3-4 times a week in addition to more advanced training to improve my speed and form. I also branched out in the running world and went to work as a coach, leading group runs and writing training plans. I had a philosophy that whether on a mountain or in life, you are either climbing or sliding, there is no standing still. I was not going to stand still. I changed the way I ran—form and efficiency became priorities. I changed the way I ate—I adopted a plant-based diet and paid attention to everything I put into my body. I also became certified as a trainer, nutrition specialist and run coach.

In past years, I had chosen to limit my running by self-imposed ceilings. "I'll never be fast," I used to say. "I start off slow and taper off," was an all-time favorite. "I would never want to run for time because it would take the joy out of it," was also on my playlist. I thought back to all the limits and restrictions I had put on myself in my struggles with addiction. They were all bullshit. Were my running restrictions also self-imposed? What if I decided that I would never be bound or restricted by fear again? What would happen in my life immediately—today or tomorrow? Could I do better at Leadville?

As I was sitting on Bear Peak looking over the Boulder and Denver skylines one morning, I felt the old familiar feeling of truth washing away the uncertainty of doubt. I knew I had to go back to Leadville. It didn't matter what happened if I went back. It didn't even matter if I was unable to finish the race a second time. I had to prove to myself I was still willing to risk. I had to face the fear of failing.

I knew I had to let go of any lingering fear, but fear isn't always as easy to see as one would believe. Fear can come to us hidden in many forms. It can be the voice of reason, "You are only going to hurt yourself if you train harder." It can be the voice of compassion, "You deserve to take today off." And the tricky thing is that these are genuine concerns not to be ignored. But if it is fear of failure that is ultimately steering the ship, we will never be able to find our potential. Much like releasing the demons of my addictions, I released the demons of fear. I was after the truth—and whatever it was, I was ok with it. "Let it go—run free and stay on top of the rocks," I would say, as I ran fearlessly down the steep rocky back side of Bear Peak. It doesn't matter what's under the rocks—worrying will only make you fall.

And what is it exactly that I was afraid of anyway? Why did I find comfort in the back of the pack? And now that you have "accepted" that you are slow, why not let it rip anyway and see what happens? What if it was a lie you sold yourself to spare yourself the pain of racing hard against the voices? I smiled at the thought. Just like when I reconstructed my broken and shattered image of myself as an addict, I tore apart my image of being a slow runner. I didn't see myself as a fast runner exactly, but I saw myself as a fearless runner... and I liked that.

To say I trained hard for the 2011 Leadville 100 would be accurate. It would also be lacking in depth. I did train hard. I took what I did the year before and added a focus and intensity that I hadn't brought to running before. I still laughed and danced my way through the trails, but it wasn't ALL fun and games this time. I started running trails that I once was forced to hike due to the steep terrain. I ran on the treadmill every night and always with the incline set high. I added yoga, cycling and strength training to the mix. and I found I gained even more enjoyment from running in the process. I also did something completely outside of the box. A friend of mine heard that a film crew was looking for a few athletes for a documentary that was going to be filmed during the Leadville 100 race that year. I emailed the producer with my story.

Kevin Morris the producer of *1 Hundred: Running the Impossible* called me one afternoon and said they might be interested in talking to me about being one of three runners featured in his upcoming film. He asked me to submit a video telling my story, and he and the other filmmakers would get back to me. I didn't have any idea what to say, so I set up the camera and just started talking. I am not sure if I mentioned running at all, but I did tell my story and spill my heart. As I hit the send button and sent my video email to Kevin, I sat at my desk and wondered what I'd gotten myself into. "Do you really want to do this?" I asked out loud. It's one thing to tell your story, another to hang it out there for all posterity. AND what if you fail? Now your failure will be immortalized. I got the word back—I was in.

In the ultra running world, the "sub 24 hour finish" is the gold standard for excellence. To complete 100 miles in one day garners you the respect of all your peers—and usually a big shiny buckle to wear for all to see. Almost every 100 mile race across the country offers runners the lure of the "sub 24 hour buckle," but due to the extreme nature and difficulty of the Leadville 100, they have historically offered a "sub 25 hour buckle." And the buckle itself is in true Leadville style—huge, shiny and one of the most sought-after awards in all of ultra running. I set my heart on earning this accolade.

Runners are notorious for hedging their bets and having multiple goals for races. The reality is every runner knows exactly how fast they want to run; they just don't want to put it out there and make the race a "pass or fail" event. Usually we have a minimum standard goal (the time needed for the race to not be a bust), the goal we share with our friends (one that is ambitious but realistic), and the actual goal (the reason we are racing at all and torturing ourselves). I was no exception to this superstitious and strange dance. But this time I was going to walk the walk and talk the talk. I told my crew and pacers my true "secret goal" for the Leadville race. And I even shared the goal with the world on camera before the race. I wanted to finish the Leadville 100 over 4 hours faster than I had the years before—I wanted to get back to the finish less than 24 hours after I started.

After a strange pre-race week in Leadville that included a camera crew following me around town and filming me eating breakfast, it was finally time to run. I went out like a banshee from the start. I wasn't playing any games this time—I was here to work hard and suffer. I made it to the first aid station way ahead of schedule and ran in and out with hardly a stop. I ran the entire uphill climb after the first checkpoint and made it past the long line of runners opting to hike up this steep trail. I ran down the Powerline sections just like I did a year ago—only this time I was at the 25-mile point of the race in less than 4 hours. I was hanging it all on the line for a fast finish and I was starting to wonder if I had bitten off more than I could chew.

Only a quarter of the way into the race, my legs were already cramping and starting to feel fatigued. Naturally, the demons took the chance to chime in and tell me there is no way I could go another 75 miles when I was already suffering. I didn't care what they said—they were liars. I ran hard. I was having trouble standing up and getting out of the chair at the 40-mile point, and my crew was a little concerned (so was I). I tried to play it cool for the cameras that had been following me all day, but I was in a lot of pain.

On sheer will and grit I forced my legs to carry me over Hope Pass, and even though I was dealing with a lot of physical pain, I noticed that my time was still proving to be fast. I was exactly on my sub 24 hour pace, but I knew I was going to be slowing down as the race went on. I made it to Winfield on shaky legs and smiled for the cameras. I sat down long enough to change my shoes. I was trying every trick I knew to stay in the moment and out of my mind. If I gave any real consideration to how my legs were going to feel going back over Hope Pass. I would quit. I simply smiled and was thankful that I wasn't in the same dark place as I was last year at this point.

"Pain only hurts," I told my pacer as we once again rallied over Hope Pass and made it back to the 60-mile point of the race while the sun was still shining. I lowered myself into the chair and changed my shoes for the last time. I told the cameras that I thought the 24-hour goal was out of the picture, as I'd lost a little of my projected pace. I was still going for the big shiny Sub 25 Hour Buckle, though. I was all in—and I just didn't care how much it hurt. "Slowing down will not make me hurt less," I kept telling myself. It's another lie. The only thing that will make me feel better is if I do myself proud and run this thing as best as I can. If I don't get a big buckle at that point, who cares. I continued to run as fast as I could and my legs kept on carrying me, despite the throbbing pain.

I started to feel the pull of the finish even though it was still 40 miles away. I drew strength from every place I could find it—my pacers, my crew, the spectators, and my brother Chase to whom I had dedicated this run. I had his name written on the inside of my arm. Chase, who was such a big part of my race last year, was at that moment in rehab fighting his own demons. We were both in an all-out fight for life—each of us battling against voices telling us to quit, to opt out, or just give up. But there was no way that was happening today. I didn't need to be strong forever—just one day, just today. As I left the last aid station at May Queen, I pointed to the camera and said "Chase." I meant my brother's name, of course, because I had been carrying him with me every step of the day. But I also thought as I turned my back and ran that I was no longer afraid of anything that was behind me. I wasn't being chased any more—I was running exactly where I wanted to go.

I knew the math didn't work. There was just no way we could make it back to Leadville in less than 24 hours, but I was going to be damned if I let that stop me from going as hard as I could. And sub 25 was still in play. I ran, my ankle caught fire, and I walked. After a few steps I ran again. I pushed pulled, ran, hiked and moved as fast as my shredded legs would carry me. We had made up a lot of time in the last couple hours and all of a sudden it looked like it was going to be closer at the finish that we thought. As we made our way off the dirt road of "The Boulevard" once again, I knew I was close to the red carpet.

Just then, my crew appeared out of nowhere. Matt, Kathy, Nico and Jerry were all jumping up and down and yelling at me and my current pacer Scott. "You can do it!!" they yelled, "It's just up the road!" I looked at my watch and I couldn't believe it. Somehow we had run faster than I could have ever planned on doing late in a race—we had 18 minutes to make it to the finish. We took off running. It was excruciatingly painful. I cannot even describe the level of pain, but I was running almost as hard as I could. It felt like 6-minute miles but it was more like 9-minute miles.

I never wanted to stop more than I did for that long run on 6th Street towards the red carpet. It was still dark. There were no family members out cheering, as most of the field of runners was still behind me. Scott had taken the American flag down from his house before driving to Leadville to pace me. He now took it out of his pack and handed it to me as we ran. I threw the flag over my shoulders like a cape, and I smiled a deep and peaceful smile. I ran across the finish line and looked up at the clock. It said 23:50:46.

In a quick recount of such an amazing race it is impossible to describe the effort put forth not just by me, but by an entire team of selfless friends who dedicated themselves to supporting me, holding my hand, and ensuring that I didn't do anything too stupid during the race. To run the Leadville 100, much less in the time that I did, would have been impossible for me without Kathy Jambor, Matt Gant, Nico Brooks, Scott Miller, and way too many others to mention.

I wasn't going to ever doubt myself again. I knew I would fail, I knew I would take on more than I was capable of doing in the future, but never again would I shackle myself with the chains of low expectation. As fate would have it, a month-and-a-half after my second Leadville race, I was at the starting line of another ultra, the 12 Hours of Boulder. This race features a 12-hour event and a 24-hour event, as well as the 100-mile event. It was at the 100-mile event that I attempted and failed in my first 100-mile attempt after my back surgery a couple of years earlier. On a total whim and at the very last minute, I signed up for it so I could return to the scene of my "ultra demise." The course is the same no matter which event you are in, the runners do a 7.17-mile loop until the time is up. Whoever has run the farthest after the allotted time wins that event.

At the start of the race I had my goal and I wasn't afraid to share it with my friends. "I am either going to win this thing, or I am going to blow up trying—either way, it should be fun to see." I said. So I ran as hard as I could for as long as I could. It was a battle for about 6 hours, and then I pulled away. I was 15 miles ahead of any other runner at the 10-hour point. So my prediction was correct—I did, in fact, win the 12-hour race. I ran 71.17 miles in 12:02 minutes, setting the course record.* The most ironic part of this is that I ran the exact distance that I stopped at in 2009 when I failed to complete my 100-mile goal—only this time I ran it 8 hours faster.

I want to say for the record that this race is a very low-key event. It is not nearly the same thing as winning a large event with the world's best runners competing, but the victory meant as much to me as winning any race possibly could have—because I ran well. And I left it all out at the Rez, where I failed so miserably before.

Superman

I organized my outreach to the recovery world though a foundation I started. The group called "The Superman Project" is a small support and coaching resource for those who are using sports and endurance events as a means to finding sobriety. We write training plans, do counseling, and generally try to support all groups out there promoting a healthy lifestyle. The inspiration for the name of the group came from my son Davey who told me he thought I had turned into Superman. I told him I was most certainly not Superman, but we can all be really strong if we need to be. We all have a Superman inside waiting to "fly."

I took every chance I could to promote the power of change. The parallel between running an ultra and battling addiction is uncanny, and I used every opportunity I could to spread the word through running events. If the newly-sober addict tries to imagine a life without his precious drug of choice, he cannot see a life worth living. Similarly, if you try to hold the weight of running 100 miles, it will fold you up and crush you. One step at a time, relentless work and faith will get you to the finish. That is how sobriety is first discovered and how ultra running is done.

I wrote blog posts, I dedicated races to those struggling, and I ran 24 hours on a treadmill at a local gym for youth alcohol awareness. I managed to get on the news to talk about change and addiction. I wrote articles for blogs, I donated my time to coaching sober athletes, and I spent a considerable amount of time talking to people about weight loss, substance abuse and the mental struggle of change.

One day I heard someone use the term "recovery run." It's a very popular term used to describe a very low-intensity run on tired legs to promote healing after a tough race. The word "recovery" resonated with me, however. My brain started to turn and I began to think of how I could use this wordplay to do something big to get the word out to those who were struggling. I decided I would do an epic run for those in recovery—or those looking to find it. After batting around a few ideas, I settled on running across the state of Colorado. In the ultra running world this is not so unusual; in fact, many people have run across the entire country. But I was going to do something totally unique, in my mind. I was going to average an ultra marathon (50k or 31.10 miles) per day for 10 days. To truly make it a run about recovery I decided to revisit the 12 Steps of AA during my run.

In the two days leading up to the start of the "300-mile Recovery Run," I completed the first two steps of Alcoholics Anonymous. Then each day for the next 10 days, I was going to do a step in my mind while running all day. At night after the run, I blogged and shared my personal thoughts in hopes that the fearless inner journey of my own demons might speak to someone in need. Day in and day out I ran. People came out to join me each day along the way and the support I received was beautiful and overwhelming.

The route I chose was along the Continental Divide from the Wyoming border south all the way to New Mexico. The route was at an average elevation of over 8,000 feet and went over many mountain passes. At first my body started to break down under the strain of running 30 plus miles a day on the hard and unforgiving roads, but by the time we finished, I felt strong and fit. I felt as if I could keep going for months—another testament to the power that humans have to adapt.

When it was over, I was forever changed in far too many ways to list. The vast undertaking of running so far was hard to digest. And the support and outreach I received every day as people followed the run online was too heavy to carry. Also weighing me down was the emotional strain of digging into the dark corners of my own life once again. My heart was very heavy as I purged my soul mile after mile.

By May of 2012, my personal life had withstood some severe blows over the last few years. On the road alone with my personal faults (not to mention doing another fearless inventory), I was faced with the many things I had tucked away and hidden from view—not the least of which was my divorce. During my years as a drunk and a selfish husband, my wife and I had grown apart as a couple. After years of hiding from this obvious but painful truth and years of sleeping in separate rooms, I eventually strayed from the marriage. I am not proud to mention it and, in fact, I have tried to employ every trick I could think of to find a good reason to leave that fact out of this story, but sometimes the truth demands the light of day. I will forever be ashamed of my actions, and I am surprised that I could be so weak, but it is not something I am prepared to hide from. I did the very best I could to repair things but it was too late. The only thing I could do is be the best father I could be and try to live by example for my children. When we screw up, we don't quit. We own our shit and we move forward. I consider myself lucky to have made it through the aftermath with my sobriety intact. Today my ex-wife and I are great friends and I continue to try to be there for her as we share the custody and the lives of our amazing children.

People ask me why I would so unashamedly share all the worst moments of my life. They ask why I would openly wear my weaknesses in public as if they were medals of honor. The answer is pretty simple: because walling myself away and trying to control what people thought of me, was in many ways, what put me in a cage in the first place, I no longer choose to be locked up. I live my life as if everything I have ever done or will ever do is public knowledge. And in doing so, it has brought me a level of peace that I could never explain. I am not always proud of my actions, but I own myself and everything I have ever lived. If you want to sleep well at night I recommend this highly. So what if what I feel and say isn't always comfortable for myself or other people to hear? It's what is in my heart and I am no longer afraid to put myself out there.

I think that people are all capable of miraculous strength—it is our very nature to adapt and survive all the elements. We are predators and prey, lovers and fighters, and as a race or species we have done unexplainable things when we have needed to. This power is in our DNA, yet many of us live our entire lives without ever touching it. I suppose that might be ok for some. It means they never got too low or had to deal with horrible struggle—they never needed that strength. But for those of us who have spent time in the gutter, those of us who have found a new life having endured the loss, the pain, the hopelessness of addiction—we know we got lucky. We know if we hadn't cleaned up on that one day, sobriety might have never come, and we would be dead or still out there struggling.

We know that by some strange twist of fate, we touched that evolutionary trigger that allowed us the superhuman strength to stop using, even though every cell in our bodies cried out in protest. Somehow we made it a minute, an hour, a day without using. And the strength stayed. We made it 30 days, then a year, and we even managed to find a whole new way to live life. It was a miracle. And there isn't a sweeter view to take in than the simplest of moments from a clear mind, a mind that was once ravished and tortured by demons. It is a vision of the world through a set of eyes that are old, but seeing things as if just born.

Doing something like running 100 miles might seem extreme, but for me that is the very reason that it should be done. If I can push myself to the brink of me, to the edge of my own sanity, to the point that doing something as mundane as taking a single step forward seems impossible; if I can persevere in that moment, and fight off every demon or instinct that tells me to quit, if I can tell my body to move, even though my brain says I am spent, then I know I will be fine. If I can will my mind to be still, even as it races for a way out of hell, I will be fine. And if I can come out on the other side still moving forward, it will be because I have once again accessed that hidden power that lifted my drunken body to safety—the power that brought my children back to me, that restored my sanity. If I touch that place again and again, I know my sobriety is no fluke. Above all, I know I can reach that power for my own recovery if the day of temptation to use ever comes back.

It sounds crazy, and people tell me I am sick to run like I do. And no matter how hard I try to describe the inner workings of my old addict's brain, they will never get it; if they did, they would be running along the same trails that I do. Hell, I even call myself crazy sometimes. But most of the time I tell people, "I'm not crazy—I'm just out there."

Badwater Race Report

My Blog: Part 1

Death Valley, July 15th, 2013

"This ain't no pillow factory," I said as I finished retching and heaving on the side of the road. I was in Death Valley and I felt like it. The temperature was 102 degrees but strangely it felt almost cool. Well... cool compared to the 124 degrees I was running in a few hours earlier. No sooner had I finished my strange roadside dance of regurgitation, than I was running again. The sun was coming up and I had been going for almost 19 hours already, but I had been here before. I had completed 5 races of exactly 100 miles in length— but usually I could see the finish line by now. On this day, though, I was only beginning. I was at mile 75 and I still had 60 miles to go.

Some things just speak to us. We don't know why, and rarely can we explain to others in a meaningful way what we see when our souls are moved to act. The first time I heard of the Badwater 135, I was speechless. The race puts runners on a 135-mile run across Death Valley on the hottest day of the year. And if that's not enough, to get to the finish, runners must climb three mountain ranges (including Mt. Whitney) to get to the finish line. As I watched a documentary about the event called *Running on the Sun*, I felt a combination of disbelief, confusion and anxiety. I think the disbelief came from the simple observation that people could actually do something like this without dying. The confusion perhaps came from wondering why I was so moved by witnessing it, and the anxiety was still harder to define, for by this time, I had run many difficult courses. Maybe it was a precognition of sorts, a vision that I may find myself out there in that very desert one day with the ultimate question ringing in my ears, "Can I make it to Mt. Whitney?"

After a couple of years of learning about and running ultra marathons, my resume was peppered with what seemed, at least to me, like a lifetime of experience. I had the thrill of winning a small local ultra and almost setting the course record; I had AG wins in a few races and placed top 10 in a couple of bigger events. And of course, I had been tempered by the pain of a DNF (Did Not Finish) or two. I had run 24 hours on a treadmill for charity, and I had even run an ultra (50k) every day for 10 days, carrying me all the way across the state of Colorado. I was certainly no Marshall Ulrich, but I was no longer the fat guy with the drinking and drug problem, either.

I was at Starbucks having coffee with some friends after a Saturday morning run when my life changed forever. My phone vibrated and I opened it up to receive the most thrilling and sobering email of my life: "Congratulations, you have been invited to compete in the 2013 Badwater 135."

Later that morning driving home from Starbucks, I started to cry. Most people know my story as one of redemption and second chances, and to be sure they are right. But they might also be surprised to learn of my lifelong inner struggle to know if I am better than the sum total of my rocky childhood—a story I rarely share with anyone. You see, my inner demons go beyond those of food and substance abuse and are, in fact, rooted in a much deeper place—a place that causes me to doubt my very worth. It pushes me to places that seem cruel and masochistic to some, but to me simply serve as a temporary answer to a rhetorical question, "Am I just a white trash kid who grew up in the back of truck, or do I have something special inside?"

Well, it seems I was going to receive the ultimate gift, a chance to see for myself if I could accomplish something truly elite in my mind. Could I become one of the only 566 people to EVER complete what *National Geographic* calls "The Toughest Race in the World"? If I could do that, maybe I could put to bed some of those old doubts once and for all.

I started Badwater training within a few days of my acceptance email. I knew there were a thousand things that could come up and bite me in the ass during the race, but I was going to do my best to make sure it wasn't going to be something obvious, like lack of preparation. I did the work. I put in the hours in the sauna. I ate well. I ran the miles, and I did everything I could think of to be the best and strongest version of me I could muster. The months ticked off the calendar in a whirlwind of 50-mile races, gluten free/vegan meals and hours and hours of solitude in the sauna. And then it was July, just like that—and the race was here.

Pre-Race Check In

To be at Furnace Creek the day before Badwater is to be welcomed into a family. And you can't help but be taken in by the extreme nature of the people you are surrounded with—everyone with their own unique reason to make the pilgrimage to Death Valley on the hottest day of the year. Addicts, amputees, soldiers, yogis and seekers of their own personal truths. Each with unique lives and experiences, yet all the same inside—willing to expose themselves to the toughest of conditions in order to connect the dots of their own picture. And whether you are runner or crew member, we all had the same thing on our minds—to get the team safely from the Badwater Basin at 283 feet below sea level and across the 135 miles, down the road to Lone Pine and to the Whitney Portal at the base of the highest peak in the contiguous U.S.

As I walked into the check-in room at the Furnace Creek Inn, I was taking it all in like a kid on Christmas morning—only the gifts I was receiving weren't of the "toy train" variety. Instead, they came in the form of all the faces I had come to know from magazines, ultra movies and being a fan of the history of this race. As I made eye contact with those veteran runners around me, I could see they recognized me, just as I knew them. It seems Facebook has made even the rookies such as me famous, and that was clear here at runner check-in. To say I was made welcome would be a horrible understatement. I felt like I was returning home from a long trip away. I could see Marshall Ulrich, Dean Karnases, Charlie Engle, David Goggins, Cheryl Zarkowski, Lisa Batchen-Smith... and the list goes on and on—all here with their crews to once again complete this, the ultimate trek. Even the crews had big names in them: Rich Roll and Ferge Hawke, just to name two champions who were here not to run the race themselves, but to work for their runner as pacers.

My crew was comprised, not of wily Badwater veterans (save for my crew manager and his lovely partner), but was an assemblage of people I knew I could trust—people that I respected, loved, and people I knew I could never let down. I knew that even if I wanted to quit, I simply couldn't do so in the presence of these souls.

My Crew

Emily Booth. She is brave and tough, yet has a tenderness that is overwhelming to me at times. She has done multiple Ironman triathlons, 100-milers, marathons and cycling events. She is a rock, and I knew that if I needed her to, she would take every single step of the course with me. Emily has carried me to some of my greatest ultra performances, including my first-ever win and two separate 100-mile PR's.

Nico Brooks. The face of selflessness. Nico has been there for me for everything that I have ever done of note. From my first ultra, to my 24-hour treadmill run, all (save 2) of my 100-milers, my run across Colorado... you get the picture. He always seems to say or do the exact right thing when I need it. He is a very experienced and very accomplished trail runner. I look forward to the day that I get to return the favor and work for him as he has for me.

Scott Miller. We call him "Big Miles" but we really should call him "Big Heart." He is the kind of friend that would drop everything and come to your rescue no matter the time. He has done several marathons, and a couple of his own ultra adventures. He has paced for me before, and he brought me home to the finish in Leadville. In my best Ken Chlouber I would say, "He is stronger than he thinks he is, and he can do more than he thinks he can..."

Brian Remington. Tough. Sober. Determined. Brian is no stranger to the demons of addiction and near-death experience and he is fearless because of it. I have seen him become a great runner in a short period of time, and I knew he would turn himself inside-out to get me home. Brain has run over 50 half marathons and 2 ultras, including a 50k and a marathon on back-to-back days, and he has only just started.

Carmella House. As smart as they come, a Naval Academy grad and an ultra runner in her own right. I met Carmella for the first time the day before runner check-in, but I could tell right away she was good people. We shared much time together on the course at Badwater, and she will always be considered by me to be a dear friend. You really get to know someone well when you blindly trust them to take care of you and they don't let you down.

Jimmy Gabany. Jimmy and I were Facebook friends before we ever met in person, which happened only a week before the race. Jimmy did everything I could ask a crew manager to do. He paced, he drove, he planned, he logged my nutrition and he got me to the finish. He supplied his own vehicle to the cause, he stayed awake for days on end and he fricking held an umbrella over my head at the pre-race meeting, for Godsakes! Seriously, to do so much for someone you have never met says a lot about the character of a human being.

The Race: Day One

There are three waves for the start of The Badwater 135, and I was put in the 8 am wave. As I stood at the starting line, I was strangely calm. I won't say I was feeling confident because that wouldn't have been exactly accurate. It was more of a peace or mild curiosity that in the hours to come I was going to learn more about myself than I had ever known. I hoped that meant I was going to make it all the way to the finish that lay so far ahead of me, but I wasn't feeling the need for any false bravado or temporary motivational-speak to psyche me up. I was ready. And the only fear I felt was an understanding of the level of commitment I had made to myself before getting here. I knew that for me to quit, I was going to have to experience a level of pain that I couldn't imagine. In the hotel room the night before I told myself that I was moving forward on this course until I finished or ran out of time. If that meant I had to get on my hands and crawl an inch at a time towards Lone Pine, so be it.

As the national anthem played, I closed my eyes and gave silent thanks to the brave men and women who serve our great nation. I was thankful for them, thankful to be born here, and thankful that I didn't kill myself with drugs and alcohol before I made it to this special place. The next thing I knew, Chris Kostman, the race director, was counting down "3... 2... 1..." and just like that, I was officially a runner in the Badwater 135.

The athletes must run the first 17 miles of the race without a pacer, but the crew is allowed on the course to ensure that proper hydration and nutrition are available to the runner. I started out with a very conservative approach to the first section of the race. Due to the heat, the first 50 miles of the race are where most people get into trouble, and with my training taking place in Colorado, I had no idea how my body was going to respond to the extreme weather. I put in the time in the sauna, but there is simply no replacement for actual running in the heat, and this was to be my first time running in anything over 100 degrees. I made it through the first 17 miles and into the Furnace Creek checkpoint on schedule. I was on top of my nutrition and hydration, and even as the temperature was skyrocketing, I felt good. Emily was my first pacer and it was amazing to have her out there with me. We just looked at each other and smiled. "Badwater," we said at the same time. Then we just did what we do... we ran.

The miles were ticking away and I was getting a new pacer about every 3 miles or so, which kept everything new and exciting. In Badwater the pacer cannot be next to or in front of the runner to shield the wind or sun, so my pacer was almost never in my sight, but I felt their presence nonetheless. Jokes and politically incorrect-speak were in abundance. The crew car would leapfrog me about a mile up the road at a time to check in and see how I was fairing in the hostile environment.

I was reminded about the intensity of the heat one time when I stopped to get sprayed down with cold water and have ice put in my bandana. The water from the sprayer had actually turned hot in the 10 minutes that went by since my last spritz. I was greeted to a nice blast of hot water in the face. Welcome to Death Valley. And the heat radiating off the pavement felt like I was standing over a campfire... where are the marshmallows?

I heard after the race that Dean Karnazes said the thermometer hit 130 at Stove Pipe Wells. That seemed about right. As I came into the 42-mile checkpoint at Stove Pipe, I was still feeling pretty good and that was comforting. In all my race planning I assumed that if I was going to get my ass kicked, it would come in the most intense heat of the race. I was wrong. Up to about the 45-mile mark, the terrain is mostly flat and as we put that section behind us, I was looking forward to some climbing. We started a 17-mile climb up Townes Pass, which goes up to 4,936 feet in elevation before dropping back down to sea level. As we started the climb, the temperature started to drop and the wind started to roar. Before I had time to even know what was happening, I was leaning forward into a 25-mph headwind and just trying to keep from getting blown off the shoulder of the road. So much for running this hill hard, as was the plan. Something else also started to make its presence known in my conscious thoughts—my abdominal muscles were hurting. When did that start, I wondered? I didn't feel sick or nauseous. I felt more like I had been doing sit-ups. I really didn't pay too much attention to it until it started to intensify over the next hour or so. All of a sudden it was all I could do to keep moving forward while my stomach muscles wrested and clinched almost in synch with the unyielding wind.

I thought I had experienced almost all there is to experience in an ultra, but this was new. I thought about how much distance I still had to cover as the mile markers slowly approached me. It was as if I were standing still and the ground was moving towards me on its own slow schedule. The most troubling thing was not the pain itself, but more that I couldn't figure out how to fix my body. Usually, no matter how bad I feel late in a race, I am flying soon enough.

The dark thoughts began to creep in.

I didn't think about quitting, but for the first time I had a lingering doubt as to whether I could make it 80 miles more like this. I quickly put the negative to rest. As a former addict, I am no stranger to battling my demons and I made quick work of these for now. I decided to do the best I could to get over the pass and into the next checkpoint at Panamint Valley (72 miles). There I could see if a quick rest might allow my system to reset. It was becoming apparent that my body was in shock.

I crawled into the checkpoint around 4 am and into the back of the crew Jeep in a state of confusion and concern. I was afraid of stopping, and even more afraid of sleeping, as this was all new territory for me and I didn't know how I would feel after a rest. But I was willing to try anything to stop the assault on my mid-section. I lay in the back of the SUV with the rear gate open. I could hear people coming over to the truck to ask how I was doing. I heard Emily and other crew telling the story of the last 20 miles, I could hear the gas pump clicking on and off at the only gas station for miles, and I heard the voices in my own head—and those were getting loud. After about 15 minutes I couldn't take it anymore. I had to get back out on the course. Only now, I had a new commitment to myself... run as hard as you can, because it wasn't going to get any better. "This ain't no pillow factory," I said as I jumped out of the truck.

"Is your stomach better?" someone asked.

"No," I replied, "but let's get up this hill anyway."

We were at the base of the next big climb, a 15-mile trek up a 7% grade to Father Crowley Vista Point, and I was anxious to get to work. It looked like the sun was going to rise while we were climbing—and it seemed appropriate. I felt a renewed energy. My stomach was still dancing as the gravel started to crunch under my shoes, but I didn't care anymore. As I started to run, I started to retch. I kept running anyway—day one was in the books.

My Blog: Part 2

No sooner than I hauled myself out of what could have been memorialized as the "Jeep of DNF" and proclaimed that the Badwater 135 Ultramarathon was, in fact, not a manufacturing facility of sleep products, I started the steep climb up Father Crowley. For good measure, my body decided to check in and make it clear that it still wasn't happy. Here's a nut shot for you, buddy—have fun.

Sometimes it is my stubborn nature that can be my biggest ally in an ultra, and this was one of those occasions. I'm sure my buddy and pacer Brian laughed a little as I yelled "Fuck this!" and took off running up a grade that I probably should have been walking, even if I felt fresh and light. In a pretty cool video taken by Brian, you can see me stop running long enough to heave along the road and quickly take off running up the hill again.

I felt like a man alive again. I felt absolutely no different physically than I did before I climbed into the crew car in pain—but now I was pissed. Energized by the steep terrain and the fact that I should have been walking, I just put my head down and ran. After a few miles I caught a glimpse of some other runners up ahead. Their lights still blinking in the morning light was just another reminder that we were on day two now, and they served as a beacon. I picked up the pace and we passed one group, then another, and another. The game was afoot.

With the help of the day crew, meaning my buddies Brian, Nico and Scott, I made it up Father Crowley and to the summit or "Vista Point." I wasn't feeling much better, but I was moving aggressively and that was good enough. At the summit of the climb, I stopped for a while to chat with Marshall Ullrich, who is probably as good a person as you will ever meet. I was still hurting, and Marshall said he was glad to see I was moving again. We had spent some time on the course together over the last 25 hours and were leapfrogging for many miles. He was grabbing a bite to eat before heading out again and I was in need of a quick gear change and some calories, as well. He gave me some advice and encouragement and then went on his way. My crew switched shifts again and that meant I got to see Emily, which was cool with me. Jimmy and Carmella were also a welcome sight, and I told them that I wanted to get to the 100-mile marker as soon as possible and put the longest part in my rear view. I felt like 35 miles wouldn't seem so far if it meant the finish line was in sight... Yeah right.

Carmella, Jimmy, and Emily all took turns pacing behind me, changing my socks, feeding me what I could eat and just being amazing all the time. I had started a pattern that was working pretty well: run to one road marker, then walk for little to let my abdominal fireworks subside, then run to the next marker. We repeated this ritual for hours and hours on end. At some point, I saw Marshall up the road about a mile or two ahead strolling like he was out for a fun walk in the mall (only his fun walk is done at about 5 mph, it seems). I really wanted to talk to him for a while, if for no other reason than to just escape my brain, so I decided to try to catch up with him. It gave me a boost of energy, or at least a newfound commitment to suffer a little more for a perceived reward. So I put my head down and ran hard for what seemed like an eternity. I finally caught up to the man I admire most in the ultra world, not just for his accomplishment but because he seems to just be the genuine deal. You don't have to worry about who Marshall Ullrich is—he is always authentic. We chatted for a while as we walked. It was probably just another of many random moments for him, but it was special to me and something I will always remember. Eventually we parted ways only to agree that we would see each other soon.

As I ran, more mile markers came and went (on their own schedule it seemed, more than mine) and eventually the miracle of constant forward motion delivered me to the 100-mile mark of the Badwater 135. The time was 29 hours and 30 minutes into the race. Even though I would have been done with almost any other 100-mile race over 9-10 hours earlier, I took a certain amount of consolation in that as horrible as I felt, I would have made the cut-off in Leadville. Really, I was searching for any piece of leverage I could find to keep myself moving forward as fast as my body would allow. I didn't want to let the math creep too far into my world because it said I probably had 12-15 hours more go.

At this point my crew was waiting for me on the side of the road. Emily and Jimmy ran over to me and handed me the American flag that I had brought to carry over the finish line. The winds were whipping around fiercely as I took the flag. I turned my back to the wind and held the flag above my head and was pleased to see it cascade out in front of me. I instantly froze in place. As I saw the flag billowing up and down, I could see the mountains way off on the horizon. Mt. Whitney came in and out of view from under the flying flag. "Don't move!" Someone said. Emily and Jimmy both scrambled for cameras and caught the moment that will last forever in my mind.

From the 100-mile point of the race, there is a mind-numbing section of long road that stretches out for what seems to be forever. To make matters worse, it actually appears as if you are moving away from Mt. Whitney (off to the right) and are heading farther and farther from the promised land of Lone Pine. I did my best to not think in terms of how much time I had left, but instead, tried to look around and take in the moments that the day offered. I was trying to create as vivid a picture as possible for future recollection—the sound of the wind, the heat from the road, the sound of my shoes.

My beloved crew seemed to adopt a serious, yet relaxed attitude. They knew it was crunch time and it was getting hot again. I continued running as best as I could, stopping only when needed to walk fast and let the stomach cramps settle down a notch or two. After 10 miles or so, I was starting to experience some real foot pain for the first time in the race. The sick part of me was glad to have pain from a new epicenter, and it was with detached curiosity that I stopped to take off my shoes and socks. I wondered what I would see under there. What I saw was some pretty standard blisters, nothing to be too concerned about. "Just deal with it, dude—this ain't no pillow... yeah, I get it."

After some serious shoe modifications (cutting apart a new $170 pair of shoes so my toes could be out in the open) we were off again, and I did some of my best running in the next section of the course. At about the 110-mile point, I made a strange deal with myself. Tired of making such slow progress, I committed to running 1 hour without any stopping or walking at all. Screw it. "What's the worst thing that could happen?" I thought. So I ran—and ran hard. I clicked off a couple of 10-minute miles (which seemed world-class fast at this stage of the game), and I found that my new all-out assault on running re-energized my crew, as well.

In retrospect, I can say that I ran the first of those painful 1 or 2 miles for myself—and the remainder of the miles for my crew. They were so excited and enthusiastic that I just simply couldn't let them down. They knew nothing of the mental games and bargaining I was doing; they only saw me running and running hard. My body was screaming for me to stop or slow down. My gut was twisting in knots. My feet were on fire from blisters. But each time I passed the crew car and waived off support, my friends cheered and honked the horn in support. "It's worth it," I thought. So I kept running for them, as they had been doing for me for 2 days now.

I had fleeting thoughts of running all the way into Lone Pine and up Whitney without stopping, but that proved to be a bit ambitious, to say the least. Eventually after 6 miles or so, the pace took its toll on my body. I was broken down to the previous run/walk strategy—only now my body was really pissed off. I spent the next 3 miles in a crawl that including gagging, retching, power walking, and fighting off sleep.

"Are you ok?" I heard from somewhere that seemed at least 1,000 miles away. It seemed I was running and I was asleep—what a strange combination. "Yes, sir. I'm good," I fired back, making a mental note to try not to weave into oncoming traffic in the miles to come. We were now 120 miles from the Badwater Basin and the starting line. More importantly, we were approaching the city of Lone Pine. And we were finally getting close enough for the first thoughts of actually finishing this beast of a race to surface in my head. Those who have paced me know that I am somewhat superstitious in races and won't even talk about being done until I am within arm's reach of the finish line. Even so, my veteran pacer Nico told me he had no doubt that I was going to make it up Whitney. I was having nothing to do with it. "Don't even think it, dude," I said with a smile on my face.

It was great to see the entire crew all together just outside of Lone Pine, and I think we could all taste the finish in the air, but no one was talking about it now. Nico and I made the right turn to head into Lone Pine and ran the 2 miles to the checkpoint. From the checkpoint we were just a 13-mile climb up the Whitney Portal Road and to the end of this grand adventure. Strangely, the 5,000 feet of switchback climbs ahead were not too concerning for me. I knew I had done big climbs hundreds of times before. However, the fact that the climb included a long slow 7-8 mile grade at 9% before the steep climbing started, was playing tricks on my sleep-deprived brain. A quick scan of the math said it could take 5-6 hours or so to make it to the top and that seemed overwhelming. Oh well, this was no time to be in my head—it was time to work. I was very glad that Emily said she was going to climb all the way to the top with me. I knew that I would work even harder with her by my side.

The crew car with Jimmy and Carmella were waiting just a mile or so up the Portal road, and they were there to give me what I needed before the climb got too steep to allow for crew access. After a quick pit stop and a can of Coke, I shrugged my shoulders, looked straight ahead into the road, and started to climb as fast as I could manage to. We were not going real fast to speak of, but we were steady, and I wasn't about to slow down.

By now I had been stripped of every layer of my outside persona. Just the real me was present. No thoughts of the future. No thoughts of emails, charity projects, deadlines, expectations, or even of finishing this race. Every mental and physical resource available to me was singly focused to the task at hand—moving up this damn hill. I felt insane, as if reality was just another mile marker I'd passed on the road hours or days before. I no longer trusted any of my senses to tell me the truth. I wasn't sure if any of this was real. Maybe this was all a dream, or a drug-induced flashback. I kept thinking,

"Don't slow down," and I kept climbing.

I asked Emily if this was real. "Am I still here?" I said.

"Yes, baby. You are here," she replied.

I thought I saw giant praying hands sticking out of the rocks. I was drifting in and out of sleep without any perceivable change of state. When I "woke up" I simply took inventory of my pace. Was I still moving as fast as I could? Ok, good, keep going. I felt eerily alive. I felt like my heartbeat was connected to everything around me—every blade of grass, every rock on the ground and every star in the sky were calibrated to my heartbeat. I told Emily again that I was going crazy and I busted up laughing.

"This shit is really pretty out there, huh?" I said.

She smiled and told me I was doing awesome. "Keep going, baby. We're getting there."

The steep switchbacks had started some time ago, and I knew we must be getting close. I could start to feel the draw of the finish line like it had a weight and mass. It was as if I was no longer pushing up hill; I was being pulled by a force greater than me. I couldn't hold off the emotions anymore. "I did it," I allowed myself to croak in a weak voice. Emily started to cry. I looked up the road to see a strange shape taking form ahead of us. I could see the outline of a man. A giant light behind him made the flag he was holding appear almost ghostly. His arms were stretched out to display the flag in all of its glory. I knew it must be Brian. Emily started to cry even harder. I lost control of my emotions completely and tried to let out a yell of victory. What came out instead was a cacophony of tears, sobbing and sheer exhaustion.

I could hear Scott's voice now, as well, "You did it, man!!" he shouted. And like that I was blanketed in the flag. Brain's arms were wrapped around me and I could feel his body shaking as he cried and told how proud he was. We were all there now. Jimmy and Carmella, Scott and Brian, Emily and me, all embracing. Nico's body may have been miles away in a car driving to the airport, but at that instant we could all feel his presence on Mt. Whitney with us. "Let's finish this thing," someone said. I looked up and I could see the actual finish line only a few hundred yards ahead. We ran—together as one team, one heart, one purpose and one hundred and thirty-five miles of pure will later.

"I'm free," I thought as I grabbed the banner, lifted it to my face, and kissed it.

Acknowledgments

I would like to take a moment to thank a few of the people who made this book possible. First and foremost, I want to mention my mom and dad, Joan and Loren Clark. Without their love and constant encouragement, I would never have had the instinct to fight for a new life. In reading this book, it might be easy for people to misinterpret their journey in life and not understand how it could have gotten so bad at times. It was beyond the scope of this book for me to communicate how amazing and pure of heart my parents were in their quest to find religious truth and establish a relationship with God. And although the journey may have taken us all to places we wished we hadn't visited, we all learned more about love and life than most people do in a lifetime. You never know how rich you are until you count all the things you have that money cannot buy. In this arena, my parents made me very wealthy.

I talked much about my business partner and good friend Dan Lynn in this book. The story of my company and its rise and fall was the story of both of us, not just me. All the success we experienced was a result of a shared and mutual effort. There is hardly a thing we went through in that time that we didn't do as a team or as "brothers." It was hard for the purposes of this book to separate our journeys, but necessary in order for me to be able to tell all that was going on inside my warped brain at the time. Dan Lynn is still the only man outside of my family that knows all there is to know about me.

I have to mention Marshall Ulrich for putting his time and effort into writing the foreword for *Out There: A Story of Ultra Recovery*. I only knew Marshall in passing before I asked him if he would be interested in helping me out with my book. In the days and weeks that followed, we spent much time together, shooting the shit over lunches in Idaho Springs and sharing our stories of life, business and family. It's funny, we rarely talk about running, but we always seem to have something to say. Marshall read the entire unedited manuscript in a couple of sittings and was very honest and encouraging throughout the process. In case you were ever wondering, Marshall is the real deal—one of the most humble and genuine people I have ever met. His book *Running on Empty* is a must-read for anyone who wants to know about what a real runner goes through in plying his trade.

I would also like to thank Linda Sanders for all her kindness, emotional, moral, spiritual, and financial support for this project. Linda is a lady who dedicates her entire life to helping others, whether it's through her non-profit Hope So Bright or just from her works as a role model in the health and fitness world.

A thank-you goes out to David Adlard and Scott Kummer, as well, for all their dedication, friendship and financial support in making sure this book was published. Your encouragement was, and still is, very much appreciated.

In addition, I would like to thank my editor Nancy Hutchins who went well above and beyond the call of duty to walk me through this process, hold my hand and tell me it was going to be ok. Although I presented her with a complete manuscript to edit, I hadn't a single clue how to get it to the place where you could be reading this today.

And lastly, I must mention my many friends, family and crew that show up to support and train with me in my races and events. There simply wasn't enough time to accurately depict all the selfless work, tireless effort and pure dedication to my own selfish needs that these wonderful friends have supplied—and not just at my races, but in all the days and months leading up to the events. I could write an entire book on each of them and how they have impacted, not just my races, but my soul—and although I try to give back to all these beautiful people, I fear the balance will always be shifted to their side.

Running Highlights**

2005
CU Turkey Trot 5k 39:22
2006
Steamboat Half Marathon 2:05
Denver Marathon 4:45
CU Turkey Trot 5k 22:15

2007
Ironman 70.3 6:31
2009
Boulder 100 DNF
Collegiate Peaks DNF

2010
Collegiate Peaks DNF
Leadville 100 28:21

2011
Silver Rush 50 8:58
Leadville 100 23:50
Overall WIN 12 Hours of Boulder 71.17*

2012
Rocky Raccoon 100 20:59
8th Overall AG WIN Lean Horse 100 20:19
10th Overall AG WIN Bear Chase 50 8:31

2013
3rd Overall Run for Aurora 50
18th Overall Big Horn 50 10:11
Badwater 135 41:24

2014
Treadmill Record Run 12 Hours 73.44 miles
10th Overall Rocky Raccoon 50 7:39
2nd Overall Prairie Spirit 100 18:04

*The official distance is listed as 64.53 miles. The lap must be finished completely by the 12-hour limit to count on the official record. I was recognized as course record holder since I managed to run that distance faster than any other runner had previously. The course record has since been broken.
**Some results are from memory and not available online.

Made in the USA
Middletown, DE
27 December 2015